SOME OTHER TITLES FROM FALCON PRESS

Daniel Allen Kelley
Behind the Veil: The Complete Guide to Conscious Sleep

Christopher S. Hyatt, Ph.D.
Undoing Yourself with Energized Meditation and Other Devices
Techniques for Undoing Yourself (audios)
Energized Hypnosis (book, videos & audios)
To Lie Is Human: Not Getting Caught Is Divine
Secrets of Western Tantra: The Sexuality of the Middle Path
Hard Zen, Soft Heart

Christopher S. Hyatt, Ph.D. with contributions by
Wm. S. Burroughs, Timothy Leary, Robert Anton Wilson et al.
Rebels & Devils: The Psychology of Liberation

Christopher S. Hyatt, Ph.D. & Antero Alli
A Modern Shaman's Guide to a Pregnant Universe

S. Jason Black and Christopher S. Hyatt, Ph.D.
Pacts with the Devil: A Chronicle of Sex, Blasphemy & Liberation
Urban Voodoo: A Beginner's Guide to Afro-Caribbean Magic

Antero Alli
Angel Tech: A Modern Shaman's Guide to Reality Selection
Angel Tech Talk (audio)

Peter J. Carroll
The Chaos Magick Audios
PsyberMagick

Phil Hine
Condensed Chaos: An Introduction to Chaos Magic
Prime Chaos: Adventures in Chaos Magic
The Pseudonomicon

Joseph Lisiewski, Ph.D.
Ceremonial Magic and the Power of Evocation
Kabbalistic Cycles and the Mastery of Life
Kabbalistic Handbook for the Practicing Magician

Israel Regardie
The Complete Golden Dawn System of Magic
New Wings for Daedalus
The Golden Dawn Audios

Steven Heller
Monsters & Magical Sticks: There's No Such Thing as Hypnosis?

**For up-to-the-minute information on prices and
availability, please visit our website at
http://originalfalcon.com**

BEYOND LUCID DREAMING

The Art of Conscious Sleep

by
Daniel Allen Kelley

Foreword by
Ivan Kos

THE *Original* FALCON PRESS
TEMPE, ARIZONA, U.S.A.

International Standard Book Number: 978-1-935150-85-5
ISBN: 978-1-61869-850-6 (mobi)
ISBN: 978-1-61869-851-3 (ePub)
Library of Congress Control Number: 2020936022

First Edition 2020
First eBook Edition 2020

Cover Image: *"The Dream"* by Pierre Puvis De Chavannes

The paper used in this publication meets the minimum requirements of the American National Standard for Permanence of Paper for Printed Library Materials Z39.48-1984

Address all inquiries to:
THE ORIGINAL FALCON PRESS
1753 East Broadway Road #101-277
Tempe, AZ 85282 U.S.A.
(or)
PO Box 3540
Silver Springs NV 89429 U.S.A.

website: http://www.originalfalcon.com
email: info@originalfalcon.com

DEDICATION

For my daughter and fellow Fantastican,
Page Celeste Kelley.

May you always do what you dream.

Acknowledgements

I'd like to thank the following people for their support during the writing and production of this book:

My daughter, Page, for enduring my creative absences. Nick Tharcher, for his patience and consistency. Robert Peterson and Antero Alli, for their lovely reviews. Ivan Kos, for his wonderful Foreword. Beckie Camplin, for encouraging me to write during a dark period in my life. Tami Stronach and Greg Steinbruner, for taking the time to read my manuscript and forward it to friends. And to you, Dear Reader, I thank you for choosing me as a companion on your Quest.

TABLE OF CONTENTS

Foreword: by Ivan Kos 11

Preface: The Key to the Kingdom 13

Part One
Foundations and Framework

Chapter One: The Integral Model of Subliminal Cognition Training.. 21

Chapter Two: Lifting The Veils: States, Stages and Structures of Consciousness.................................. 49

Part Two
The Four Pillars of Subliminal Cognition Training

Chapter Three: Astral Projection: Myths and Theories 93

Chapter Four: Pellucid Sleep and Dreaming.......... 118

Chapter Five: Lucid Dreaming: Why, What, When and How... 134

Chapter Six: The Importance of Full-Sensory Dreaming (Vivid Dreaming).................................. 169

Part Three
Mentoring, Magick and Methods

Chapter Seven: Fear. Loss of Control. Children, Night-Terrors and Conscious Sleep..................... 181

Chapter Eight: Sexuality, Magick and Conscious Sleep 209

Chapter Nine: The Three-Body Fitness Program 221

Afterword: The Future of Subliminal Cognition Training 244

Glossary... 246

Bibliography 251

About the Author... 253

FOREWORD

BY IVAN KOS

When Daniel asked if I would be interested in writing a Foreword to this book, I was eager to read the manuscript he sent me. After reading it thoroughly, I am pleased to say that Daniel has written an extremely provocative and readable book. What Daniel has to say is more than just thought-provoking; it is a challenge, an invitation to personal transformation. What I really enjoy about Daniel's work is that he never markets "spiritual knowledge" as a panacea. Quite the contrary! He makes no bones about how arduous and dangerous the path of conscious sleep can sometimes be. His approach, called *Subliminal Cognition Training* (SCT), is a *living* map. It is a collection of viable landmarks and formulae culled from a vast array of timeless methodologies, and yet it lends itself readily to customization. As Daniel says, *"You cannot cut the man to fit the coat."*

Today, there are countless techniques to choose from. Many of them have been around for centuries, and yet most of them tend only to one or two aspects of the human bodymind. But when the real awakening happens, your whole life will become a process of awakening! Once that occurs, you will not have to *practice* being awake; but first, your whole life must become a process of awakening. Having followed Daniel's work for the past three years now, I can honestly say that *Subliminal Cognition Training* is an approach that honors this timeless truth. As Daniel so aptly put it, "This isn't the lazy man's guide to the subject!"

Deep meditators can accomplish the magnificent task of breaking the limited agreements that shape our reality. There comes a point when you will feel the absurdity of taking life so seriously, that is, with a melancholy mood. You begin to approach personal development in a more playful manner, and this allows you to grow beyond plateaus. Daniel has clearly walked that road, and he provides a pathway up the mountain for others to follow. He undertook deliberate actions to understand and live the mysteries of life, and he inspires others to do the same.

There is great intensity and a sense of longing in Daniel's writing. Many writers have spoken of ancient spiritual wisdom, or some great body of knowledge, and the great civilizations that produced it. Few have succeeded in combining specific aspects of this ancient wisdom with modern knowledge. In my opinion, *Subliminal Cognition Training* continues to accomplish this. Daniel takes us by the hand and leads us along secret pathways to those mysterious corners where meaning is found.

For those who prefer to know who they are, what they are capable of, and how to buttress their personal development via deliberate contact with superconscious forces, how to accomplish this while simultaneously living in the secular world represents a genuine crisis. This moment defines a transition in which a spiritual seeker becomes an individual who wants to know the Truth and enjoy the company of other seekers-of-truth. Daniel has synthesized an Integral approach that answers this lack. This book you now hold in your hands is about how to fashion your own key to unlock the mysteries of conscious sleep. As Daniel says, *"I'm going to help you discover your unique key to unlocking the mysteries of Conscious Sleep."* Over the course of his more than twenty years of involvement in the various Wisdom Traditions of the world, he has succeeded in doing just that.

— Ivan Kos, author of *Skygates of the Mind*
Saskatoon, Saskatchewan, 2019

PREFACE

THE KEY TO THE KINGDOM

What if I told you that you already possess the key to unlock the secrets of the world's great Wisdom Traditions? What if I told you that the quest for the Holy Grail begins no further away than your own bedroom? What if this key is no further than your own pillow?

This book is about how to unlock the wonders of Conscious Sleep. Although we all pass through the same door of sleep, each of us has a unique way of unlocking its mysteries. In this book, I'm going to help you discover your unique key to unlocking those mysteries. We're going to take this journey together. Lucky for us the oneironauts, mystics and sages who came before us were kind enough to leave scattered fragments of maps, road signs, and landmarks to assist us. My work is to synthesize some of these maps and methods into a practical system. I call this system *Subliminal Cognition Training* (SCT).

I offer a practical approach to the full-spectrum of Conscious Sleep. This book isn't just about learning Lucid Dreaming or Astral Projection. Rather, it demonstrates the relationships among *all* aspects of Conscious Sleep, especially as expressed in the religions and mystical traditions of the world. This approach has profound implications for meditators especially…

I've practiced many different forms of meditation for twenty-five out of my forty years on this planet. Until I discovered the connection between meditation and Conscious Sleep, I was always somewhat dissatisfied with meditation. Not that I wasn't seeing results from my meditation practices. I was! But I wasn't interested in just becoming more mindful of the tip of the iceberg, as it were; I wanted to become mindful of the greater portion of the iceberg submerged in the murky depths of my subconscious mind. In short, I wanted the light of my awareness to remain lit in all conceivable states of awareness, perhaps even in death. Meditation simply wasn't scratching that itch…

Eventually, I began supplementing my meditation practice with *Tai Chi Chuan, Qigong* (energy-work), and various forms of Yoga. Each of these disciplines conferred their own unique benefits, to be sure, but I didn't see them as being truly related to each other in any specific way. As the years went by, however, the relationship shared by these disciplines began to reveal itself to me. This taught me that the ability to carry meditation through waking and sleep states is the key to transforming meditation into something you are, rather than merely something you do. After all, if falling asleep is all it takes to destroy your meditative awareness then something's missing! And the same rule applies to, say, the insights that emerge in your nightly dreams:

If waking up in the morning is all it takes to forget those insights, what good are they?

Whether it's Astral Projection, Lucid Dreaming, Dream Recall, Dream Incubation, etc., for any of these to become accessible and enduring traits of your consciousness, the subconscious and conscious regions of your bodymind must "agree" to make that happen. In other words, conscious intention must align with unconscious capacity, and the best way to accomplish this is to carry your intention into the Waking, Dreaming and Dreamless states of consciousness.

I often refer to Sri Ramana Maharshi's famous quote to illustrate the significance of this point:

If it's not still present while you're in deep sleep then it's not real.

It took roughly sixteen years after that breakthrough for me to truly uncover the links among Meditation, *Qigong,* Yoga, Lucid Dreaming and Astral Projection. The strange thing is, I wasn't actively seeking a connection among them and, although I knew that such a connection existed, I was practicing each of these skills for purposes that had little to do with one another. In retrospect, I often wonder if I was subconsciously aware of their connection all along, as it seems something of a happy accident that I stumbled upon it. At any rate, after so many years of consistent practice, these seemingly discreet disciplines somehow merged into one unified skill-set.

It came as a shock to me! But after some time had passed, and I slowly became familiar with these connections, their relationship (reliance even!) made perfect sense. In this book, I'm going to share some of these discoveries with you so that you might apply them to your own quest. In *Behind the Veil: The Complete Guide to Conscious*

Sleep, I laid the groundwork for balanced and healthy cultivation. In that book, we learned the core module of the *SCT* system—the *120-Days Curriculum*—and by now you should be nurturing a daily meditation practice, keeping a thorough dream journal, uncovering and decoding your dream "language," channeling intensity, and aligning yourself with the tides of Nature. In this book I'm going to expand on that core module. This work essentially represents a form of "Three-Body Cross-Training" in which you'll learn how to successfully navigate the five Veils of *SCT simultaneously.*

The exercises in this book are in no particular order of importance, save that I tried to pick up where I left off in *Behind the Veil.* New readers of my work should consult that book (specifically the *120-Days Curriculum)* regarding the order of training. As we each have our own unique personalities, it's impossible (and deplorable) to make rules for everyone. Of course, there are universal guidelines from which anyone can benefit, and *SCT* is an attempt to synthesize those guidelines; but there are no absolutes when it comes to the nuances in how one learns and uses these skills.

The techniques in this book are meant to be approached in a playful manner. Although the exercises demand total commitment, the order in which they're presented isn't as important as your decision to practice them. Each of the techniques in the *Three-Body Fitness Program* are complete in themselves, as they were created and synthesized to exercise the Gross, Subtle and Causal bodies simultaneously. In this way you'll learn to traverse the *Five Primary Veils* in a single session, whereas in *Book One* you learned how to access them one at a time. Thus, you can start with any technique of your choosing. There's no absolute order to the Program.

Here are a few examples of what you'll learn from this book:

- A comprehensive system for learning how to have full-sensory Vivid and Lucid Dreams.
- A discussion of the Dos and Don'ts of Astral Projection.
- How to convert *physical* movements into *etheric* and *astral* ones using *Qigong* (Chinese Yoga) principles.
- Methods for communicating with your subconscious mind and Higher Self.

- How to use the Seven Categories of Dream to Enhance your Dream Recall.
- The relationship of methodologies from Vedanta, Tantra, *Tai Chi,* Vision Quests, the Western Magickal Tradition, and Psychedelic states to Conscious Sleep.
- The relationship of bioelectrical brainwaves to the practice of *Qigong* and Astral Projection.
- How to navigate the *Five Primary Veils* of Consciousness.
- A "Three Body" Fitness Regimen aimed at strengthening the *Physical, Etheric, Emotional, Astral* and *Causal* bodies.

While you can read this book from the first to the last page, feel free to pick a topic or exercise that interests you and dig in.

This book is divided into three parts. *Part One* deals primarily with the foundation of the *SCT* system. We'll discuss the Art, Science and Spirituality of Conscious Sleep with an eye toward a quick recap of *Book One*. Because of their importance, I've also reintroduced some of the core Taoist practices taught in *Book One,* but with additional information on how you might advance that aspect of your training.

In *Part Two* we discuss the Four Pillars of *SCT.* However, Vivid Dreaming, Lucid Dreaming, Pellucid Dreaming and Astral Projection have been listed in the reverse order of the *120-Days Curriculum* in *Book One.* This has been done in the spirit of picking up where *Book One* left off. In *Book One,* we went up the ladder. Here we go back down. This has been done to emphasize that your development as a Veiler is more like a spiral staircase than a rigid ladder. So when I say that we're going "up" and "down," I really mean that we're *spiraling* up and down. It often happens that a discovery made at an advanced level of practice sheds new light upon a previous one. The process of refinement has no upper-limit, and is anything but straightforward.

Part Three deals with some of the more peripheral aspects of Conscious Sleep. We'll talk about the role of sexuality and the magickal arts in our quest for the continuity of consciousness. We'll discuss the relationship between the occult and Conscious Sleep. We'll talk about ways you might teach children how to Lucid and Pellucid Dream to stop night-terrors and enhance creative inspiration. Finally, we'll dive into the *Three-Body Fitness Program* and bring it all together.

SCT champions a full-spectrum approach to Conscious Sleep. Each dedicated and sincere practitioner represents a unique contribution to this timeless and perennial flower.

What new discoveries and contributions will *you* make?

Part One

Foundations and Framework

CHAPTER ONE

THE INTEGRAL MODEL OF SUBLIMINAL COGNITION TRAINING

(1)
The Model of Subliminal Cognition Training: Let's Recap!

If you have not yet done so, I urge you to read *Behind the Veil: The Complete Guide to Conscious Sleep*. For the sake of convenience, though, let's take a quick look at the model I use in this series. (If you've already read *Behind the Veil*, don't skip over this part as I've added new information here.)

Over the course of my twenty years of involvement in the various Wisdom Traditions of the world, I've discovered their many commonalities despite their cultural differences. Whether we're talking about Judaism, Hinduism, Taoism, or any other *-ism* for that matter, we're still talking about people, and people have more similarities than differences. It should then come as no surprise that the myriad systems have more in common than their surfaces might suggest.

What's the common core shared by the great spiritual traditions?
ANSWER: *The Perennial Philosophy.*

Put simply, the Perennial Philosophy is the oldest and most universal developmental model in the world. The belief that the universe, including human consciousness, is composed of an onion-like series of layers or nests leading from dirt to deity, from dust to divine, is found in virtually every known culture of the world. A common theme running through most versions of the Perennial Philosophy is that each level, world, plane, body or realm is separated by "sheathes" or *veils*, much like the layers of an onion are separate and yet still comprise the whole onion itself.

The most stripped-down versions of the Perennial Philosophy tend to look something like this:

- Earth = Man = Heaven
- Ecosphere = Biosphere = Noosphere
- Body = Mind = Spirit

And so on…

I've worked with the Perennial Philosophy as it appears on the Kabbalah's *Tree of Life,* in the internal Alchemy of Taoism, the five *Koshas* of Vedanta, and of course the "Five Primary Veils" of my own system:

- the Veil of Tears
- the Veil of Breath
- the Veil of Dreams
- the Veil of Ghosts
- the Veil of Bliss

(These correspond to the *Physical, Etheric, Mental, Astral* and *Causal* realms, respectively. In *Chapter Two,* I'll elaborate on the Primary, Secondary and Tertiary Veils of SCT.)

Another important principle of the Perennial Philosophy has to do with the energetic embodiment in which we travel through and behind these respective Veils. The most basic description of these "bodies" is found in the well-known format of *Body, Mind, Soul* and *Spirit* and its many compact versions which typically look like this:

- Physical Body/Etheric
- Mental Body/Ego Body
- Emotion Body/Astral Body
- Spirit Body/Causal Body

Some systems go a step further and lump *Etheric, Mental, Astral* and *Causal* under the general heading of "subtle-body," with the Causal Body being, on the one hand, the very root of consciousness itself, and on the other hand, the subtlest aspect of the Subtle Body. Depending on how and why you choose to slice that pie, you could just as easily give a scheme of:

- Gross (not so subtle)
- Subtle (more subtle)
- Causal (very subtle)

These correspond to the three basic states of *Awake, Dreaming* and *Dreamless Sleep,* respectively. The diagram below should help clarify these basic correspondences. The upper-left quadrant represents your subjective self and its various states of awareness. The upper-right quadrant represents your objective self, namely the tangible and intangible "bodies" of your subjective experiences. The lower-left represents the "culture" or entities and characters you might perceive behind each Veil. And the lower-right quadrant represents the Veils themselves. In other words, these are the subjective and objective versions of the individual and the collective (items are listed in ascending order):

Basic Correspondences of Subliminal Cognition Training System

It's important to understand that the Subtle Body is actually a heading under which falls several other "subtle" aspects of the bodymind. Different traditions give slightly different qualifications of these. For our purposes, the Subtle Body includes the Etheric Body (*Qi,* Prana, Orgone, Bioelectricity), the Dream Body (emotional Body), and the Astral Body, respectively. Therefore, what we're calling the Subtle Body actually includes in its expanded territory the *Veil of Breath,* the *Veil of Dreams,* and the *Veil of Ghosts.* The reason for this consolidation is practical rather than theoretical. I find that this scheme is the very least that's needed for a truly holistic approach to Conscious Sleep. After all, the Etheric Body is actually a very subtle aspect of the physical nervous system—plus something extra. The Dream Body is actually a subtle aspect of the Gross and Etheric bodies—plus something extra. And the Astral Body is actually a subtle aspect of the Gross, Etheric and Dream bodies—plus something extra.

As we'll soon see, our conscious participation in all three of these primary states holds the key to consistent behind-the-Veil access. That said, how you categorize the levels of the Perennial Philosophy depends upon why you're navigating it in the first place. It all depends on which Veil you're stepping behind and the map you're using for this purpose. For example, in the tradition of Psychoanalysis, they use the triad of:

- Id
- Ego
- Superego.

In such a system, the mental aspect of the Subtle Body is of primary importance, and the Veil which separates the *Biosphere* (physical life) from the *Noosphere* (the realm of Mind) is the one being stepped behind. Because most systems tend to favor one particular Veil/Body over the others, it's often left to another system to fill in the gaps.

Take sports, for example. Most sports deal primarily with the Gross (physical) body. Of course, the mental aspect is there in the form of rules and strategy, but the bulk of athletic sports is a Gross Body endeavor. As a result, many progressive thinkers in the realm of athletic performance have begun to study "the zone," a flow-state experienced by many athletes that has meditative characteristics. Today, it's not uncommon to find football players practicing *Tai Chi,* a subtle-body exercise, or Mindfulness meditation, a Causal Body practice.

The bottom line?

If you're exercising Body, Mind and Soul, you're a complete human being; and as long as you're capable of smoothly transitioning from your Gross to Subtle to Causal bodies you're a Veiler!

One of the most significant points to bear in mind is that these "bodies" are just the limbs of one unified body. I really can't stress this fact enough. That *bodymind,* that organic unity, is the stuff you're made of. Being a "Veiler" is simply a snappy way of saying that you know how to lift the curtain to reveal the secret spaces within that mystery.

But being a Veiler is more than that...

If you wish to learn a skill, you first must possess the necessary equipment to perform it. You must have the right *anatomy* for the job, and I mean that literally. If I want to become a professional track runner, I first need strong legs, a powerful core, and a strong heart and lungs. If I don't have these fundamental requirements I'm doomed to fail from the start. It's one thing to be able to walk. For that I only require the minimum in terms of physical functioning. But to be a track runner? Well, for that I'll need a strong body. Not only that, I'll need a specific *type* of body. The body of a runner is different from that of, say, a professional bodybuilder. A dancer's body differs in many obvious ways from that of a powerlifter's body.

My first encounter with this somewhat obvious fact came when I made the transition from bodybuilding to the *Internal Martial Arts*. I planned on keeping my bodybuilding practice as an adjunct to my Internal Martial Arts training, but it was clear from the start that this was an impossibility. A *Tai Chi* body is completely different from the bodybuilder's body! So different, in fact, that they're totally incompatible. So I had to make a choice: *Tai Chi* or Big Muscles?

I chose *Tai Chi*...

The same holds true in any serious endeavor. If I want to learn to play piano, it's not enough that I have ten fingers and a piano. I need to have some degree of natural talent. I've got to have a good sense of pitch, good coordination, mental focus, and a good memory. All these requirements demand a certain physiological and cognitive make-up. Without it, you may be able to play a few chords. You may even be able to learn to read some musical notation. But you'll never be a virtuoso if you're tone deaf or missing a few fingers. In much the same way, it's not enough that you have dreams every night. To learn how to have Lucid Dreams you've got to be wired that way, either naturally or through sincere and long-term training. Lucid Dreamers and Astral Projectors have a unique neurology. Either they were born that way, or they developed it over time.

A Veiler's body is different from other bodies...

Think about it: What are advanced Yogis, Taoists, Shamans and Monks doing when they meditate, eat consciously, practice *Qigong,* or go on vision quests? They're exercising, cultivating, and in a very real sense *creating* their Subtle Body, resting in their Causal Body, and rooting in their Gross Body! That's the whole process in a nutshell.

It's important to remember that not all Veilers are the same. Admittedly, this isn't the most popular aspect of my approach. After all, assuring people that you can teach anyone how to go Astral, or Lucid Dream, or contact their dead relatives, is a great selling point. I get it! Still, it doesn't change the fact that it's simply not true. To become a proficient Veiler you need to first possess, and then cultivate, a very specific anatomy. There are many Subtle Body anatomy textbooks available. In this book, we'll be working primarily with Taoist, Tibetan and Tantric methodologies.

That's all fine and well, you say, but so what? What's the ultimate goal of being a Veiler?

The goal of a Veiler is to attain continuity of consciousness in the Physical, Dream, Astral and Causal realms.

That sounds like a tall order, doesn't it? Well, yes, it is and no it isn't. Like any skill, being a Veiler is at least 40% talent. Like any talent, certain personality types tend to have more initial success with it than others. For example, look at most artists. Most tend to be introverted, reclusive and dreamy. Now contrast that with the outgoing and extroverted personality of, say, a car salesman.

So, what's the best way to know whether you have a natural proclivity for being a Veiler? Well, first, you're reading this. Chances are you wouldn't be if not for the fact that you've got a natural interest in these topics. In my experience, the natural Veiler tends to be a little introverted, right-hemisphere of the brain dominant, emotionally dynamic, and a sensualist. This doesn't necessarily mean that other Personality Types can't learn how to go Astral or Lucid Dream, only that they'll probably have to take an unorthodox route to get there. The good news is that *SCT* contains plenty of unorthodox methods!

The following is an experiment should help you gauge your natural talent as a Veiler.

The Reality Rorschach Exercise

Most of us are familiar with the famous "inkblot test," also known as the Rorschach test. In that psychological test a subject is shown a series of patterned inkblots set against a white background. Subjects often report seeing butterflies, spiders, people conversing, and various body parts. (I'll leave that to your imagination!)

Using a similar mechanism as that of the Rorschach test, I use a simple method to gauge a student's inborn talent for skills like Lucid Dreaming. I firmly believe that Conscious Sleep, in one capacity or another, could become an evolutionary trait we all possess in the future. But not everyone has an inborn talent for it. I also fear that the collective acquisition of Conscious Sleep may be stymied by our increasing dependence upon technology. Indeed, many rarified experiences might soon be accessible technologically rather than through years of dedicated practice.

So how does *The Reality Rorschach Exercise* work?

The following test was created out of my own early-childhood experiences as a Veiler. I can recall countless sleepless nights staring out of my window at the terrifying shapes made by the silhouetted branches of trees. During the day, however, the clouds formed a happier panoply of characters. This disparity between nighttime horror and daytime pleasantness was due to the fact that I suffered extreme Lucid nightmares as a kid.

As I grew older, I marveled at this capacity of the mind to shape the external world in its image.

Like external reality, our dream world is also a mirror. This also applies to the Astral Plane, even if the denizens there act with relative autonomy. The point is that we see what we ourselves are. And this is the simple test I use to gauge talent in would-be Veilers and Oneironauts. Not only does it gauge talent, but it also predicts the quality of experience the student is apt to have.

Try this: Look out your bedroom window at night. Look at the trees. Look at the clouds, too, at dusk. What shapes do they make? What stories do they tell? Do they tell any stories at all? If they do, then you're a natural! If not, don't be discouraged, you can still learn!

I've even experimented with this technique while casually strolling along with friends. On one occasion it was dusk, and I was walking down the street with someone. Suddenly a cat came up to us and my friend picked it up. At that moment, I happened to spot a silhouetted tree in the distance and noticed that its branches formed a perfect image of a taller person standing next to a shorter person, and the shorter person was holding something. I pointed this out to my friend and she gasped in amazement. As it turns out, she and I ended up having multiple shared dreams. On one occasion, we both woke up sweating after a shared dream of a burning city. Soon thereafter the horrors of 9/11 occurred in the city we both dreamed of.

Such are the mysteries of Conscious Sleep!

(2)

A Descriptive Tour of the Five Veils of Perception as Outlined in Subliminal Cognition Training

The *Veil of Tears* is a paradoxical place. It extends to us one hand open in friendship and the other one closed tightly into a fist. It offers both the taste of honey and of sulfur in the same bite, conferring at once both promise and betrayal. From birth, we're thrust mercilessly through the Abyss, choked and cheered by our own umbilical cords, and taught the fine line which separates a strangle from a hug.

In the *Veil of Tears* we receive both lashes and love. We cry tears of joy and tears of pain. We share moments of wordless wonder. We crawl, grovel, walk, run, make love, scream, sigh, sing and dance, all in homage to that shadow-clad debt-collector, the Grim Reaper.

Welcome to Eden!

***

It was a hot day in upstate New York. The sun was completing his daily chariot-ride across the sky and was sinking slowly on the Western horizon, leaving behind a motley trail of exhaust fumes for the shy twilight stars to feast upon. My body, aching from hours of overwork, had settled into a convoluted inner snarl. I could practically taste the lactic acid pooling within my muscles as my *Qi* meridians began their nightly yield to the Circadian rhythm.

It takes roughly an hour of focused *Qigong,* stretching, and an alternating cold/hot shower to fully bolster the healing and recovery phase of the intense workout routine that is my life, but this is how a Veiler navigates the *Veil of Tears—sensitively, skillfully and scientifically.*

As I lie down to sleep, I relax my body completely. Using what I call *Mobile Mental Focus* in combination with Progressive Relaxation, I relax my physical body (Gross Body) thoroughly. By doing so, I also stimulate my *Qi* meridians and cause them to open (Etheric Body). At the same time, I allow thoughts to come and go without getting attached to or identified with them. The moment my thoughts become something I *feel* rather than something I *think,* I know that I'm fully immersed in my Etheric Body at the *Veil of Breath* and that the

Veil of Tears is falling behind me. Soon the *Veil of Dreams* will emerge from the void.

As my awareness of my physical body slowly fades, I circulate *Qi* within the *Microcosmic Orbit* around my body to cleanse my Etheric Body and loosen my Astral Body. As I feel this working, I'm grateful for my many years of dedicated practice. Soon, microbursts of dreaming flash across my mind's eye. At first, I feel myself yielding to the irrational logic of the *Veil of Dreams,* but soon the absurdity of dream stuff alerts me to the fact that I'm dreaming. Periods of dreaming and absolute stillness of mind and being alternate and vie for my attention.

But I remain unmoved…

Then, suddenly, I become aware of an intense light shining behind my eyes. Sometimes this light appears as bright flashes, at other times it resembles a pulsing lighthouse beacon. Hypnagogia swirl in psychedelic patterns behind my eyes. I focus on these for a while and then the light gets even brighter. Then…then…

BOOM!!!

I'm in my Dream Body and fully behind the *Veil of Dreams.*

Powerful vibrations course through my body like an adrenaline surge that threatens to wrench me from Lucidity, but I rest in pure awareness, the calm eye of the storm, my *Shen,* the center of my consciousness. I rest in this pure Being while voices swell in the darkness, some menacing and others benign. I can sense presences in the room around me and my body is going completely numb. My heartbeat feels erratic and my breathing has disappeared. I ignore these sensations and focus on the emerging dream scenarios.

As I move deeper into the dream realm, I am confronted by people and places both familiar and foreign. I find that some of them are trying to teach me something. Sometimes I'll be given the solution to a creative problem which has eluded me for some time. Other times I'm given entire poems or book titles. Then there are the premonitions: those strange dreams in which I'm shown the future. I've predicted car accidents, political elections, social situations and natural disasters in this way.

In the dream realm, I can do whatsoever I want provided I'm psychologically prepared to embrace it. If not, then Dream Control will not happen. I can have mind-blowing sex, breathe under water, fly, defeat monsters and talk to angels.

The Laws of Physics don't apply here!

Then something unexpected happens, something both terrifying and exhilarating at the same time.

The dream is shaken suddenly like an earthquake is in progress. My entire being feels as though it may be swallowed up by the event-horizon of some invisible black hole. The very universe feels like it's speeding up to an impossible pace all around me, and yet I can't move. I can't breathe. Powerful waves which resemble an electrical current pulsate and throb through my Etheric Body. Popping and buzzing sounds explode all around me and voices are heard whispering in the dark. This reaches a feverish pitch and then…. Then….

WHOOSH!!!!

I'm hovering two feet or so from my body. At first, I panic but quickly manage to center myself in my Causal awareness and all becomes still. I can see, but darkly. I can feel, too, but everything feels ballooned and disproportionate. I can hear, but everything sounds like I'm listening while submerged under water. I can even hear someone breathing! Who's here?!

Oh, wait, that's just me. Phew! My breathing sounds like it's echoing down a long metal tube.

I manage to Astral travel to the kitchen and get a glimpse of the digital stove clock: 5:00 am.

I travel back to my body and, for a moment, dream scenarios blend with Astral perception. I center my awareness and I'm nowhere to be found all at the same time. I feel like I'm resting in the calm heart of heaven itself! I know this to be the *Veil of Bliss,* that coveted treasure of innumerable sages and buddhas. I then feel a throbbing ache slowly spreading over my feeling-awareness and I feel heavy, very heavy. I can feel the pressure of my bed pushing up on the joints of my physical body and it dawns on me:

I'm back to the *Veil of Tears.*

Back to that darkly splendid world of perpetual whining and hades wrapped in clouds. Where ecstasy dances with agony in a comic and cosmic waltz of wonder and rage, death rattle and orgasm, love and hate.

And I stand here more fully aware of it and more eager to embrace it than ever before.

(3)
The Goal of Subliminal Cognition Training

As I tried to make clear in the description above, the goal of *SCT* is to learn to fully occupy the Gross, Subtle and Causal bodies *all the time*. Granted, there are times when one Body is emphasized over the others. For example, when in deep Dreamless Sleep the Causal Body takes center stage. While dreaming, it's the emotional part of the Subtle Body. While awake, the Gross Body is most active. Regardless of which of the three Bodies you're occupying in a given moment, your aim is to realize the interconnectedness of all three Bodies as limbs of one unified bodymind. The health of the Gross Body affects the health and functioning of the Etheric Body (*Qi*, Bioelectricity, Prana, Orgone); and this mutual dependence flows both ways, which is why Acupuncture, *Qigong*, Breathwork and the various forms of Yoga are so effective for physical health.

Emotions, too, and their projected expressions in dreams (Lucid, Astral, both or neither), are simply the *feeling* component of the Etheric Body which, in turn, is the bioelectrical *(Qi)* component of the Subtle Body.

Finally, at the "center" of all of these is the Causal Body. The Causal Body is the headquarters and command-center of the Gross and Subtle bodies. It's the pure Witness of all experience and the root of the "I" thought. Although the Causal center can be inhabited to the point where root-canal can be performed without anesthesia, it's still subject to disease and death. It's just the case that what immediately affects the Gross and Subtle bodies takes a longer time to reach your Causal Body. Depending upon your degree of skill, much of it won't reach you at all!

As we're presently going to learn, every single Wisdom Tradition known to man targets one or more of these three Bodies. Some of them even focus on cultivating all three Bodies, which makes for a complete Yoga, and *SCT* is one such system. The emphasis in *SCT* is on the Subtle Body—and its Emotional, Etheric and Astral subsets—and the Causal Body which functions as the *stabilizer muscles* of the Subtle Body.

After so many years of studying the Wisdom Traditions, I finally found a way to consolidate them in a practical and comprehensive manner, thanks to the Integral approach. I can assure you that these great traditions are all meaningfully connected, and if you want to skyrocket your training in one you should engage the others in some way. For example, not too many people would think that a connection exists between *Qigong* and Astral Projection, but I know for certain that the connection isn't just there, it's right under our noses! Not too long ago, for instance, nobody would believe you if you said that dreams have a bioelectrical equivalent in and around the physical body. It wasn't until the year 1924 that a man named Hans Berger laid the groundwork for *Electroencephalography*, which culminated in the creation of a machine capable of detecting and recording these electrical brainwaves as they appear on the human skull (EEG).

Consider also the recent discovery that dreams are largely a *memory consolidation* function of the nervous system. This research has uncovered a connection between increased **REM** (Rapid Eye Movement) sleep and the digestion of new skills. In other words, people who are constantly learning new things have more of an intense dream-life than people who live in the same daily routine.

Other compelling research has revealed a connection between OOBE (Out of Body Experiences) and proprioception (spatial orientation). The structure of the inner-ear has also been shown to play a role in OOBE. This Gross Body interpretation of a Subtle Body phenomenon has sparked umbrage from the Astral Projection community, the members of which tend to lean toward a completely metaphysical interpretation of the issue. But this antipathy is totally unnecessary! For when you stop to think about it, of course there's a physical-neurological dimension to OOBE! Just as the experience of, say, feeling happy, finds its biochemical equivalent in the neurotransmitters *serotonin* and *dopamine*.

This isn't a war; this is a wedding!

The goal of *SCT* is the attainment of the continuity of consciousness throughout all conceivable states of awareness, but especially Waking, Dreaming and Dreamless sleep. There are many ways to achieve this goal, and *SCT* always strives to include many diverse methods to cater to as many types of mind as possible. However, because my own background consists mostly of Hermetic, Buddhist, Taoist and Tantric methods, those are the ones I teach. Wherever possible, I try to fill in the gaps left by my own limitations by referring students to other reputable teachers, books and traditions. I myself am a work in progress, and I learn something new every day! One of the core tenets of *SCT* is to bring together as many teachers, systems and methodologies as possible; find out what their core contributions are, learn them and then teach them to others.

I hope you'll join me in this exciting adventure! If this gets you as excited as it does me, let's begin our quest by looking at the science behind it all.

(4)
Surfing The Waves: The Science of Being a Veiler

Conscious Sleep is arguably the most fascinating skill you can learn. It's almost ironic, really, because sleep is largely a process of memory and skill consolidation. Why is that ironic? Well, first of all, sleep is thought by most people to be an eight-hour period of inactivity, but is actually anything but. By the time you've entered the second phase of sleep (90 minutes in), your brain and nervous system have been very busy. While you were busy snoring, your brain was constructing neural connections to house new skills and information. Those piano lessons you had yesterday afternoon? Check! Those elective courses you took yesterday evening at school? Yup, your brain made room for those, too.

And that's happening whether your sleep is conscious or not!

The most ironic part of *conscious* sleep is that you're learning a skill which employs the very same mechanism that learns new skills. Dreams, being largely the consolidation of new skills, are now the skill you're attempting to consolidate! It's the neurological equivalent of what happens when two mirrors are facing each other: It generates an endless hall of unending reflections that you experience as Lucid Dreaming, Astral Projection, Remote Viewing, and much more.

Isn't that far out?

Your dreams are at least 70% composed of people, places, things, emotions and sensations you've experienced at some point in your life. The remaining 30% is, well, something extra. That "something extra" isn't personal or biographical. We experience these extras when we have Out of Body Experiences, Astral Dreams, Precognitive Dreams, and so forth. We'll talk more about that later. For now, just note that

Conscious Sleep, even though much of it is a theatrical reenactment of your diary, is unique in that it's a new skill that uses old skills to refine itself.

Reflections within reflections within reflections...

For example, imagine for a moment that you're having an OOBE. You wait until you reach the second phase of sleep and induce the OOBE by conjuring up the feeling of riding a rollercoaster. Suddenly, you feel yourself rocking back and forth. Heavy vibrations flood your body, and a buzzing sound fills your ears. Before you know it you're up and out! You look around your room and everything is as it should be, save for the occasional appearance of a dream scenario. There's just one problem:

You can't seem to fly away from your physical body!

The reason you're anchored to your mortal coil may be any number of things. In this case, your subconscious mind presents you with a dream image of a vast body of water. You approach it and begin swimming. Suddenly, you find you're able to fly! The water vanishes and you're soaring high above the roof of your house.

What's happened is that, because you've never actually flown before, the closest activity your mind could conjure that resembles flying was the act of swimming. So you used your former experience with rollercoasters to get up and out, as it were. You then used your former experiences of swimming to fly away. Or, to put it more technically, you used the process of consolidating skills (dreams) to tap into learned skills to support the learning of a new skill. In this case it was OOBE.

Reflections within reflections within reflections...

But what's going on inside your brain when all this is taking place? In *Behind the Veil*, I discussed the *Five Basic Brainwaves* and their corresponding subjective experiences. Here, I'd like to focus on three specific brainwave phenomena called *K-complexes, Sleep-spindles* and *PGO-waves*. Since I'm not a sleep specialist, 1 won't be tangling you up in convoluted dissertations on synapses and neural firings along calcium channels in the brain (ahem, and so forth). Instead, I'll limit my focus (as always) to the experiential aspects of these things. After all, that's where all the fun is!

What are K-complexes?

According to the book, *Neurology Secrets (Fifth Edition),* a *K-complex* is a high-voltage diphasic slow wave that may be preceded or followed by a spindle burst, maximally expressed in the frontocentral regions of the brain bilaterally.

In layman's terms, this means that a *K-complex* is like the trough of a wave and a *Sleep-spindle* is like the crest. We'll discuss *Sleep-spindles* in a moment. For now, let's take a closer look at *K-complexes* and how they might be experienced by a Conscious Sleeper.

When brainwaves are recorded on an Electroencephalograph (EEG), *K-complexes* appear primarily during the second stage of Non-Rapid Eye Movement (**NREM**) sleep, and are more prevalent during the first two sleep cycles in a night's rest. At this time, the brain is still responsive to external stimuli and *K-complexes* tend to multiply in the presence of external sounds, touch and changes in light patterns. Should you awaken someone at this phase of the sleep cycle, the subject may insist that he or she wasn't asleep. Some scientists speculate that *K-complexes* evolved to be responsive to external stimuli in order to serve as warnings of approaching predators while sleeping.

Another theory holds that *K-complexes* perform a sedating function, effectively turning off the analytical mind so that the brain can begin its process of consolidating memory. My own experience bears this out and, in just a moment, I'll offer my own take on this theory.

At any rate, once the sedative power of *K-complexes* takes hold, the process of memory consolidation begins. This neurological construction project begins with the appearance of *Sleep-spindles*.

What are Sleep-spindles?

Here's what *Tuck Sleep* has to say about *Sleep-spindles*:

> "Researchers believe Sleep-spindles represent periods of time where the brain inhibits mental processing in order to keep the person in a tranquil state. By keeping the person in a tranquil state, the sleep cycle can continue, and the person can transition to the next stage of deep sleep." (TuckSleep.com)

That sounds an awful lot like the function of *K-complexes*, yes?

Though I'm not a sleep specialist, I strongly believe *K-complexes* and *Sleep-spindles* are two parts of the same movement. They are the *Yin* and *Yang*, the valley and the peak, the trough and the crest of the same brainwave phenomenon. In my own experience, I've noticed a pattern during stages one and two of my own sleep cycle. This pattern convinces me that my theory is correct, but its credibility ultimately relies on future scientific research. I'll discuss the experiences that led to my theory in just a moment. In the meantime, let's hear more of what recent science says about *Sleep-spindles*:

> "Fast spindles (13–15 Hz) occur in the centroparietal part of the brain, while the frontal brain produces slow spindles (11–13 Hz). Increased spindle activity occurs at the onset and outset of light sleep." (TuckSleep.com)

For those who have no idea what these egghead scientists are talking about, here's a short list of the basic functions of the Frontal and Parietal areas of the brain:

Frontal lobe

- Personality, behavior, emotions
- Judgment, planning, problem solving
- Speech: speaking and writing (Broca's area)
- Body movement (motor strip)
- Intelligence, concentration, self-awareness

Parietal lobe

- Interprets language, words
- Sense of touch, pain, temperature (sensory strip)
- Interprets signals from vision, hearing, motor, sensory and memory
- Spatial and visual perception

With me so far? Yes? Good! Let's hear more from the eggheads:

> "Sleep spindles begin to develop once an infant has reached six weeks of age and may explain why babies twitch in their sleep. EEG typically will display sleep spindles immediately after muscle twitching." (TuckSleep.com)

Since the *Sleep-spindles* located in the Frontal brain tend to be slower, could it be that their function is to sedate the analytical part of the brain? In other words, the part of the mind that is capable of *Lucidity*. And could it be possible that the *Sleep-spindles* found in the Parietal area of the brain are faster because their function is to discharge residual kinetic energy to prepare for *Sleep Paralysis*?

I believe this may account for why the first and second stages of sleep are the most potent times for OOBE. Energy that would otherwise be spent in Gross Body activities can now be employed in dream activities, and even OOBE (if you know how).

Whereas *K-complexes* "stun" the sleeper, slow-wave *Sleep-spindles* "sedate" the sleeper. This paves the way for fast-wave *Sleep-spindles* to release excess kinetic energy and do a quick run-through of recent data to consolidate. In my opinion, this accounts for microbursts of dreaming experienced during light sleep (e.g., hypnagogia, hypnic jerks and twitches).

As an aside, I refer to the subjective experience of *K-complexes* and *Sleep-spindles* poetically as *The Sleep Serpent*. Like a snake with potent venom, these sedating brainwaves render dream Lucidity impotent. This is not to imply that these brainwaves are toxic, only that you have to learn how to surf them. Just as you can gradually become immune to snake venom by injecting small amounts of it, so too can you become immune to the sedative power of *K-complexes* and slow-wave *Sleep-spindles*. The secret is, in my experience, a mystery pertaining to the adrenals, hormones and retraining of attention. But that's another story…

Before I share the experiences and experiments which led to these theories, there's one more brainwave we need to discuss.

What are PGO-waves?

It's difficult to find a straightforward definition of *PGO-waves*, at least one that doesn't leave you cross-eyed. Generally speaking, *PGO-waves* occur at the tail-end of **NREM** sleep and at the start of **REM**. *K-complexes* and *Sleep-spindles* have accomplished their stun-and-sedate mission, and your physical body is now completely paralyzed. This is a necessary step for both Conscious and Unconscious sleep. With your physical body out of the way, its projected double can come out and play. This neurological doppelganger is called the Subtle Body.

At this phase of the sleep cycle, a group of cells, called *Cholinergic* cells, begin firing upwards to the higher regions of the brain and down the spinal cord. The net effect of this neurological tango is twofold. On the one hand, the emotional and sensory areas of the brain become activated. On the other hand, the nerve-plexus responsible for physical movement are stimulated. Despite this kinetic stimulation, however, the body is now in sleep paralysis. Besides a few myoclonic twitches and hypnic jerks, the Gross Body is dead to the world. Instead, the motor impulses are now passed on to the Subtle Body and you can now run, fly, have sex, and breathe under water. Why? Because you've now passed the *Veil of Tears* and have entered the *Veil of Dreams*.

PGO-waves also appear to play a role in image-stabilization. Not just in dreams, but in creative visualization, fantasy and hallucinations. *PGO-waves* strobe rapidly, kicking up a dust cloud of paradoxical images and emotions. This is fertile soil for creative inspiration, spiritual epiphany, and psychological insight. Evidence suggests that many poets, painters, musicians and even schizophrenics spin their webs using *PGO-waves* for yarn.

My Little Experiments

The moment I learned about *K-complexes, Sleep-spindles* and *PGO-waves* I immediately intuited what they were. I plan on one day recording and submitting my findings using my very own EEG machine.

In the meantime, I've carefully monitored my sleep cycle over the years and have achieved a good working knowledge of its architecture. I can tell, for example, when I'm entering the first and second phases of sleep. Depending upon factors such as how hard my workday was, how stressed I am, or how much caffeine or alcohol I've consumed, I can even consciously access the third stage of sleep fairly regularly. But before I could consciously access stage three sleep successfully, I spent about five years tapping into it by accident during the hypnopompic phase of sleep (beginning stage of waking).

I'll never forget the first time I experienced *PGO-waves* consciously. It was about 3:00 or maybe 4:00 am. I became Lucid in the middle of a dream and noticed, to the left of me, a field of sunflowers. The dream started shaking and I stabilized it by employing what I call *The Hitchhiker Method.* This works by fastening your attention onto a dream-object, sensation, sound or smell and holding onto it for dear life. This allows you to surf the already present *PGO-waves* and assists them in their purpose of stabilizing dream images.

The next thing I knew I was taken up into a blizzard of fantastical images. These oscillated at a frequency that resembled the rapid flicker-rate of a strobe light. Lucid Dreams blended with OOBE and I was able to control every nuance of the narrative (Dream Control).

I've had similar experiences during the hypnagogic phase of sleep, but that pesky Sleep Serpent often bested me in battle.

K-complexes and *Sleep-spindles* are, in my opinion, responsible for the mind's tendency to believe the absurdities of many dream scenarios. *PGO-waves* have also been shown to be responsible for this confusion. However, due to the fact that **REM** sleep resembles wakeful consciousness, it's easier to become Lucid while dreaming than Pellucid during **NREM.** In fact, scientists refer to **REM** sleep as "paradoxical sleep" for this reason.

As the years rolled on, I gradually learned to detect the signs of approaching *K-complexes, Sleep-spindles* and *PGO-waves.* For example, have you ever seen flashes of light behind your eyes as you're falling asleep?

Those are *PGO-waves…*

Have you ever felt like you were falling, only to snap out of it with a sudden jolt?

Those are fast-wave *Sleep-spindles…*

Or perhaps you've felt yourself "drifting off" into reverie. You're still vaguely aware of your surroundings, but you feel disembodied.

Those are *K-complexes…*

Have you ever been to a hypnotherapist? You know that part where the doctor says, "Your eyelids are getting heavier…"?

Those are slow-wave *Sleep-spindles…*

I've gotten to the point where I'll bring myself to the threshold of light and deep sleep. From there, I'll consciously alternate between light and deep sleep, or awake and asleep in general. My purpose in doing this little dance is to acclimate myself to the subtler nuances of these transitions.

The cool part about learning how to consciously surf these bioelectric brainwaves is that it amounts to a sort of Tao of Conscious Sleep. It's *Sleep Yoga* at its most scientific. It's *Qigong* at its most scientific. If we can honor the insights and practices of the ancient Wisdom traditions and wed them to modern scientific research, we'll be left with an Integral approach that honors the discoveries of the past, the technologies of the present, and the breakthroughs of the future.

In such a world, what more proof would you need of the magical and miraculous? Speaking of proof, let's take a look at some of the more common experiences that we're likely to share with them.

(5)

Conscious Sleep: Some of the Experiences You Might Have

Merging States of Awareness

It's impossible to make rules for everyone, but there are some very common experiences shared by all Veilers. One thing you can expect to experience is an ever-increasing merger between your sleep and awake states. To give one example, you'll notice that you're no longer prone to believe dream-stuff the way you used to. The typical scenario of having a profound dream which we believe to be real, regardless how absurd the dream might be, begins to fade, and you stop buying into them so easily.

It's difficult to describe this transition if you haven't experienced it for yourself. You could be having a dream in which you're flying and suddenly start to fall to the Earth, for example, but instead of waking up in a cold sweat you'll probably become Lucid and wake up calmly. This is the result of having familiarized yourself more with the in-between states between waking and sleeping. Whether Lucid or not, your consciousness gradually becomes seamless, and these so-called altered states of awareness become much like changing into different clothes, but clothes from your own wardrobe.

You'll also notice that 'reality checks" start to happen of their own accord, both in your dreams and while awake. That is, you'll spontaneously scan your environments for signs that you might be dreaming. You might also begin to notice which foods and supplements positively and negatively impact your Conscious Sleep.

Another common occurrence for Veilers at the intermediate skill-level is what I call *Dream Reticence.* On the most basic level, *Dream Reticence* occurs when Lucidity has been achieved, but the dreamer has trouble taking an active role in the dream narrative. This isn't to be confused with Pellucid Dreaming, although they're related in some fundamental ways.

Pellucidity is a function of the Causal Body and *formless* state. Even when dreams are present, the Pellucid sleeper is content to rest in the energetic root of the dream itself rather than its various contents. *Dream Reticence,* on the other hand, finds the dreamer conscious enough to want to participate in the dream, but unable to do so. Bluntly speaking, it's a form of Subtle Body lethargy.

People who play lots of video games often report this problem. Because they're so accustomed to viewing an alternate reality in the third-person, this spills over into a "gamer's" dream-life. Of course, this is only natural, as sleep is itself a necessary form of reticence. Because the brain and nervous-system aren't accustomed to the paradox of being awake and asleep at the same time, the sleeper is either pulled into unconsciousness, pushed into full wakefulness, or somewhere in between. That in-between state is what I'm calling *Dream Reticence.* Furthermore, this phenomenon isn't restricted to Lucid Dreaming, but also occurs during Astral Projection and even some psychedelic states (i.e., the "Astral Anchor" effect).

Lastly, as you progress to the more advanced levels of skill, you may also notice that, despite the presence of full Lucidity, you suddenly can't bring all five senses to bear on the dream or Astral experience. This began happening to me after about ten solid years of training. The only reason I can think of to explain this is that, precisely because your brain now knows that you're no longer situated inside your physical body, it sees no point in drawing a connection to it. For example, I used to enjoy having very powerful sexual experiences in my Lucid Dreams. These were so real that I was having "wet dreams" all the way into my late thirties! Then, suddenly, they stopped. I was still having Lucid Dreams that featured sexual encounters, but I suddenly couldn't feel the sensations associated with physical contact (bummer). When this happens, the dream either abruptly ends and I wake up, or I slip into an Astral Projection, or else I fall deep into the Pellucid state. To be sure, this doesn't always happen, and I still enjoy full-sensory Lucids and Astrals, but the Causal Body seems to become more and more prominent as the years progress. Then again, coming from a solely spiritual perspective, that's the entire point!

By far the most common complaint in the Oneironaut community pertains to the haphazard nature of Lucid Dreaming and OOBE. That is, someone will start their training and immediately have, say, a few Lucid Dream experiences, but then the whole thing comes to a screeching halt. What gives? Well, this is largely an issue of ingrained habit versus building a new one. In short, it's a *neuroplasticity* issue. We can think of this innate resistance to bringing awareness into the sleep cycle as two separate gardens located in two different places: one in the East and the other in the West.

Let's imagine that the garden in the East is facing West and gets exposure to sunlight only when the sun is setting, so the plants within it tend to grow toward the West. On the other hand, the garden in the West faces East and gets its sunlight mostly during the morning hours; its plants consequently grow toward the East. Both gardens are part of the same Earth and receive nourishment from the same sun but, due to their opposite locations, they each contain plants which grow in quite different ways.

Similarly, our neuropathways grow toward the sun of our awareness. Because our awareness is shining in different locations while we're asleep and awake, our neuropathways for each of these broad states are very different. However, when we attempt to merge conscious awareness with unconscious sleep, we run into this disparity and feel it as resistance. The art of being a Veiler has much to do with getting the gardens of our nervous system to grow toward the sun of our awareness *at the same time* and in the same direction.

Archetypal Themes

While reading the following section, I recommend you bear in mind *The Seven Categories of Dream* I discussed in *Behind the Veil*. We'll also discuss later how to use these categories to enhance your ability to remember your nightly dreams. For your convenience, I'll include the seven Categories here:

- The Hedonistic Dream.
- The Physio-Etheric Dream.
- The Premonitory Dream.
- The Biographical Dream.
- The Archetypal Dream.
- The Educational Dream.
- The Astral Dream.

The Terror at Shillry Hall

Another thing you're almost certain to experience is the emergence of Archetypal themes in both your Lucid Dreams and Astral adventures. These are universal themes shared by all humanity from time immemorial. Examples of Archetypes are *The Mother, The Father, The Guide, The Wise Old Man or Woman, The Lover, The Devil, The Hero, The Creator, The Trickster,* and so forth. What follows is a true account of such an Archetypal encounter during one of my own Lucid Dreams.

***

"This is what you get when you mess with my treasures!" the voice said from out of the dark. It was a man's voice, deep and hoarse. "Yeah, someone else's money!" it shouted.

This was how last night's Astral terror began. I became Lucid in my dream somewhere in the middle of the last phase of my sleep cycle, and I was walking down a hallway with my five-year-old daughter. She was holding my right hand and was carrying a toy in the other. I'd never seen this place before. When the hallway led us out into a spacious room with nothing in it, I knew we were lost.

Then the lights went out…

My daughter squeezed my hand because she's afraid of the dark. I knew this wasn't my real daughter, but a dream version of her. But at that moment I was awoken by my real daughter's erratic breathing.

She was having a nightmare…

I shook her lightly and kissed her cheek. She smiled and fell back asleep. I lay back down and reentered the Lucid Dream. I was right back where I left off! Only this time my wife was there, and my daughter was playing with the toy she was previously carrying. My wife was walking frantically back and forth, and the mood of the room was menacing.

That's when the dream version of my daughter started crying...

"Something's wrong, Papa!" she exclaimed. "Why are people acting weird here?"

I ran to her and held her tight and said, "This isn't real, honey. It's just a dream."

Then the lights went out again...

My daughter was yanked away from me violently. I knew it was a dream, but this disturbed me greatly. I tried to wake up but couldn't. I was in sleep paralysis.

"SHIT!" I yelled.

For a moment, I wondered if I had said that aloud in my sleep. I wanted my wife to wake me up. But then, I heard the dream version of my daughter crying, "Papa, where are you?!"

Laughter came from the dark, somewhere in the middle of the room. And then a woman's voice in broken English said, "This no dream. This real." Disembodied laughter again. "No it isn't. This is just a nightmare," I responded. "Papa. My heart hurts!" said my daughter, from the dark. "I'm coming, baby. Wait for Papa."

Just then, I came to my senses and realized that wasn't my daughter. The was a dream, after all. No sooner had I thought that than the voice changed into a little boy, singing:

"I can be whatever I want. I can do whatever I wish. But not you, no you're no good. So you're gonna stay right here."

I heard the sound of metal falling to the floor. The voice said, "Wanna play Pennies?" I stood up and strained to see in the darkness. Then I said (and it makes me laugh thinking it now), "What the fuck are you talking about?" The man's voice replied mockingly, "Here, have a fucking plum!"

Then it clicked:

These are all Plutonian themes! The treasures, the pennies, the fruit. So I responded, "What's next, a pomegranate?" I then heard a little boy laughing and a man call him from somewhere to the right of me, "Stop it, Joseph! There are rules at Shillry Hall."

I was then awoken by the extremely loud sound of a woman's laughter. I sat straight up in my bed and whispered loudly, "Leave me the fuck alone you bastards!" My wife startled and said, "It was just a dream." But I could see, using Auric sight, ink black blobs of energy darting all over the place. The bedroom door was open, and I could see my living room clearly. Dark blobs of light all over.

I lay awake for the rest of the night…

I pondered the symbols of the dream. It was what I call an Astral Dream, with Astral (impersonal) elements blending with personal (dream) ones. The obvious Plutonian theme startled me. Even the name "Shillry Hall" sounded like "Shilling Hall", a "Shilling" being a form of currency.

Stewart Bell's Remote Viewing Experience

It's also extremely common to have experiences that are not explainable using the currently accepted scientific model: predicting the future (premonitions), reading another person's mind, seeing auras around living and inanimate objects, being in two places as the same time (bilocationality), and so on.

To give a personal example, the man who wrote the *Foreword* to *Behind the Veil* had a "remote viewing" experience in which he saw me at my place of work. He was in Europe at the time and I was in upstate New York! He had an Astral vision of me standing in front of a big white house shouting, "City?! I'm crawling down the big black suit?!"

Sounds like nonsense, doesn't it? But here's the amazing part:

The day before I was in fact standing in front of a big white house. I was doing the drywall inside the house. The key broke inside the lock to the front door so I went to the back of the house and crawled into the basement to look for stairs leading up into the house.

There were none…

There were also no lights. Just a small dark sooty, creepy basement. I shouted aloud, "Really?! I'm crawling down this black sooty basement right now?!"

Sounds an awful lot like, "City?! I'm crawling down the big black suit?!"

Energy connects us all to each other like an invisible web. Establish a connection or uncover a previous existing one and the possibilities are truly endless. Luckily, we have a direct pipeline to these connections. It's been called by many names in many tongues throughout history. Regardless what name you choose to call it, you can directly encounter the source of these subtle connections through Conscious Sleep. In the following section, we'll explore what it means to redefine the act of sleeping as a sacred act.

(6)
The Temple of Your Bed: The Sacred Ritual of Sleep

Whether you do or don't experience any of the phenomena described above, it's important to cultivate an attitude of sanctity around the act of sleeping. This empowering art of Conscious Sleep seems lost to modern man, but is an integral part of life in many ancient civilizations.[1] Arrange your sleeping space in a manner that reflects this attitude. Whether it's saying a prayer before you retire for the evening, performing a protection ritual, placing a dream-catcher or religious icon over your bed, or what have you:

Make it a habit to approach those eight hours of rest with joy, respect, gratitude, and even excitement.

Also, whenever possible, clean your sleeping space thoroughly. Treat it like a temple. It is! In fact, you could do worse than to decorate it as such. Incense, essential oils, and the positioning of your bed; all of these are excellent ways to signal to your subconscious mind that you intend to take a Sabbath for the next eight hours.

One of the (shall I say?) tragedies of the current Lucid Dreaming craze is that the many ways even non-Lucid dreams can be used get swept under the rug. For example, even non-Lucids can be used to speed up the learning of new skills. To give one example, let's suppose you're learning a new language. If you can make it a point to increase your Dream Recall via journaling and other methods, you'll soon discover that your dreams are communicating insights that make

---

[1] In Ancient Greece, Egypt, and the Middle-East "sleep temples" existed as hospitals for the soul. Ruins of these dream temples can still be seen today in the UK.

learning the new language much easier.[2] Dream Recall is the first step to becoming Lucid. Not only that, but if you take dreaming completely out of the equation and focus on the **NREM** phase of sleep (non-dreaming), you're left with an extremely fertile area for healing, reprogramming, and even spiritual enlightenment.

It's also important to get into bed consciously. Before you lie down, make sure that the bedroom isn't too hot or cold. Whether you're sleeping on an incline, as per some of the exercises in this series, or simply lying on your back (recommended unless health issues prevent it), bring all of your senses into the act. Feel your mattress becoming warmer with your body-heat. Be mindful of your body-weight giving in to gravity and assist this process by surrendering all muscular tension with each exhalation of breath (breathing naturally). If you're burning incense or oil, be sure to use a calming scent such as lavender or sandalwood. Also, keep your bedroom temple as dark as possible, as light will suppress the production of the sleep-hormone, *melatonin*.

A question I am asked a lot is, "Should I fall asleep to music? Or should my bedroom be completely silent?"

The answer is: *It depends upon your goal for the night.*

Sometimes I fall asleep listening to an audiobook and incubate my Lucid Dreams to fit the narrative of the story! On other nights, I put earplugs in my ears, make my bedroom as dark as possible, and focus exclusively on Pellucid Sleep. Music, if I do decide to listen to it as I fall asleep, is typically classical or instrumental movie scores. My own experience has taught me that music that contains lyrics serves more as a distraction than an aid to Conscious Sleep of any variety. Still, and as always, experiment on your own and see what works best for you.

---

[2] The *SCT* method of enhancing Dream Recall utilizes the Seven Categories of Dream (listed earlier in this section and elaborated fully in *Behind the Veil*). Because dreams are mostly biographical, it's best to begin your attempts at recall by scanning the prior night's dreams for personal themes. Once you've caught the "scent," you may then proceed to cycle through the other six Categories.

CHAPTER TWO

LIFTING THE VEILS:
STATES, STAGES AND STRUCTURES
OF CONSCIOUSNESS

(1)

The Primary, Secondary and Tertiary Veils of SCT

In *Chapter One,* we learned that the *Five Primary Veils* may be
thought of as the cognitive sheaths that separate your egoic awareness
from the "worlds" experienced by your Gross, Subtle and Causal
"bodies." I put "worlds" and "bodies" in quotation marks because

these Worlds are really just *perception zones*—environments of greater or lesser subtlety your "I" navigates while occupying any of the Three Bodies. To the extent that they're actual Worlds apart from perception remains to be seen. In the meantime, the three Bodies may be thought of as the vehicles we use to navigate the five Worlds represented here as five Veils. Furthermore, these Bodies are really not three distinct bodies, but rather limbs of an organic and unified *bodymind.* For example, your dreams aren't separate from the rest of your mind, your mind isn't separate from your brain, your brain isn't separate from your physical body, your physical body isn't separate from your vital force (*Qi*), your vital force isn't separate from your breath. And so forth…

It's worth repeating that the apparent mathematical discrepancy between the *Five* Primary Veils and the *Three* Bodies is one of convenience and personal preference. It's just my preferred way of slicing the pie, as it were. The discrepancy centers around how to qualify the Subtle Body. You'll recall that the Subtle Body is a blanket term for the subtler aspects of the Gross Body and includes the *Mental, Astral, Dream* and *Etheric* aspects of the overall bodymind. Some systems prefer to delineate these as bodies in their own right, and they have their reasons for doing so. In my own system, I choose to include these aforementioned items under the blanket term "subtle body," and I do this because it's far more convenient and truer to the experience of most people to say that anything not directly accessed via physical motion is of a *subtler* nature, but not entirely separate from the Gross (physical) Body. Also, when you consider the fact that these Veils and their commensurate Bodies are really just different shades and grades of a singular process, it becomes clear that different systems slice that pie to accommodate the specific area of experience with which they deal. My system deals mostly with the Subtle Body, and I've sliced the "pie" accordingly.

There are as many versions of the Veils as there are systems, and some have more or fewer Veils depending upon how much ground is covered by a system. The *Five Primary Veils* and the *Secondary* and *Tertiary* veils of *SCT* are the ones with which I'm personally familiar—that is, I've experienced them in concrete and consistent ways throughout my life.

The *Five Primary Veils* represent the "holonic" structure of *The Perennial Philosophy*. Arthur Koestler was the first to coin the term "Holon". Basically, a Holon is a whole that's also part of a larger whole. To give one example, a quark is part of a particle which is part of an atom which is part of a molecule which is part of a cell which is part of an entire organism. These all transcend and include each other, like a series of nests within nests. This is what distinguishes a *Holarchy* from a *Hierarchy*. A Hierarchy is a ladder, whereas as Holarchy isn't just a ladder; it's also the wood the ladder's made from. The universe is one of Holarchy, not Hierarchy.

The *Five Primary Veils* and their corresponding Bodies are also *Holarchical*. As such, each Veil transcends and includes its predecessors. The *Veil of Breath* transcends and includes the *Veil of Tears*; the *Veil of Dreams* transcends and includes the *Veil of Breath* and the *Veil of Tears,* and so on down the spectrum.

It's important to understand that the Gross, Subtle and Causal Bodies also constitute a *Holarchy*. As I've pointed out, the three broad states of Waking, Dreaming and Dreamless Sleep that these Bodies generate, respectively, can be experienced while one occupies any of the three Bodies. Still, each of these three broad states of awareness has a Body to which it's particularly suited. The wakeful state is usually (but not always) limited to the Gross Body. The dreaming state is usually (but not always) limited to the Subtle Body. And the dreamless state is usually (but not always) limited to the Causal Body. As should by now be obvious, the goal of *SCT* is to awaken to and within all three Bodies and Veils. Once this begins to happen, the student can then venture into the various combinations and nuances of these existential modes of being. What are these other modes, you ask? They are the *Secondary* and *Tertiary Veils*.

The Secondary and Tertiary Veils

The *Secondary Veils* are really just the subtler expressions of the *Primary Veils*. They represent a further descent down the Rabbit Hole found in each respective World. Not only that, but they also represent the more intermediate to advanced talents of the Three Bodies. When they first appear, they do so in an uncontrolled and haphazard fashion.

But with time and practice, these capabilities will become stable traits of your overall consciousness as a Veiler.

Because the *Secondary* and *Tertiary Veils* are really just extensions of the *Primary Veils*, I find it useful to illustrate them as the cognitive echoes and refinements of the *Primary Veils,* issuing from them like waves, streams and rivers (see diagram below). Although they may not necessarily represent a Holarchy in their own right, the *Secondary* and *Tertiary Veils* may in fact become so in time. This seems to be how novel "emergents" occur in Evolution. As more and more people utilize and co-create these areas of the bodymind, posterity inherits them as part of their own anatomy and potentialities.

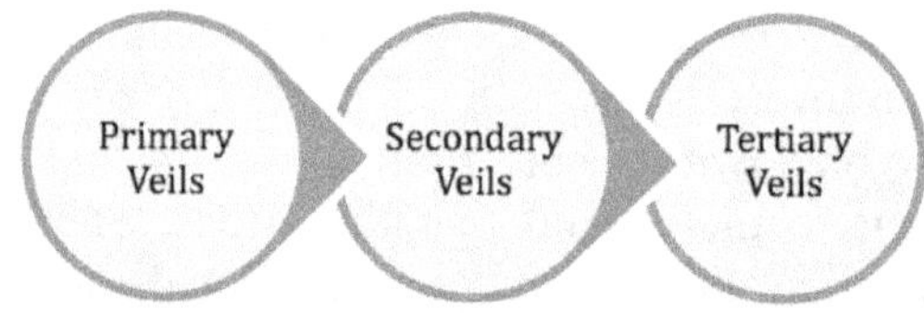

So, what type of experiences are found on the *Secondary* and *Tertiary Veils* that aren't found on the *Primary Veils*? Well, for starters, the phenomenon called "false awakening" is a common *Secondary Veil* experience. False Awakening occurs when you awaken inside a dream, believe yourself to be actually awake, only to discover that you're still dreaming. That's an example of a *Secondary Veil* extending from the *Veil of Dreams.* Or, when you discover how to alter your biochemistry with the force of your mind or Will: that's an example of a *Secondary Veil* extending from the *Veil of Tears.* Or, when you access, not only the "real-time zone" during OOBE, but also the Astral Plane: that's a *Secondary Veil* extending from the *Veil of Ghosts.* Or, when you access the so-called Akashic Records and acquire information about the past, present and future of the world: that's a *Secondary Veil* experience extending from the *Veil of Bliss.* Or, when you have a Kundalini experience, or a peak-experience during sex: that's a *Secondary Veil* experience extending from the *Veil of Breath.*

Secondary Veil experiences are oftentimes (but not always) the direct result of one or more of the *Primary Veils* intruding upon and influencing the Body you happen to be occupying at the time. For example, the experience called *déjà vu* is the result of the *Veil of*

Dreams briefly opening up and intruding upon the Gross Body behind the *Veil of Tears.* Another example is found in "premonitions," or the ability to divine the future. These most often occur in dreams and are therefore the *Veil of Bliss* opening up and intruding upon the Subtle Body behind the *Veil of Dreams.*

It's important to understand that the phenomena associated with the Veils, Bodies and States all flow both ways, with the *Veil of Bliss* often erupting into the *Veil of Tears* or the *Veil of Dreams.* Similarly, the *Veil of Dreams* often erupts into the *Veil of Ghosts,* and so on. In the same way, the *Secondary* and *Tertiary Veils* often erupt into, and are largely influenced by all the other Veils and Bodies. We experience this whenever our thoughts affect our mood, our mood affects our digestion, and so forth. The scientific term for this is Upward and Downward Causation, and this mechanism can even be the cause or cure of many diseases. So the Veils and their corresponding Bodies represent a spectrum of *states* of consciousness and the environments they generate and inhabit. The goal of *SCT* is to turn them into stable *traits* of consciousness.

(2)
STATES versus TRAITS of Consciousness

The three broad states of Waking, Dreaming and Dreamless Sleep are like the weather or seasons of your consciousness. Just as the four seasons of Nature progress and circle back around again every year, so too do the three states of Waking, Dreaming and Dreamless Sleep cycle and repeat every twenty-four hours in a healthy human being. Like the four seasons, the three general states of consciousness don't really develop or evolve. That is to say, they tend to be pretty discrete states of consciousness without any real developmental trajectory. There is, of course, the occasional merging of states but, for the most part, they're taken for granted and cycle in a fairly predictable fashion.

What research does seem to suggest, however, is that once these states are handled *consciously,* they do show a definite pattern of development. That is, in everyone who actually makes the effort to make these states *conscious,* the three states tend to evolve. For instance, look at the very structure of Buddhist meditation. The Sanskrit word, "buddha", means "awakened one." Thus, Buddhism can be translated as the religion of *wakefulness*. Literally every sect of Buddhism has this emphasis on wakefulness in common. Whether meditation is performed on one's breathing, or being alert to everything one says and does while awake, or focusing wakefulness on one's dreams, wakefulness is the very heart of Buddhist discipline.

When you focus on the wakeful state and try to be more alert to it, the developmental pattern might proceed as follows: First, you might become more efficient in your everyday tasks. From there, you might become more in tune with your physical organism and detect sickness before it manifests as physical symptoms. From there, you might become more socially engaged and, perhaps, a better listener. In extension, when you apply that wakefulness to the dream state, the first thing that might happen is better Dream Recall. That is, you can remember your nightly dreams when you wake up with more efficiency and accuracy. The second thing that might happen when you bring awareness into your dreams is you may start Lucid Dreaming. And then you may proceed to being able to control your dreams and decide what dreams you'd like to have (dream incubation). From there, you may start to have what I call "astral dreams," which are really just out of body experiences within the dream Realm. Finally, when you apply this wakefulness to Dreamless Sleep, the first thing you may notice is that you can witness your dreams and have astral forays into the dream plane without getting caught up in them (Pellucid Dreaming). From there, you may notice that you're completely absorbed in pure Being: *consciousness without content.* Lastly, you may begin to experience true OOBE into the "real-time zone"—that is, instead of Astral forays into the world of dreams, you might experience the actual physical environment.

After many years of experience, I've noticed that this development flows both ways in a *top-down* and *bottom-up* fashion. For example, when dreams enter the waking state, you might notice an increase in creativity. Then you might notice that your psychic gifts are increasing. Or, if the Dreamless Sleep state starts to erupt into the Awake state, you might notice a background feeling of deep contentment and emotional tranquility.

Each one of these developing states of consciousness are no longer *states* once you occupy the three bodies that correspond to them. In other words, by consciously engaging the three states of Waking,

Dreaming and Dreamless Sleep, you've begun to transform passing *states* of consciousness into enduring *traits*.

Also worth mentioning is that these three developing states/traits of consciousness have their own unique pathologies. For instance, if the dream state erupts into waking consciousness, you might have a psychotic break if you're prone to mental illness. Or, if the Dreamless Sleep state erupts into waking consciousness, you may start to experience Dissociative Personality Disorder (DPD). I believe that one of the guiding intuitions that led to scientific experimentation with psychedelics as a means of studying schizophrenia was the hunch that schizophrenics are probably dreaming while awake.

The four points I'd like you to remember are:

1. The three broad states of Waking, Dreaming and Dreamless Sleep are transitory. Think of them as three "seasons" of consciousness.
2. The Gross (waking), Subtle (dreaming), and Causal (dreamless sleep) Bodies are capable of development.
3. These three general states of awareness can flow both ways and interact with each other.
4. Each of the three broad states of awareness contain their own potential for pathology.

If you look closely at any system of spiritual development, any sport, psychology or practice, you'll soon notice that they all focus on the cultivation of one of these three basic states of consciousness. Sometimes a system will focus on all of them, or only two in combination, but they all focus on the creative and conscious development of either Waking, Dreaming and/or Dreamless Sleep. In other words, any given system of *State Training* emphasizes either the Gross, Subtle or Causal Body (or all of them).

Perhaps a few examples will clarify this point.

1. **Athletic Sports**: These place an obvious emphasis on the Gross Body (waking state). In rare cases, an athlete will borrow from another state of consciousness to bolster Gross Body performance. Examples of this are prayer, meditation, guided imagery, and semen retention (accumulation of sexual energy). Some athletic sports, such as *Taijiquan* or Judo, contain the entire spectrum of states in their regimen.

These martial arts represent a complete Yoga, including all three Bodies in their disciplines.

2. **Mysticism and Psychology**: Shamanic traditions, the mystical branches of many monotheistic religions, and even transpersonal psychology emphasize the Subtle Body (dreaming and astral experiences) in their work. Vision Quests, Astral Projection, Spirit Guides, and communion with God or Goddess are all examples of Subtle Body exercise. Oftentimes these, too, will borrow from other Bodies. Examples might include dietary observances (Gross Body), mindfulness meditation (Causal Body), and so forth.

3. **The Arts**: Dance, music, painting, sculpting and poetry are just a few examples of how the Arts utilize and express the three broad states of consciousness. Zen painting and poetry, for example, attempt to capture the serene reflection of the Causal state in both image and word. Dancing hardly requires an example of how it works in terms of states of consciousness and the Bodies that house them. Sculpture, too, often amounts to an attempt to capture in form something from the Waking, Dreaming or Dreamless Sleep states. Music, by far the most ethereal and diaphanous of the Arts, attempts to do the same thing. Each of these arts emphasizes a specific state of consciousness, and often has to "borrow" from one or all of the others to make it work. After all, you can't play a piano unless you have fingers! And the music won't be worth listening to if you don't have a deep emotional or spiritual well to draw inspiration from. The same goes for any art you can think of.

SCT aims to train all three states of awareness by focusing on Gross, Subtle and Causal Body *fitness*. If you've practiced the *120-Days Curriculum* featured in *Behind the Veil,* you're already acquainted with this approach. If, however, you're new to *SCT,* the *Three-Body Fitness Program* offered in this volume will introduce you to this holistic approach to Conscious Sleep in an "Integral" fashion. In other words, you'll learn to exercise the Gross, Subtle, and Causal bodies at the same time.

(3)

The Benefits and Dangers of Conscious Sleep

As you gain proficiency as a Veiler, side-effects are common. Some are blessings, others can be rather unpleasant. In this section, I'd like to list some of the benefits and dangers associated with Conscious Sleep. Please remember that the following list of side-effects are generalizations, and everyone will experience some, none (rarely), most, or (rarely) all of them:

Wet dreams (urination and orgasm). Dizziness and a feeling of unreality during the day. Enhanced psychic abilities (auras, "spirits," clairaudience, clairvoyance). Enhanced internal dialogue. Increased sensory phenomena. Night-terrors. Feelings of oneness and bliss with no external cause. Reading other people's thoughts (yes it happens). Tremors and skin-crawling. Vertigo. Altered proprioception.

After I crossed the "psychic moat" in my twenties these things came back full-force. I had them in early childhood, seemingly from birth, but chronic fear and social alienation slammed the door shut by age sixteen.

In my many conversations with Oneironauts, Near Death Survivors and Psychonauts, I've encountered mixed feelings when it comes to the supposed dangers of Conscious Sleep. As you might expect, this isn't the case when discussing the many benefits of these practices. On the one hand, this is due to the fact that many individuals and groups gravitate toward Conscious Sleep in an almost religious way. Like most religions, you can't very well list the many dangers of a particular creed to its adherents without provoking their irritation. Similarly, many people are seeking the very opposite of danger when they approach, say, Lucid Dreaming or Astral Projection. These folks are, in fact, looking for an escape from pain and suffering through these practices. While I understand this plight, I most strongly disagree with it. Any attempt to altogether avoid the suffering of daily life—by any means—should serve as a red flag. It's one thing to use Conscious Sleep as a means of enhancing your life, but when used as a means of *escaping* life? Beware!

I'm reminded of an article my wife wrote about this type of spiritual escapism. The message contained in the essay is so pertinent to our present discussion that I'm compelled to share the entire article.[3]

Seeking the Spiritual Goody
by Christina Sportiello

The storms we face within are never stilled for very long. This fact becomes especially apparent when we attempt to silence them through various forms of meditation, Lucid Dreaming, Astral adventures, drugs and so forth. I used to love the power granted me through meditation and the cultivation of psychic abilities. I was addicted to it really, but now I see the whole thing in a different light. So earth-shattering has this realization been that part of me feels silly writing about it! Having said that, I still enjoy meditating. In fact, I enjoy it even more now that I'm not using it as a means, but rather, as an end in itself.

You realize some interesting facts when you travel to the moon and back. One such observation I have made is that *preferred* states of being will always be a divider within us. Let me repeat that, because it is at the heart of what I want to share:

Preferred states of being will always be a divider within us!

Why do we seek fulfilment somewhere other than right now? To put it bluntly, what makes us believe that our happiness is found in some preferred state of consciousness other than the one we occupy in this moment? The typical answer is: because we imagine that such a state will ease our suffering or boredom, and *that* is more important to us than finding meaning right where we stand! We will find it too, because we always find what we imagine we should when we search hard enough for it. Not only that, but when the desired result comes, it always seems to come from the Beyond, out of nowhere, but that is only an illusion. Nor does our preferred state of being belong to our individual selves alone. On the contrary! Our preferred state of being also belongs to others who are going, and have gone through a similar process. From time immemorial, human beings (and other animals) have been devising ways of escaping the suffering inherent to life. We

---

[3] Article used with permission.

then keep a record of what works, and pass it down to posterity orally, through the written word, through art, and our DNA. You have an "I", that is to say, YOU exist (like it or not); but there is also potential to be something other than what you currently are, but this "something other" is not divorced from who you are right now. In fact, when the new YOU arrives, it will happen in the Now; *tomorrow* always comes a *today*!

There is a timeline and, paradoxically, there is no timeline…

The simple but profound truth is that we seek a preferred state of being because there is an "escape artist" within us that dislikes suffering. Consequently, we feel peaceful for a time when we truly believe that we are separate from that which causes pain; when we are the immortal Atman, or soul, or the transcendent Witness. This is always the Escape Artist speaking, whether we know it or not. Realizations are not needed, rules are not needed. Rather, they are *conjured.* Why do we conjure something? Well, because we imagine we lack something! However, do we really lack anything in the moment? That is, when it comes to being alive and conscious, is anything other than that required for growth? Of course we need food, shelter, good health, and so on; but psychologically, spiritually, are we not already rooted in the very soil from which all growth occurs?

We are the one who watches even when we are not the one who watches…

This statement is not a realization. It comes from pure BEING. There cannot be one or the other. If you are anything at all you are still all of it, *preferred* or not. Valid or not. If you believe a lie, what matters is that you believe the lie. What matters is why you believe it. What matters is the symptom, valid or not. Making it unreal by choosing a preferred state changes nothing because we have negated the symptom, and more so, the cause. Yes, it can all change. Yes, it is transient. They do not have to be seen *as you* nor do they have to be seen as *not you,* the Observer or the Observed. If you are truly here-now, the question of where to find it never arises. Are you the watcher? Well, if you are really here, why does that even matter? Why does it matter if we are the actor or the stage? More importantly, why do you believe the answer or the role your mind comes up with? No matter what you come up with, it will not fix what you are trying to fix, not for very long anyway.

We cannot only be the part that manifests peace at the exclusion of discomfort. If we continue to choose only our preferred state of being then we will never discover our true nature, which is at once both individual AND collective.

Let us turn our faces to the wind and to the reality our minds produce when we do so.

(4)
The Tao of Conscious Sleep: Embryonic Breathing, Microcosmic Orbit, and Channeling Intensity

(**NOTE**: The following is a recap of four core practices of the *120-Days Curriculum* featured in *Behind the Veil*. These practices are Trance, Embryonic Breathing, Microcosmic Orbit, and Channeling Intensity. Because of their importance, I include them here, especially for those who are approaching my work for the first time.)

The Importance of Trance: The Wuji State of No-Extremity

The word "trance" immediately conjures up images of hypnotized subjects following the suggestions of a hypnotist. Or perhaps some Indian holy man sitting cross-legged in a cave, endlessly chanting mantras. However, the Trance that I'm referring to here is a transcendental state brought about by a cessation of the willful mind combined with a steady flow of attention.

What does this mean?

In the Zen Buddhist tradition, there's a practice known as *Zazen* that serves as a perfect example of what Trance is and how to enter it. Zazen is usually translated as "sitting for Zen." What exactly is Zen? Well, to put it plainly, Zen is the state where there's no separation between what you're doing, what you want to be doing, and who and where you are. In other words, if you're washing the dishes, then that's exactly what you're doing: *you're washing the dishes*. There's no hankering to *not* wash the dishes. In fact, you're so absorbed in washing the dishes that you *are* the act of washing the dishes.

The British philosopher, Alan Watts, once described Zen by giving the analogy of a rider and a horse. A good horse and a skilled rider are almost one body, and it's sometimes hard to tell who leads and who follows. Similarly, when you're practicing Zazen, you're literally *just sitting.* You're not "meditating" or "practicing" or "trancing" or really doing anything at all. You're just sitting there with whatever is or isn't arising in the moment. You're just *being.* If thoughts and emotions arise, you don't engage them, but rather you simply sit with them until there's no difference between you and what's arising. The Indian sage, Jiddu Krishnamurti, was referring to Trance when he advocated what he called "choiceless awareness" as "the first and last freedom," although he himself would probably shudder at the association. Still, if you can do this perfectly, then you enter the Trance state. From there, lots of interesting things can be done!

Acquiring the skill of Trance is not easy, and mastery depends upon a variety of factors. The two most common obstacles to entering Trance are physical discomfort and mental restlessness. Oftentimes a more creative approach is needed before one can "just sit." This is where "mindfulness meditation" can help.

In the mindfulness approach, you don't just sit passively like an immovable mountain of attention, but rather you actively notice and feel into all that's arising. In mindfulness methods, you bring an active curiosity to your thoughts and feelings without getting swept away by them. For example, if you feel restless and irritable during a meditation session, the mindfulness approach is to allow the restlessness without any censorship or attempt to eliminate it. Instead, observe the feeling of restlessness with an active and almost tactile curiosity that, without words, asks:

- Where is this restlessness arising?
- What effect is this restlessness having on my body?
- What conditions are giving rise to this restlessness?

And so on with anything else that arises during meditation.

Success in meditation of any variety is won the instant the practitioner stops trying to see the meditation session from the *outside.* What this means is that one ceases to objectify the moment, the *Now,* which is where meditation takes place. At first, depending upon the type of meditation you're doing, this requires an orientation process on the physical, mental, emotional and spiritual levels. It's like learning to drive a car. At first, you've got to be very aware of the stick-shift, the pedals, the steering wheel, and the rules of the road. After a while, though, you get to a point when you can just focus on driving the car, maybe listen to the radio, or have a conversation with someone in the passenger seat. Similarly, once you become accustomed to the physical posture of meditation, the proper breathing, the correct mental attitude, and so on, then you can simply meditate. Then you can focus on things like storing and circulating Etheric energy, deeper levels of absorption, and other forms of Subtle and Causal Body work. In Taoism, they call this the stage of "regulating without regulating." This simply means that now you can truly begin to meditate without having to check in to see if you're doing it properly, which only serves to divide your attention and, therefore, your energy.

However, you decide to enter it, the beauty of Trance is that it's just another word for meditation. Unfortunately, the word "meditation" has been given dozens of conflicting definitions. Truly, most of this confusion stems from a one-sided view of what meditation is and what its purposes are. The type of meditation you do depends upon your goals. For our purposes, there are two sides to meditation: A *Passive* side and an *Active* side. In other words, there's a *Yin* and a *Yang* to meditation, and doing one without the other is like eating without digesting your food.

So, the first tenet for acquiring the skill of Trance is *non-doing,* and there are a few ways to create the situation for non-doing to arise. In Taoist *Qigong* this is known as the "Wuji" state of No-Extremity. Another way of putting this is to say that energy isn't moving outward, but rather is pooling within and around your body. Because you're *being* rather than *doing,* your energies come to rest and begin to accumulate. Furthermore, when you successfully enter the Trance state, the Etheric part of your Subtle Body is *stimulated,* and your Astral Body is *loosened*; and once your Etheric energy is stimulated, it can be made to move and *breathe*! This is important, because when you lie down in preparation for Lucid Dreaming or Astral Projection your success is dependent upon your ability to enter this Trance state successfully and with minimal effort. If you make too much of an effort, then you'll interfere with the Trance state. If you make no effort at all then you'll just fall asleep. Remember, this isn't an unconscious state we're talking about here. Quite the contrary:

The state of Trance is like a flame of attention burning in a windless room.

When trying to grasp the Trance state it helps to know that *intention* isn't the same thing as *effort*. An intention carries its own energy, and that energy has a movement all its own. Effort, on the other hand, is a form of tension. Obviously, there's a place where effort is needed, but when it comes to attaining Trance, manipulating *Etheric Force,* or going Astral, effort only gets in the way.

Another way of looking at non-doing is that it loosens the grip of the **BETA** brainwave and allows for the smooth transition to **ALPHA, THETA, DELTA** and **GAMMA** brainwaves. In other words:

Trance is the key to behind the Veil access.

There are many situations when we enter Trance *naturally*—which is really the only way to enter it when you stop and think about it. Trance can't be contrived or premeditated, and it's only when this fact gets through the ego's thick head that one can truly begin to meditate. If you've ever lost track of time listening to the sound of the rain or staring at a sunset or into your lover's eyes, then you've experienced one version of the Trance state. The only difference is that, in meditation, you're including in this global attention your own thoughts, feelings and consciousness itself. So, the passive side of meditation is just a training in developing a deep enjoyment and appreciation for consciousness itself, for the simple feeling of being, for the mystery of being aware in the first place. Take this heightened feeling of "I AM" deep enough and you'll attain the continuity of consciousness.

Lastly, success in meditation is dependent upon your lifestyle. This includes your diet, your social life, your job, your overall well-being, and even how much sex you have! Like any other aspect of being a Veiler, meditation is an integral and holistic affair. If you truly want to access the deeper secrets of the following method, then there are a few things you'll want to seriously ponder and implement. Please note that everyone is different. Do your own research and experiments to find the right balance for your needs.

The first thing is diet. The best diet for the Etheric side of Subtle Body development is organic, non-GMO, gluten free, and low carbohydrate. Depending upon factors such as how labor-intensive your job or workout routine is, small but well-rounded meals are ideal. Also, too much caffeine is a no-no. Many seasoned Veilers will tell you that OOBE can be stopped in its tracks due to excessive caffeine intake.

I'm not saying that you've got to give up your morning cup of Joe; I love coffee myself! But if you're going to have a second cup, make it green tea instead. Alcohol doesn't tend to negatively impact dreaming, but it does delay it. Since alcohol has been proven to delay **REM** sleep, your dream work will begin later in the sleep cycle if you consume too much alcohol before bedtime. Not only that, but excess alcohol consumption also ties you to the lower Astral Planes. I find that if I go Astral after consuming alcohol, the exit-symptoms tend to be more pronounced and uncomfortable.

The second thing is your social life and the overall environment you find yourself in. Toxic relationships, an overly stressful lifestyle, lack of personal space is detrimental. This is a no-brainer. After all, too much on your mind distracts you from the moment, and lack of solitude means lack of training space. It also muddles your energy. As for your job, that's obviously a little more complicated and most of us can't just quit earning paychecks. So, the job thing is something we've all got to decide for ourselves.

Lastly, and this one's especially important for men past the age of thirty, too much ejaculation of semen drastically weakens the Etheric Body. I know, bummer, right? Be that as it may, it's quite true. Still, notice that I said it's *ejaculation* that weakens the Etheric force? I didn't say that *sex* weakens it! It took me a few years to grow to a point where I could enjoy sex without having to ejaculate every time or go without sex entirely for a prolonged period. Traditionally, a man must wait at least ninety days without sex before he can begin the following practices. Unfortunately, I'm not sure how—or if—this applies to women. The standard for men seems to be no more than two ejaculations in a thirty-day period, but everyone's got a different level of sexual force. Taoists call this natural level of Libido *Jing.* Some Taoist and Buddhist masters even claim to be able to orgasm without ejaculation!

As far as *Channeling Intensity* goes, you'll want to preserve your *Nerve-Force* because, one, the practice opens your energy channels. You want flow to match capacity. Two, Channeling Intensity can sometimes drain you. You want to reach a point where it does the exact opposite. That's when you know you've attained the goal. In the meantime, however, you'll want as much reserve energy as possible to recuperate. Let's begin!

Embryonic Breathing: How to Gather and Store Etheric Energy

In this section, I'm going to teach you the fundamental skill of gathering and storing *Nerve-Force*. This isn't necessary for all aspects of Conscious Sleep, but it's crucial for Astral Projection. It also plays a part in how lucid your Lucid Dreams are. Equally important is Embryonic Breathing's power to ground your energies and set the stage for Microcosmic Orbit practice which, among other things, serves to loosen your Astral Body and rebalance *Etheric* energy after experiencing powerful emotions. So let's get started!

Below are the instructions for Embryonic Breathing practice. Be sure to take your time, and don't expect quick results. If you follow the instructions to the letter, then you're sure to have success. Like all skills worth cultivating, Subtle Body development takes time, patience, perseverance and an indomitable will. I've been practicing Embryonic Breathing for ten years now and can personally attest to its power. I learned it from Dr. Yang Jwing Ming and highly recommend his work if you wish to cultivate higher levels of this skill. Please note that there are elementary, intermediate and advanced levels of these two practices, and two separate volumes would be required to fully discuss them. Here, I'm simply offering you the basics.

The Practice

The practice of Embryonic Breathing begins with the correct sitting posture. Proper posture—as well as the care and attention you give to it—accounts for at least half of the health and cultivation of your Etheric force. Therefore, a good Chiropractic adjustment to your spine can help to realign your Chakras. Please note that you don't have to sit in full *Lotus Posture* or bend yourself into a human pretzel to reap the benefits of this exercise, but if you're capable of Full Lotus then by all means use it. Just know that you'll be sitting in that posture for upwards of forty minutes or more. The following picture will give you an idea of how to sit for this practice:

Notice that the spine is straight, and the legs are crossed. Whenever possible, your hips should be elevated slightly above the level of your knees. Placing a cushion under your butt can accomplish this. This helps keep your spine straight by forming a tripod out of your torso and lower body. Your spine mustn't be held rigid or ramrod straight. Rather, the chest is slightly concave, and the thoracic region of the spine maintains its natural curve. Be sure that your tailbone is straight and in line with the lumbar region of your spine and not jutting out or collapsing inward. Your mouth should be closed, and your jaw drawn gently inward toward your throat. Your head should feel as though it's suspended from above by a string. This takes the weight of your head off your spine. Your shoulders should be in line with your hips and relaxed downward naturally. The tip of your tongue should gently touch the upper palate of your mouth. This connects the *Governing* and *Conception* Meridians, helps to silence inner chatter, and generates saliva to swallow at the end of the session. (Certain healing enzymes are generated during Embryonic Breathing that infuse the saliva, which is then swallowed for healing purposes.)

Your forearms should rest on your thighs and your hands should be placed in front of your navel.

If you're left-handed, place your left hand under your right, and *vice versa* if you're right-handed. The hands should feel relaxed and comfortable with your thumbs very lightly pressing each other. If you find this hand posture uncomfortable, you can simply let them rest folded on your lap. Folded in this manner your hands create a circuit of energy and helps to keep your awareness on your lower abdomen where Embryonic Breathing takes place. At first you may keep your eyes open slightly if you experience eye-twitching and other symptoms of a restlessness mind. Zen monks will sometimes meditate while facing a blank wall, looking at the floor a few feet in front of them, or focusing on the tip of the nose until the mind settles at which point they close their eyes.

That's it! Now you're ready to begin Embryonic Breathing meditation. When possible, face East while meditating in the morning and West when meditating at night. Later, as you advance in skill, you can practice while lying down in alignment with Earth's magnetic field. (For books offering a complete discussion on orientations for practice, see the *Bibliography.)*

Now that you're in the proper posture for Embryonic Breathing, the next step is to regulate your breathing. During this time, you still regulate your body to make it more and more relaxed. Be sure that you don't slouch or hunch over as this destroys the energetic integrity of the posture, puts undue pressure on your internal organs, increases the likelihood of falling asleep, and distracts the mind with discomfort.

Start by entering the Trance state by accepting all that is arising in the moment with a deep and total *YES* from the very core of your being. Really feel as though every problem has been solved and there's nowhere to go and nothing to do. Next, become aware of your breathing. Don't do anything with the breath at first, but simply watch its rhythm. Eventually, as your body adjusts to the training, you'll slowly deepen your breathing and establish a rhythm that's deep, silent, steady and slow. For now, simply breathe naturally and focus on *freeing* the breath by relaxing the physical structures around your lungs and diaphragm. Scan your body for any feeling of tension and, with every exhalation of breath, feel the tense areas relax and melt downward, following gravity. Do this until you feel completely relaxed. The attitude that you adopt here is very important. It should be one of alert curiosity as well as love and care for your bodymind.

Next, and without any force or rigidity, try to feel yourself becoming more and more physically motionless. Without sacrificing the relaxation and integrity of your posture, remain motionless like a stone Buddha. Focus on this stillness for a few moments while maintaining awareness of your breathing. Pay attention to the full course of breathing, including the turning points when inhalation becomes exhalation and when exhalation becomes inhalation. When your mind wanders (and it will), *gently* bring your attention back to your body and breath.

You'll probably notice that by simply becoming aware of your breathing you change its pattern. Allow this to happen. Take note of where your breathing is occurring—that is, are you breathing from your chest or from your abdomen? If you're breathing from your chest, try to relax your chest, upper back, neck and shoulders with a few natural exhalations. Remember, the goal here isn't to force your breathing into a certain pattern, but rather to relax and open the physical structures of your body to *allow* the breath to return to the same pattern seen in sleeping babies. This is especially true of the muscles, fascia, ribs, etc., surrounding your lungs and diaphragm. You want to relax these areas to allow your breathing to move from your chest to your abdomen without forcing it to do so. You want your lungs to be still and silent and to breathe using just your diaphragm. This takes a lot of practice and should *never* be forced.

(To help relax the physical cage surrounding your lungs, diaphragm and other internal organs, I suggest you purchase a quality magnesium supplement. The health benefits of magnesium are profound and its ability to assist in breathwork can't be overstated.)

Go ahead and enjoy this relaxed state for a few moments. Then, gently, and without "searching" for it, simply become aware of the fact of your *beingness,* your "I Am," the very fact of your consciousness itself. If there are any thoughts floating around in your mind at this point, notice that *you're not your thoughts.* Rather, you're the space in which thoughts are arising. Maintain awareness of your breathing and simply rest in the wonderfully obvious fact of your own presence. Most people feel this "I Am" in the center of their head. In Taoism, this is called the "Upper Dantian" and the location of *Shen* (spirit). Do this while focusing more on the inhalation phase of your breathing. This condenses *Qi* inward toward the *Yin* center of the Upper Dantian. Taoists call this spot the "Mud Pill Palace," which refers to the Pineal Gland. When you exhale, simply relax your concentration and allow the air to expel naturally.

The rhythm you're seeking to establish is a concentrated awareness of your "I" upon inhalation, and a relaxing of that concentration upon exhalation. Eventually, you'll begin to feel as though you're breathing from your Upper Dantian. This is called "Spirit Breathing" in Taoist *Qigong*. Continue this for a few moments and then, while maintaining an awareness of your "I" at the Upper Dantian, include in your awareness the center located at your sternum, called the Middle Dantian. Continue to focus more on the inhalation phase of breathing. This cools down the fire *Qi* located in this region as well as condenses *Qi* inward.

At this point, both your Upper Dantian and your Middle Dantian are breathing. Your "I" is concentrated upon inhalation with a simultaneous awareness of the center of your sternum. Upon exhalation, you relax your concentration. This should be done gently and without strain. Continue this for a few moments and then move your awareness downward to a point two finger-widths below your navel and about three finger-widths inward toward your spine. After you become proficient in this practice, you'll be able to locate this area due to the heat generated there. This area—called the Real Lower Dantian—is the place for storing Etheric energy and is classified as *Yang*. The Lower Dantian is the *Yang pole* and the Mud Pill Palace in the Upper Dantian is the *Yin pole*. They're in two different locations, but they function as one, much like the two poles of a battery.

Your attention must be 100% in the Lower Dantian for *Qi* to begin to accumulate there. Eventually, you'll come to feel that your whole body is breathing, condensing into your Lower Dantian with each inhalation. This process can also be reversed. That is, when exhaling, you expand Etheric force outward from the Lower Dantian. This is known as "Girdle Vessel Breathing." For now, though, we're interested only in storing *Qi* in the Lower Dantian. The sure sign of success is this: *As soon as you feel your physical breathing disappear and your Etheric Body starts breathing, this is true Embryonic Breathing.*

Now that you've successfully condensed *Qi* to the three Dantians, there's one more important thing you must do. There's a point on the pelvic floor between the genitals and anus called the *Huiyin* cavity. We in the West know it as the *perineum* and it's where we find the PC (pubococcygeus), BC (bulbocavernosus), and IC (iliococcygeus) muscles used in sex, urination and bowel movements. The *Huiyin* cavity is the meeting place of all four *Yin* vessels in your Etheric anatomy. The very word, *Huiyin,* means "meet *Yin*" in Chinese, and is the point of extreme *Yin* in your *Qi* network. In Embryonic Breathing practice, there are subtle movements of the *Huiyin* that assist in the storing, releasing and circulating of bioelectricity. The movements must be done correctly; otherwise *Qi* will stagnate there or else be released and used up instead of stored and circulated. This is one of the reasons why the ancient Taoist documents refer to *Huiyin* as "the Tricky Gate." There are two methods for *Huiyin* and breathing coordination: the Taoist method and the Buddhist method. The method which I'm going to teach you is the Buddhist method.

First, you need to locate your *Huiyin* muscles and learn to move them properly. To do this, stop the flow of urine in midstream. The goal is to use the *minimum* force required to do this. Once you've got the feeling for it, the next thing you'll need to do is carry that feeling over to your Embryonic Breathing practice and coordinate the movement of your *Huiyin* with your breathing.

The Buddhist method is more relaxed whereas the Taoist method is more aggressive. Because relaxation is so important when working with Etheric energy, it's best to begin with Buddhist breathing and then slowly advance to Taoist breathing methods.

In the Buddhist breathing method, your abdomen expands on inhalation and contracts on exhalation. At the same time, your lower back expands on inhalation and contracts on exhalation. The *Huiyin* cavity gently pushes down on inhalation and is gently held up on exhalation. The entire movement of the abdomen, lower back, and *Huiyin* is like that of a gently expanding and contracting balloon in coordination with your breathing. Breathe naturally and avoid strain or too much effort.

At this point, your attention should be completed absorbed in your Lower Dantian. Do not *concentrate* on your Lower Dantian, but rather allow your awareness to come to rest there. Please note the distinction. A good analogy is that of a pool of muddy water (the mind). If you disturb the water (with too much effort) then it'll only get muddier. If, on the other hand, you allow the mud to settle on its own, then the water will eventually become clear and you can drink it.

At this point I'd like to bring something important to your attention, as it holds the key to Lucid and Pellucid Dreaming: The state of awareness accessed in Embryonic Breathing practice is rooted in your Causal Body! This means that the state of Trance is just deep dreamless sleep, but with one major exception: You're aware!

The Indian Sage, Ramana Maharshi, used to say of the search for the true Self that if *it's not present in deep dreamless sleep then it's not real.* Well, since literally nothing is present in deep dreamless sleep, what could Maharshi possibly be referring to?

He's referring to the Causal Body...

The ability to remain conscious in deep dreamless sleep literally represents a fourth state of awareness. Since the basic three states of consciousness are Awake, Dreaming and Dreamless Sleep, then being aware during dreamless sleep is clearly a fourth state of consciousness. Not only that, it's the true key to achieving stable access to both Lucid and Pellucid Dreaming! Why? Because the Causal state is quite literally the root of your Self. If you can raise consciousness there, then you can raise consciousness in the Dream and Awake states as well. This is what the Zen classics mean when they say, "One simply sits quietly, doing nothing, and the grass grows by itself."

The "grass" is a reference to the Taoist concept of *Shen.* In Embryonic Breathing practice, you "raise your *Shen,*" for only then can your mind truly direct Etheric energy. For many years I had no idea what *Shen* was or what it referred to. After many years of practice, I slowly began to understand. On the one hand, you can't do anything directly to raise your *Shen,* as we've seen. Any form of *doing* isn't the root of your being. How could it be? The root of your being is just that: *being*! However, raising and protecting your lifeforce can assist in *feeding* your *Shen,* as we've already discussed. However, your *Shen*—which, in this context, is just another way of saying Causal Body—can't be approached directly by your ego. You can't will yourself to a heightened awareness of the Causal Body, but you can, by way of Trance, drop down into the ever-present ground of your consciousness like a stone falling to the ocean floor.

So how do you know when Embryonic Breathing has occurred? Anyone who's remained conscious during the transition from Awake to Asleep knows that awareness of one's breathing vanishes during the transition. When your breathing goes silent, and yet a tiny flame of awareness remains burning, then that is successful Embryonic

Breathing. At that point *Qi* begins to accumulate. Then it can be circulated. This is the beginning of Microcosmic Orbit practice.

Lastly, if you can get used to the pungent taste, I recommend you purchase *Shilajit* resin and place a small amount of it under your tongue before beginning Embryonic Breathing and Microcosmic Orbit practice. The spot under the tongue where saliva accumulates is known in Taoism as "Heavenly Pond." When saliva accumulates there, swallow it and the *Shilajit.* It's not necessary, but it's a powerful stimulator of *Yang Qi* and assists in its circulation. Be sure to get authentic *Shilajit!* Avoid powdered forms and stick to the natural resin form. Also, *Ashwagandha* works to relax the body, boost hormones, and enhance the effects of *Shilajit.* Pertaining to nootropics in general, understand that some of them help *raise* your *Shen* while others merely *excite* it. It's important to understand this distinction because, depending upon your purpose, you may want to raise but not excite your *Shen,* or *vice versa.* For example, *Ashwagandha* and *Shilajit* raise *Shen.* This is ideal for Embryonic Breathing meditation as you wish to have a raised but calm *Shen* for this practice. On the other hand, having a raised and excited *Shen* is ideal for Lucid Dreaming. By "excited" I don't mean hyper. Rather, an excited *Shen* is a *stimulated* subconscious. Therefore, nootropics and entheogens such as *Mugwort, Vinpocetine, Huperzine-A, Salvia Divinorum,* etc., are appropriate nootropics for those endeavors.

Microcosmic Orbit Meditation

Research being conducted on the **GAMMA** brainwave has proved that it's the wave experienced by Lucid Dreamers. Well, the pathway this bioelectrical current travels is the same as the Microcosmic Orbit. In Taoist terms, the **GAMMA** wave follows the so-called "fire path," also called the *Governing Vessel.* As we've seen, *Qi* (bioelectricity) travels this route up the back of the spine, over the head, and ends at the nose-tip. What this means is that the Microcosmic Orbit is in complete alignment with the **GAMMA** brainwave! Personally, I don't think this is a coincidence. What I'm proposing is that this ancient practice has the power to initiate, cultivate, and strengthen, not only Lucid Dreaming, but all forms of OOBE.

Now that you're familiar with Embryonic Breathing and have learned to store Etheric energy in the Real Lower Dantian, it's time to circulate that energy in the Governing and Conception Vessels. There are a few ways of doing this. The two methods which I'm going to share are known as the *Fire Path* and the *Wind Path.* The former method follows the path up the spine, around the head, and ends at the nose tip. The latter is simply a reversal of the Fire Path and moves upward from the Lower Dantian, up the front of the body and over the head, down the spine, and ends at the *Huiyin* cavity. The Fire Path is used to make the Etheric Body more *Yang* whereas the Wind Path is used to make it more *Yin.* Both methods, however, may be used to cleanse all twelve *Qi* Meridians.

The primary goal of Microcosmic Orbit is to strengthen the *Qi* Meridians. Quite literally, Microcosmic Orbit practice is a Subtle Body workout. A strong Etheric anatomy implies that your Gross Body is also strengthened by the practice, as the two are intimately related. This is why Etheric medical practices, such as Acupuncture, work to heal the physical body even though they operate on the Meridians. For our purposes, we're using Microcosmic Orbit to cleanse, strengthen, and open the Meridians to fuel our behind-the-Veil activities. We're literally making our Subtle Body muscles stronger and more flexible.

There are a few different ways to begin Microcosmic Orbit. I was taught to begin the circulation process at the location of stored energy: *The Lower Dantian.* It's important that your Lower Dantian feels warm before initiating the Microcosmic Orbit, as this signifies that *Qi* is abundant and ready to spill over into the Fire Path. The Fire Path is the natural route of *Qi* circulation in the Governing and Conception Vessels of your Etheric system (meridians).

Before you begin, be aware that there are three locations on the Fire Path where *Qi* tends to stagnate. These are the tailbone, the middle of the spine at level with the heart, and the back of the head directly above the neck. In Chinese, these are called *San Guan,* literally "Three Gates." Because of the narrow musculature of the tailbone area, *Qi* easily gets stuck there and can cause all sorts of trouble. The gate at the middle of the back is dangerous because of its proximity to the heart. If *Qi* deviates from its path, and goes to the heart instead, it can cause palpitations and even a heart attack. Finally, the gate at the back of the head is dangerous due to the narrowness of its location. Because it can be difficult to feel where *Qi* is moving here, it can deviate and go to the brain, causing vertigo and mental imbalance.

The key to avoiding the dangers of the Three Gates is to cultivate the skill of regulating the mind to be still, calm and concentrated. Also, as you learn to circulate *Qi* in the Microcosmic Orbit, these gates will widen. The trick is to proceed gently, patiently and above all, to *be relaxed.* Mental and physical tension causes *Qi* to stagnate.

Here's a diagram showing the Microcosmic Orbit along with the locations of the myriad cavities found on the Governing and Conception Vessels. As you can see, the practice can be done while sitting in a chair. However, it's best to practice with legs crossed as this prevent *Qi* from escaping into the legs.

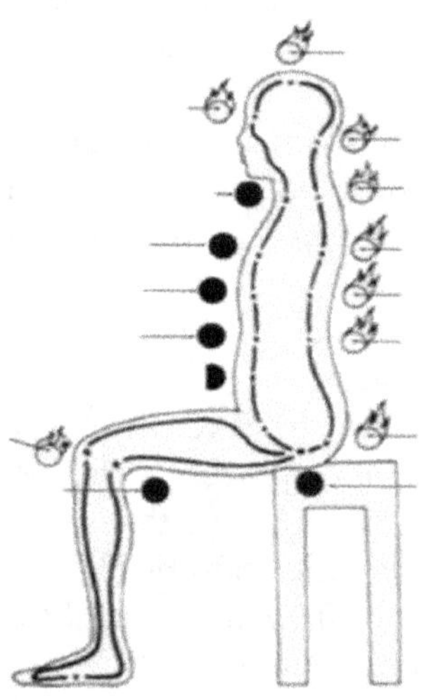

(In advanced levels of the practice, the "small circulation" of Microcosmic Orbit expands to become the "grand circulation" of the entire body. There are many versions of Grand Circulation, but they don't concern us here. For our purposes, we'll be following the Small Circulation paths of the upper body.)

The Practice

Before beginning Microcosmic Orbit circulation, you should first build up Etheric energy at your Lower Dantian by practicing Embryonic Breathing for at least ten minutes. As soon as you feel heat or trembling in your Lower Dantian, begin circulating this abundant *Qi* in the Fire Path. For this beginner-level method of the practice, it isn't necessary to feel all the *Qi* Cavities located on your Governing and Conception Vessels. Instead, your first goal is to learn to feel the Path itself. In other words, you must first feel the two *Qi* Vessels involved in the Microcosmic Orbit before you can learn to feel the Cavities. As your capacity for feeling develops, and the *Qi* Gates widen, you'll soon begin to feel the various Cavities of your Etheric system.

So, how do you use your inner feeling to locate the Governing and Conception Vessels?

As soon as you feel that *Qi* has reached an abundant level in your Lower Dantian, place your awareness in both your Lower and Upper Dantian at the same time. Remember, the best way to locate the *Yin* center of your Upper Dantian is to become aware of your "I Am," your very sense of consciousness devoid of all objects of perception. This will lead *Qi* to the *Yin* Center of the Upper Dantian, your Pineal Gland. Simply relax for a few moments and breathe in and out of these two Dantians. Don't forget to coordinate the movement of your *Huiyin* with your breathing! Also, keep the tip of your tongue to your upper palate for the duration of the session.

Next, while keeping your awareness situated in your Upper and Lower Dantians, inhale naturally and become aware of the front and back of your torso. The correct way to do this is through *feeling* rather than visualization. For some people this will be easy. For others it may take some time. At any rate, feel into the back and front of your torso and observe any sensations that arise. Pay special attention to the midline of your body: your spine, head, face, throat, chest, abdomen, groin and perineum *(Huiyin)*. Feel especially for such things as temperature, tingling, movement, etc., as you'll be using these sensations to keep track of how and where *Qi* is moving in the Microcosmic Orbit. You want to be sure to keep your mind in this midline area for the duration of the practice. If your mind deviates from this Path, then *Qi* may be led to the wrong Path and cause trouble. At the very least, you'll waste the goal of your practice. Remember:

Where attention goes Qi flows!

Now, there should be three things included in your awareness at this point: your Upper and Lower Dantians, the coordination of your *Huiyin* and breathing, and the midline of the front and back of your torso. Because we're using the Buddhist breathing method for this practice, it should now feel as if your entire upper body is expanding with every inhalation and contracting upon exhalation.

Upon your next inhalation, try to feel outward into the space that surrounds your body. Feel into the space beneath you as well, as though the ground beneath you has disappeared. Do this while keeping your awareness rooted in your Upper and Lower Dantians. This simultaneity of awareness is very important to the cultivation of your Subtle Body. Personally, I find that using body temperature as a guide for feeling-attention works well to expand my awareness into my Etheric system. After a while, you'll begin to know the difference between your body heat and the feeling of your *Qi*. The latter feels like a sort of "nerve force" with parallels to an electrical current or field. Sometimes it creates body temperatures ranging from cool to warm to extremely hot.

Once you can feel into your Meridians to a workable degree, become aware of the heat in your Lower Dantian with a simultaneous awareness of your "I Am" in your Upper Dantian as well as the surrounding aura of your Etheric force. Even if all you can do is practice this simultaneity of awareness in a given session, it's perfectly fine! I know that it seems like a lot of things to attend to at once, but I assure you that it gets easier with time and consistent practice. If you're ready to continue, let's move on to the next step.

Okay! Now that your attention is firmly rooted in your Etheric system, it's time to circulate the *Qi* you've gathered at your Lower Dantian. How to do this? Well, there are a few ways, but through trial and error, I've discovered that the best way is to first inhale and lead the sensation of heat in the Lower Dantian upward to just behind the navel and then outward from the stomach and downward to the *Huiyin*. This should be done on an inhalation of breath while gently pushing your *Huiyin* down. You want to time it in such a way that the sensation of heat reaches the *Huiyin* point at the end of your inhalation.

Next, as you exhale, sweep the sensation of heat past your tailbone, up your spine, and around the back of your head, ending at the point where the tip of your tongue touches your upper palate. Your awareness should reach this point at exactly the conclusion of your exhalation. It's important that you keep part of your feeling-awareness at least three inches away from your body while doing this. If you have 100% of your awareness inside your body while circulating Etheric force, then it's almost sure to stagnate. In fact, in the higher stages of practice, your Gross Body seems to vanish entirely, and your *Qi* is all you're aware of.

Finally, upon your next inhalation, sweep your feeling-awareness down the front of your body, starting at your throat, then your chest, your abdomen, and your groin, ending at your *Huiyin*. The timing is very important, and you must reach *Huiyin* at the end of inhalation and gently push it down and out. Remember to breathe naturally. Your awareness and timing should follow the natural flow of your breathing, not *vice versa*. In more advanced levels of practice, you'll deepen and slow your breathing down. For now, stay natural, start simple, and practice as much as possible. Your main goal is to become aware of your Etheric force and increase your capacity for inner-feeling.

Continue circulating *Qi* in the Microcosmic Orbit until the entire process becomes seamless and smooth. Remember the following rules and you'll stay on the correct path of practice:

- There should be no pauses in the circulation of *Qi*.
- Your feeling-awareness should be about three inches away from the physical body, with an emphasis on the midline of your body.
- The simultaneity of attention must be trained until it becomes one unified and global awareness: rooted in your Upper and Lower Dantians, circulating in your Governing and Conception Vessels, with breathing and *Huiyin* coordination trained until you no longer need to be aware of them.
- Train your feeling-awareness until you can circulate very far away from your Gross Body. Eventually, you'll also include circulating *within* your Gross Body *and* your Etheric energy at the same time.

- Lastly, guard and maintain your Etheric force always. Avoid unhealthy foods, toxic environments and, if you're male, too many ejaculations of semen. If female, avoid practicing during menses.

That's it! You've completed the Small Circulation of Microcosmic Orbit! Congratulations. If you've come this far you deserve to be proud of yourself. As far as Subtle Body cultivation is concerned, the two treasures of Embryonic Breathing and Microcosmic Orbit represent a real milestone and achievement.

Lastly, remember that the circulation of Microcosmic Orbit can also be reversed and made to follow the Wind Path. Some people find it easier to circulate *Qi* in this Path than the Fire Path. Be that as it may, you should practice both methods to maintain the balance of *Yin* and *Yang* in your Etheric and Gross Bodies. The Fire Path follows the natural flow of *Qi* in the Governing and Conception Vessels. The Wind Path reverses this flow thereby calming the excess Fire *Qi* generated in the Fire Path circulation. Once you become proficient in Embryonic Breathing and Microcosmic Orbit, you've laid the foundation for serious Subtle Body work. I say "work" but really, you're going to have more fun than most people can imagine. Literally…

Channeling Intensity Exercise

Many people make the unfortunate mistake of assuming that powerful *visualization* skills are all that it takes to have Vivid or Lucid Dreams. While in a certain sense this is true, the word "visualization" pertains to only one of the five senses: the sense of *sight*. However, unless all five senses are involved in the dreaming process then you really can't call it Vivid or Lucid Dreaming. You may be able to call it *visual* dreaming, sure, but Vivid? No. Lucid? Not really.

All five senses must be involved in the dream experience for it to be authentic Vivid and Lucid Dreaming!

So how does someone cultivate the skill of Vivid Dreaming?

Well, I once heard a great quote from the spiritual teacher, Ram Dass, in which he expressed shock at the number of individuals who are attempting to have out of body experiences. He suggested to such people, wisely, that they should first learn to have a complete *in the body* experience.

I couldn't agree more…

The following technique will enhance your capacity for sensory experience in both the dream *and* awake states. Further, this method is designed to sharpen your imagination, relaxation, and concentration to such an extent that you may even have a Lucid Dream while awake!

Yes, it's possible…

The following technique requires a willingness and capacity to open yourself to powerful emotions, energies, and thoughts. If you're patient and persevere, I promise you'll be well rewarded. Many people have a profound breakthrough while practicing *Channeling Intensity*. This may serve to inspire you and let you know that you're on the right track.

I'd also like to point out that *Channeling Intensity* not only increases your capacity for full sensory dreams, but it also flexes your Astral muscles, so to speak. By learning to alter your perception and involve all five senses in the process, you're teaching your subconscious mind that it's okay to set aside your normal way of perceiving in favor of another possibility. The first thing you'll probably notice is that a doorway to spontaneous Lucid Dreaming is opened by the exercise I'm about to share with you. Since Lucid Dreaming is itself a form of OOBE, the Astral Projection experience is just right around the corner.

Now let's get started!

This first exercise is the foundation for all the other skills that you're going to learn. You should continue practicing it until it becomes as natural as breathing. I first came across it in a Tantric document called the *Vigyan Bhairav Tantra*. I began practicing it in 2004 and was blown away by the results. When I first began, I didn't realize what was in store and the level of commitment required, the doors that it would open, or the unpredictable effect that it would have on my Astral development. First, you must understand that the ways by which you can open, expand and educate your Astral Body are legion. There truly is no "right" way to do it. However, regardless of which method(s) you choose, you must proceed cautiously, patiently and perseveringly. Remember this important point:

Your Astral Body is intimately connected with your emotions.

The technique that I'm about to share with you has the power to give you conscious and creative control over that connection, so you should practice it even while learning the other exercises in this book.

Certain Tantric and Tibetan schools have called this exercise the "Mahamudra" or "Supreme Gesture." I'm referring here to the *One Taste* teaching of *Mahamudra*.

What? One taste? What's that?

Well, the Indian Sage, Gautama Siddhartha (Buddha), used to describe his experience of enlightenment with analogy to the salt water of the sea. Just as every inch of the ocean, no matter where you find it, has the same salty taste, so too does enlightenment have "one taste" no matter who's experiencing it. What does this mean?

The following exercise will answer this question for you. Properly understood, the following technique has the power to:

- Get you in touch with your Astral Body.
- Enhance your overall sensitivity to Etheric energy.
- Deepen your emotional intelligence.
- Sharpen your senses.

Why is it called the *Supreme Gesture*? To answer this, you must understand that most of us live in a sort of waking dream. The average person believes that this little thing called "ego" is a concrete and living thing. It's understandable, too, since we need to develop a strong and healthy ego from an early age to survive in this world—which would be fine were it not for the fact that we mistakenly believe that our little self is all that there is to us.

The fragility of the ego is revealed in moments of exasperation and overwhelming emotions, when we react in ways that contradict our self-image. We may be the very picture of poise and calm when things are going smoothly for us, but just a tiny bit of friction and immediately the mask falls off. Whenever we lose our temper, allow the environment to push us around, or respond in a knee-jerk fashion, we're showing our true colors, our "side B," the beast in the basement… To be sure, there's nothing wrong with these repressed urges and thoughts. In fact, once you strip them of their cultural taboo or remove the moralistic and judgmental weight that holds them down, you're left not with anger or calm, or love versus hate, and so on: *You're left with raw energy!*

That's right. Any conceivable thought or emotion you possess is energy, first and foremost. Just think about how many uses electricity has, to give but one example of energy. But electricity is just natural energy. It's not trying to help or hurt anyone. Then, Nikola Tesla comes along and turns it into something productive and transforms human experience forever. Then, Alfred P. Southwick, using the same energy, creates a monstrous device called the electric chair! In much the same way your joy, sadness, excitement, sexuality, creativity, and so on, can be used creatively or crudely.

Another important point to understand is that an enormous amount of energy is wasted in this compartmentalizing of our emotions and thoughts. Each time we suppress a thought or feeling we deem taboo or shameful, we're needlessly chasing our own tail and consuming vast quantities of energy. We do this because we're employing *morality* to do a job that only *intelligence* can do properly. The fact is that most of our emotional reactions, and then our reactions to those reactions, are largely borrowed from the environment we're raised in. Truly, for many of us, we take for granted that we're not behind the wheel at all! Our parents, teachers, leaders, doctors and priests are speaking through us.

The practice of *Channeling Intensity* reconnects us with the greater portion of our energies so that we can reclaim them as our own.

So, let's begin!

The Practice

The fastest route to grasping the knack of *Channeling Intensity* is through the skill of Trance. The Zen practice of "just sitting" is the same thing, only it can be done anywhere and anytime, not just while sitting on your meditation cushion. In fact, to be truly understood, you must practice it always. After all, there aren't too many emotional triggers present while sitting in a dark and quiet room with your eyes closed.

Just as Zazen is the art of *just sitting, Channeling Intensity* could rightly be called the art of *just feeling.* It's one of the most difficult practices you'll ever commit to, but also one of the most transformative experiences you'll have, I promise!

It starts with a firm resolution to surrender to the process and open yourself up to the full breadth of your emotions.

So, here's what to do:

You start by being vigilant and alert to yourself, particularly to your *feeling* self. I don't just mean your emotions, but *all* your feeling. This includes the pain you feel when stubbing your toe, the sensation of an approaching sneeze, your emotional reactions to a movie, the sensations you feel while making love, or the anxiety you feel when giving a public speech. All of it!

Next, don't criticize, censor or otherwise label what you're feeling. Just allow it to be fully present without any preconceived idea of what you should or shouldn't be feeling and how it should be dealt with. Also, notice any knee-jerk reactions to your feelings. Notice the almost instantaneous desire to repress, blame, express, hide or excuse what you're feeling. Simply let all those reactions flower and self-liberate in your inner space. Metaphorically speaking, this is how you take the base lead of your emotions and turn it into the gold virtue in the fire of raw awareness. This is inner Alchemy!

Once you've got a feel for how to do this, notice that an interesting paradox arises here. In one sense, you've removed the barrier between your persona and the greater portion of your being submerged beneath it, and yet now there's *more* space between you and this energy. You've become raw awareness, like the bright summer sun shining on the storm clouds. The more you shine your light on all that arises within you, the more inner-sky you have available to you.

The keys to successful practice are:

1. Be very present and alert to your bodymind. This is like the relaxed alertness you'd have while fishing or waiting to spot a shooting star. When you experience powerful emotions or sensations, feel into them and follow their pathway through your body. Watch them as you would a passing storm.

2. Start small and gradually move on to more intense emotions. For example, begin by channeling your emotional reactions to a moving song or film. After some time, you may move on to more emotionally challenging situations like a lover's quarrel or a feud with a coworker.

3. Be sure to *breathe* through the entire process. Don't do anything with the breath! Simply include your breathing in your awareness.

Eventually, you'll be able to regulate the effects that strong emotions have on your *Qi* Meridians with *Embryonic Breathing* and *Microcosmic Orbit.* For now, simply breathe while *Channeling Intensity.* At first, when channeling a very powerful emotion, it helps to exhale completely and stop breathing for a moment. In other words, you come to a complete STOP inside, so the emotion can be sublimated. At intermediate levels, you'll be able to breathe into and with the powerful energies coursing through you.

We often take for granted that our emotions are pure energy…

Continue with this practice until it becomes second nature. Remember, the real attainment is won when you achieve the stage of *regulating without regulating.* In Taoism, this entire process is known as regulating the *Xin,* or emotional mind. They refer to the *Xin* as "monkey mind" because of its wayward and impulsive nature. The Taoist term for that part of the mind used in *Channeling Intensity* is the *Yi,* or wisdom mind, which they liken to a horse because of its noble goals and perceptiveness. Once the *Xin* is regulated by the *Yi* through Channeling Intensity, the *Shen* (union of subconscious/conscious mind) can be raised, and *the grass grows by itself.* Once this becomes second nature, then practices like *Embryonic Breathing* and *Microcosmic Orbit* become something you're always doing in much the same way as your normal breathing goes on whether you're aware of it or not. At this stage, your Subtle Body development has reached an advanced level of cultivation. I can't tell you what happens at that stage because I'm still working on it myself! Rest assured, the possibilities are probably endless.

One of the remarkable experiences you're likely to have at this stage of cultivation involves increased intuition. This often presents itself simply as increased accuracy in your "hunches." It's also common to encounter the figure of a Wise Man or Woman in your dreams, or perhaps the voice of an angel or of the Creator of the universe!

In the following section, we'll discuss the appearance of *The Guide* as an archetype in dreams. I beg your indulgence here, as the importance of this attainment can't be overstated. For many Veilers, the appearance of *The Guide* is the most pivotal moment in their development.

(5)

Encountering Your Spiritual Guide in Dreams

In *Behind the Veil* I qualified *Seven Categories of Dream* and we'll be revisiting these Categories throughout this book. For starters, these Categories serve as a kind of inner radar or rolodex, mapping common patterns and themes found in dreams. The first benefit of this is an increased ability to remember your nightly dreams (Dream Recall). Not only that, but you'll discover over time which of the *Seven Categories* you dream of on average. This can put you into the right ballpark for profound self-exploration, and can even serve as a kind of language shared by you, your subconscious, and your Higher Self.

One of the Categories is the *Archetypal Dream Type*. Briefly, "archetypes" are formless, primordial psychic patterns that house the forces and universal experiences shared by humanity everywhere since the dawn of our species. They're said to exist within the individual and collective mind (collective unconscious) of mankind.

Some common archetypes are *The Mother, The Father, The Trickster, The Devil, The Judge, The Hero, The Wise Man or Woman,* and *The Guide.* In this section, I'd like to discuss *The Guide.*

Before I begin, let me point out that I personally don't believe that these archetypes are lifeless concepts floating around in the collective unconscious. Quite the contrary, actually. The archetypes appear to be co-opted by the human psyche and given such forms as can be understood by mankind. By way of analogy, imagine the human psyche as a glass bottle with various other glass bottles tucked inside it—an onion-like configuration of bottles within bottles. Moreover, each bottle is of a different shape, color and size. Now, imagine that water is then poured into each of the bottles. Naturally, the water will take on a different mold, size, and hue in each of the individual bottles. All this and yet the bottles are all composed of the same glass and are filled with the same type of liquid. In much the same way, the human psyche appears in a similar form and structure no matter where on the globe you find it. Surface structures tend to vary, but deep structures are everywhere almost identical. Therefore, the archetypes take on an almost identical shape when "poured" into the psyche at birth (or whenever the unconscious regions of the psyche are fully formed).

I'm often asked whether I believe the archetypes to be independent entities and intelligences. That is to say, are they merely inherited symbols, or are they individual beings in their own right? To answer this question, we must remember that archetypes don't always manifest as personalities. In fact, and as I mentioned above, the archetypes often appear not as beings, but as places. Sure, it can be argued that archetypal beings could possess the ability to appear as a place, person, idea and so forth, and personally I do feel this is quite possible. That said, in my experience, most archetypes that appear in dreams are NOT individual entities, but rather are forces that take on the form of universal themes. That's not to say that I fully dismiss the possibility that deceased loved ones or beings from other planes of reality can appear in dreams. It's just that such occurrences are probably the exception and not the rule. Still, it's not uncommon for an archetype to emerge in dreams, and for it to have very real effects upon not only the dreamer's life, but also upon the lives of those around him.

The Archetype of the Spiritual Guide as it Appears in Dreams

One of the most rewarding consequences of consistent Dream Work is an increased appearance of one's spiritual Guide and the language He, She or It speaks. For me, my Guide appeared first in dreams as a presence, then as a voice, and finally as an entire cast of different personalities. Eventually, my Guide became a living part of my daily and nightly existence. At times, She's appeared as an apparent enemy—a poisonous snake, for example. At other times, She's manifested as written words on a page. She's also appeared as an artist, writer, actor or musician for whom I have the highest respect. At other times, conversely, my Guide has appeared as someone or something that I loathe.

However your Guide appears, one thing's always certain: there's an important lesson to be learned in the how and why of your Guide's appearance in a specific form. There's a reason why your Guide appears as friend or foe, animal or angel, and it's up to you to figure out what that reason is. Sometimes your Guide may appear as a hostile or threatening figure because it's time for you to face your fears. Or your Guide may show up as a famous celebrity because it's time for you to discover and own your talents. Perhaps your Guide shows up as a Wise Man or Woman because it's time for you grow up or find the answer to a perplexing riddle.

An archetype often manifests as another archetype to drive a certain point home. It's not uncommon, for example, for *The Caregiver* archetype to manifest as *The Wise Old Man/Woman.* Or you may encounter *The Rebel* archetype wearing *The Joker's* clothes! In any case, these archetypal combinations provide much food for thought. After some time you may notice, as I did, that your Guide appears less and less as a figure in your dreams. This is because you've begun to listen to your dreams more seriously, and therefore your *dreams* have become your Guide!

One of the most rewarding types of Lucid Dream is the one in which your Guide is featured. After all, being present and conscious enough to engage your Guide in an active dialogue is a very rare event! In such Lucids, I've learned many of the techniques I'm sharing with you in my books. Not only that, I've learned proper finger positions for playing certain songs on piano, physical exercises, and even entire poems and book titles from my Guide in Lucid Dreams.

So how do you begin looking for your own Guide in dreams? Well, besides the obvious scanning of your nightly dreams for archetypal appearances, you can actually evoke *The Guide* through creative means. My favorite method is to listen to an audiobook as I'm falling asleep. That's right! It can be that simple. All you need to do is make sure that the story is replete with archetypal imagery, one of which, naturally, should be the archetype of *The Guide.* Good examples of such stories are *The Lord of the Rings, The Arthurian Tales,* and so forth. Such tales are literally bursting with archetypal characters. They stimulate their appearance in dreams by resonating with themes that are alive in your psyche at the time of reading or listening to them.

Make it a habit to "call out" to your Guide before falling asleep every night. Also, make the sharp command to your subconscious mind that you wish to become conscious in your dreams. It's important that you are very sincere and clear with this command, and then you must *know* that it will happen. I say "know" and not "believe" it will happen because *belief* still has doubt as its shadow. *Knowing,* on the other hand, is certain and final; it therefore carries much more power behind it than mere belief.

The Guide with a Thousand Faces

> "Both myth and dream are symbolic in the same general way of the dynamic of the psyche. But in the dream the forms are quirked by the peculiar troubles of the dreamer, whereas in myth the problems and solutions sown are directly valid for all mankind."
>
> — Joseph Campbell, *Hero with a Thousand Faces*

The quote by celebrated Mythologist, Joseph Campbell, would've seemed abstract to the younger version of me. Today, however, after many years of being a Conscious Sleeper, it reads almost like common sense. What Mr. Campbell is saying is that dreams are personalized myths, and myths are depersonalized dreams.

If you want to study archetypes in their "pure" forms, look to the myths of the world. If, on the other hand, you want to see how the archetypes apply to your own life, look to your nightly dreams. Once time has acclimated you to the language of the archetypes in both myth and dream, you'll soon notice that the former tend to remain stable in their narratives while the latter rarely do. For example, the archetype of *The Wise Woman* in most myths of the world tends to be just that: *A Wise Woman.* But let's imagine that a young American feminist dreams of *The Wise Woman* archetype. In this case, that archetype may appear as a Warrior who also happens to be a Wise Woman! Why? Because the young feminist is preoccupied with empowering the feminine archetype in general, her Guide may manifest in such a way that's easily understood by the young feminist's mind. Conversely, if a young man dreams of a warrior-like Wise Woman, his psyche might add a sexual dimension to the archetype. Similar examples can be multiplied endlessly, but I trust you get the point.

Put simply, just as there can be a "Hero with a thousand faces," so too can there be a Guide with a thousand faces. Our task as Veilers is to recognize our Guide when it manifests. More difficult still is learning to tease apart the meaningful merging of archetypes from the meaningless interference from our own primal urges. For example, is our Guide pointing to a deeper issue by, say, merging *The Lover* archetype with *The Guide* archetype, or is *The Lover* archetype a form of static in this instance, interfering with the true voice of our Guide? Unfortunately, there's no universal method for distinguishing one from the other, and this confusion can follow you all the way to enlightenment. This is especially confusing when applied to one's Guide. After all, if you can't decipher the true voice of *The Guide* from the siren-like voices of your own primal urges or ego, then you're literally flying blind for much of your journey! So what's the solution?

This is where Pellucid Dreaming comes into play. By the end of this book, you'll see the importance of including Pellucidity training into your regimen. Without it, you're more at risk to get stuck, confused and even psychologically disturbed by your excursions behind the Veil. Remember, Pellucidity is literally meditation carried into the sleep cycle. As such, it grants the Veiler a clarity unknown to many Oneironauts. Not only that, but Pellucidity lifts the Veil leading to true Astral Projection; this is the ideal place to commune with your Guide directly and not merely through symbol or myth.

The Brahmamuhurt: Breakfast with the Buddha

In India, the best time for communing with God (*The Guide* in its most sublime form) is said to be in the hours directly preceding sunrise. They call this time the *Brahmamuhurt*.

Like anything worth possessing, tapping into the power of the *Brahmamuhurt* requires a bit of effort. First, you need to be capable of waking up shortly before sunrise without giving in to the urge to fall back asleep. Second, you need to sharpen your capacity for Dream Recall, as this is the best time of day to scan the prior night's dreams for any messages from your Guide. This requires at least an intermediate level of skill in mindfulness meditation. Eventually, at advanced levels of skill, you'll be able to access this state without even getting out of bed! In the beginning, the danger is that you'll fall back into unconscious sleep, thereby losing the goal of training.

As I've said, Pellucidity is a synonym for meditation carried into the sleep cycle. Unlike Lucid Dreaming, in which you take an active role in the dreaming process, Pellucidity requires that you remain detached from the dream narrative, a *passive* Witness of the dream. At intermediate to advanced levels of skill, you'll be capable of taking the role of *active* Witness of the dream. This is the ideal stage of skill, as you'll then be able to actively engage the Source of your dreams, rather than passively witnessing or actively getting lost in the dream itself.

What all of this means will become more clear as we proceed. For now, simply note that the "sweet spot" for communing with your Guide (the envoy of your Higher Self) is between the hours of 4:00 am and 6:00 am. These times are, of course, generalizations. The point is to isolate the hours shortly before sunrise, and then to find and maintain the delicate balance between Asleep and Awake.

The *Brahmamuhurt* is so important that I advise students that they first get aligned with their Circadian rhythm. Once this rhythm has been established, I then advise students to begin waking up shortly before sunrise to practice sitting meditation. Oftentimes, this is all that's needed to begin reaping the benefits of the *Brahmamuhurt*. For instance, after practicing sitting meditation at this time for about one month, it's not uncommon for students to have spontaneous Lucid and Pellucid Dreams when they decide to sleep in on the weekends. This is due to the fact that the nervous system is now trained to be Lucid during these twilight hours. The bodymind, being the creature of habit that it is, begins to apply this Lucidity to the dream state in the early morning hours. Be sure to record any results in your Dream Journal! (For details on how to format a Dream Journal, see *Behind the Veil.)*

It's important to note that the *Brahmamuhurt* features a unique balance of Awake and Asleep biochemistry. This is quite literally the *Yang* and *Yin* of Conscious Sleep! Such a balance between these cosmic forces and biochemistry serves as fertile ground for communing with one's inner Guide, and is the most potent time for any experiment in Conscious Sleep. In short, the *Brahmamuhurt* is when the Veil is at its thinnest. Why not take advantage of it?

Part Two

The Four Pillars of Subliminal Cognition Training

CHAPTER THREE

ASTRAL PROJECTION: MYTHS AND THEORIES

(1)
Oneironauts and Astral Projectors: Angels without Wings

With all the hype surrounding Lucid Dreaming and Astral Projection nowadays, it's only natural to find a great deal of disagreement among enthusiasts of the movement. By far the most widespread of these disagreements is found in the Astral/Lucid debate. For the sake of theater, let's call this spectacle *Team Astral vs. Team Lucid.*

Team Lucid believes that Astral Projection is just a synonym for Lucid Dreaming. To these folks, what was hitherto regarded as the soul leaving the physical body to ride the waves of the seven *Aethers* has been scientifically proven to be Lucid Dreaming in the form of Dream Control. *Team Astral,* on the other hand, thinks that *Team Lucid* is only half right. Lucid Dreaming, while similar to Astral

Projection, isn't the same thing. Rather, Lucid Dreaming is the Astral Body navigating the Etheric Plane. So who's right?

First, let's stop for a moment and acknowledge the elephant in the room, shall we? What's really going on here? I mean, what's this fight *really* all about? Is it necessary to go into the historicity of the terms "Astral" or "Etheric" or even "Dream" for that matter? Do we really need to split hairs over this or can we grab hold of Occam's Razor and cut right to the heart of the matter?

The source of this feud between *Team Astral* and *Team Lucid* is really a feud between science and mysticism, between Existentialism and Metaphysics. If you're in doubt, go ahead and tell a member of *Team Astral* that his recent conversation with the Archangel Gabriel was just a Lucid Dream, the interpretation of which might revolve around learning how to play the trumpet. Yeah, you might want to run, or risk being strangled by a Silver Cord!

Conversely, try to tell a member of *Team Lucid* that you've personally experienced Astral Projection, and that you even verified the things you witnessed while "out of body." The verdict will come hard and swift that all you really experienced was a Lucid Dream in which your subconscious showed you something you'd already seen but forgot; and if that explanation doesn't work then your experience will be chalked up to coincidence.

The reason for this opposition is found in that most recognizable hallmark of Postmodernity: *The war between scientific reductionism, on the one hand, and spiritual elevationism on the other.*

You see, you can't tell *Team Astral* that their experiences aren't proof of life after death any more than you can tell *Team Lucid* that their experiences are just mental masturbation. Telling *Team Astral* that what they do is just a dream is to basically strip all wonder and meaning from what they do. Similarly, telling *Team Lucid* that they're just doing a neat little cognitive trick that will be erased by the Grim Reaper is to alienate them completely.

Personally, I take an Integral approach to the whole thing. I don't think that there's any real disparity between Astral Projection and Lucid Dreaming. In fact, I think that they're too related to be at war. Astral Projection is probably Lucid Dreaming *plus.* In other words, we're looking at two different functions of a single mechanism:

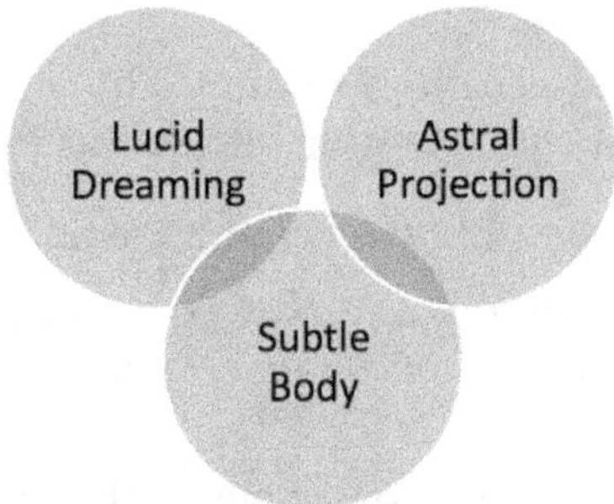

Now it may be that this "plus" doesn't make Astral Projection more important than Lucid Dreaming. It may be that Lucid Dreaming is more fundamental and Astral Projection is more significant, in much the same way as an acorn is fundamental to an Oak Tree. To be honest, I don't know! Hopefully someday I *will* know so that I can share it with you. What I can tell you is that I regularly experience Lucid Dreaming *and* Astral Projection. What I've learned is that they're both two aspects of the same phenomenon, much as jogging isn't unrelated to walking, even if they do look a little different.

I don't see any conflict between interpreting a Lucid Dream either in terms of neurotransmitters or in terms of archetypal manifestations. They're both important facets of the experience! This is also why I don't use the term "Oneironaut" to describe all aspects of a Conscious Sleeper. I prefer the term "Veiler". I find that this term fits Lucid Dreaming, Astral Projection, Pellucid Dreaming, Meditation, and other psychic gifts without favoring any particular aspect. In my opinion, we need an Integral approach to Conscious Sleep, one which respects each manifestation of Conscious Sleep without reducing or elevating either of them to fit our own personal or cultural bias.

Let's face it: being a Veiler is spiritual, scientific, artistic, poetic, sexy, meaningful, exhilarating, terrifying, enlightening, hedonistic and includes the entire spectrum of emotion and wonder. After all, that's what life is. That is, if these things are part of your life.

(2)

**Transcendental Viscerality Training. The Shared Mechanism
Behind Lucid Dreaming and Astral Projection**

I'd like to take a moment to reiterate an important point:

*Just because I point out that there's a biological equivalent of
rarified experiences doesn't mean that the latter is being reduced to
the former!*

I can't begin to describe how common this misunderstanding is.
This fear of material reductionism is rampant in the New Age community. Still, as justified as that fear may be, it flies in the face of the
counter-argument. What counter-argument, you ask? Well, let's state
it with the same candor we applied to the above reductionism:

*Just because I point out that there's a spiritual equivalent to
rarified experiences doesn't mean that the latter is being elevated to
the former!*

That's right. If it's a mistake to *reduce* all rarified experiences to
biology, then it's also a mistake to *elevate* them to the realm of Spirit.

And now that we've gotten that out of the way, I'd like to say that
this understanding of the Integral nature of rarified phenomena isn't a
neutralizing or marginalizing of rarified experiences. Quite the
contrary! To see that all experiences behind the Veil have a *subjective,
behavioral, cultural* and *systemic* equivalent is to truly be in the Tao
of Conscious Sleep. To practice, interpret and research in this fashion
is to skyrocket your development. It's what separates the Oneironaut
from the Veiler.

Educating Your Parietal Lobe

I know, I know! The "parietal lobe"?? That must be a typographical
error. Besides, didn't we already discuss this in *Chapter One*? Surely,
I must've meant to say the "pineal gland," right? Wrong…

As important as the Pineal Gland is to a Veiler (it regulates sleep/
wake cycles), when it comes to truly mastering Lucid Dreaming and
Astral Projection, you must also train the Parietal Lobe. As this area
of your brain becomes more adept participating in the Lucid Dreaming
or Astral Projection experience, the real "third eye" opens of its own

accord. Don't believe me? Well, good! I don't want to produce "believers," but rather, "knowers." Luckily for both us, you don't have to take my word for it. Commit the following information to memory, and then apply it to the *Three-Body Fitness Program* in the final section of this book, and you'll see for yourself that this approach places your feet squarely on the *Astral/Lucid* crossroads. From there, you can begin your own verification experiments, and put to rest any confusion regarding Lucid Dreaming and Astral Projection.

Before we begin, I'd like to point out that this approach isn't something new. Rather, it's a new spin on an ancient methodology. It's an *Integral* spin—one that attempts to use ancient wisdom in the light of modern science. Furthermore, it's an attempt to anchor this knowledge in a holistic framework designed to strip Astral Projection and Lucid Dreaming down to their common essence. Once you learn to cultivate them, you're free to interpret these abilities in any manner you choose. So let's get started!

For those unfamiliar with brain anatomy, the Parietal Lobe is responsible for your overall sense of balance and spatial orientation. The scientific term for this is *proprioception*. For the scientist reading this, I know that this is a very general description of the function of the Parietal Lobe. However, for our purposes, proprioception is the function that matters most.

I've discussed the role of the Parietal Lobe already, but now I'd like to demonstrate its pivotal role in initiating OOBE and dream Lucidity. The Parietal Lobe looks like this:

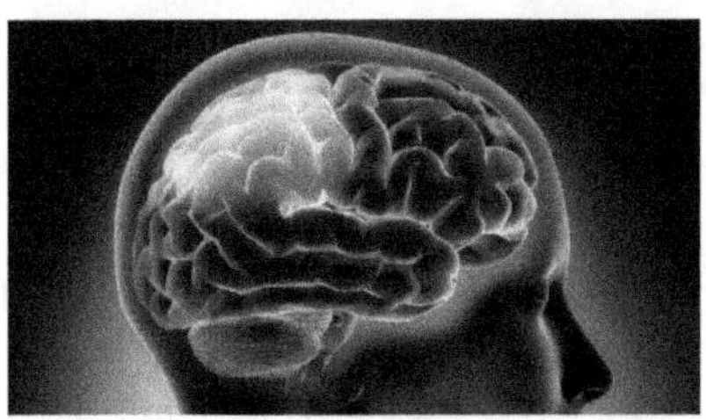

So what does contemporary science have to say about the role of the Parietal Lobe in Lucid Dreams and Astral Projection? Well, for starters, let me be clear about my current stance on this issue:

In my nomenclature, Deep-phase Lucid Dreaming *is* an Out of Body Experience (**LD-3**). Of course, it's only one version of OOBE, one which is "projected" into the Dream Plane *(Veil of Dreams)*. As This type of OOBE/Lucid Dream often blends with elements from the Collective Unconscious, forming what I call the *Astral Dream Type* (one of *The Seven Categories of Dream)*. But this type of OOBE must, in my opinion, be separated from Astral Projection proper. That is to say, genuine Astral Projection is an Out of Body Experience into what Robert Bruce calls the "realtime zone" and I call the *Veil of Tears.* That genuine Astral Projection shares much in common with deep-phase Lucid Dreaming should come as no surprise as they both require Sleep Paralysis to occur. For this and other reasons, I refer to Astral Projection as *Lucidity-PLUS* (LD+). As we'll presently learn, this kindred relationship between Lucid Dreaming and Astral Projection is best experienced by utilizing what's now known as the **WILD** technique (Wake Induced Lucid Dreaming).

That said, here's what current science says about OOBE:

Dr. Arvid Guterstam is a pioneering neuroscientist at the *Karolinska Institute* in Sweden. He's also the co-author of a study published in the journal called *Current Biology.* Dr. Guterstam's research centered on reproducing in test-subjects the various sensations associated with OOBE. Each of these sensations have in common the basic feeling of owning a body. In the doctor's words:

"The feeling of owning a body is a very basic experience that most of us take for granted in everyday life."

NOTE: This is precisely why I refer to the Gross, Subtle and Causal bodies as "embodiment zones." Really, the primary element that decides whether you're having a Lucid Dream, a hallucination, an OOBE, a "samadhi" or "satori", or if you're dead or alive, is your overall feeling of embodiment and spatial orientation.

In previous experiments, scientists created in test-subjects something akin to the "phantom limb" effect. The latter often occurs in amputees who, for a while after losing a limb, can still feel it as though it were there. In such experiments, a test-subject wearing video goggles sees a rubber hand being stroked. At the same time, a researcher strokes the subject's own hand (which is out of sight), producing the feeling that the rubber hand is the subject's own hand. Scientists have used a similar technique to produce the feeling in test-subjects of having a manikin's body, or no body at all! Dr. Guterstam's own research comes on the heels of these studies.

Guterstam's experiments also follow on the discovery of "GPS Cells", a scientific breakthrough that earned the researchers the Nobel Prize in 2014. Experiments on rodents proved that these *GPS Cells* are involved in navigation and spatial orientation.

So how does Dr. Guterstam's research prove that OOBE involves the Parietal Lobe? Well, here's how the study was conducted:

The test-subjects lay in an MRI scanner while wearing a head-mounted display assembly streaming video from a set of cameras located elsewhere in the room. The cameras were positioned to gaze down on the body of a stranger, while an image of the test-subject's own body lying inside the scanner was visible in the background.

To produce the sensations of OOBE, the researchers touched the participant's body with a rod while also touching the stranger's body in the same place, in full view of the cameras. For the test-subjects, this produced the illusion that their body was in a different part of the room than where it actually was! In Dr. Guterstam's own words:

> "It's a very fascinating experience. It takes a couple of touches, and suddenly you actually feel like you're located in another part of the room. Your body feels completely normal—you don't feel like it's floating around."

Then, the researchers analyzed the brain activity in the Temporal and Parietal Lobes of the test-subjects. Based on this brain activity, Guterstam and his colleagues were able to decode how the participants perceived their physical location.

The researchers also discovered that the Hippocampus, a region of the brain where *GPS Cells* have been found, is involved in figuring out where one's body is in space. They also found that the area of the brain called the Posterior Cingulate Cortex is what reconciles the feeling of where one's "I" is located with the feeling of being embodied *per se*.

You may recognize in Dr. Guterstam's experiment what I call "bi-locationality" and "mobile proprioception." Unlike Dr. Guterstam's biofeedback method, however, you're going to learn how to alter your spatial orientation at will. To this end, we'll be employing biofeed-back methods of a nature different from those used by Guterstam and his colleagues. Furthermore, we'll also bring our emotions to bear on our efforts. Not only the emotions of joy, elation, sorrow, love and so forth, but the visceral emotions, too—that is, the kind of emotions you feel when riding a rollercoaster, or scuba-diving or skydiving. In this and later chapters, we're going to learn how to reproduce these sensations spontaneously. Lastly, let's give this methodology a fancy name. Let's call it: *Transcendental Viscerality (TV).*

Transcendental Viscerality Training

I was perhaps twelve years old when I received my first clue as to how OOBE can be induced. Throughout the years, long before I even considered writing about this topic, I used to advise the doubters around me to induce OOBE themselves. Personal experience is, after all, the fastest way to remove all doubt. Naturally, the question of how to induce OOBE arose. Thus, in an effort to pinpoint the essential mechanism behind OOBE, I began with the following question:

Have you ever been on the verge of falling asleep, when you're suddenly gripped by the feeling of falling off your bed?

Almost every time, the person's eyes light up and they exclaim, "That happens to me all the time!" One memory immediately comes to my mind: I was working on a large construction project. Because the job was a good distance away from where I lived, the crew and I had to share a hotel room. One night the conversation turned to the topic of Astral Projection. I was describing my many adventures behind the Veil when my boss, reclining on the twin bed next to mine, gave a chuckle and said, "Hogwash." To which I said, "Yeah, I'd probably say the same thing if I'd never experienced it for myself."

Fifteen minutes later, as I was asking the other guys if they've ever felt themselves falling off the bed while drifting off to sleep, my boss gave a sudden start. He sat up in his bed and cried, "Whoa!" At first, I thought he was having a joke at my expense, but his face was flush, and I could tell by the look in his eyes that something had happened.

"Are you okay?" I asked him. He then looked at me with a bewildered expression on his face and said, "As you were talking about the sensation of falling or sinking as you drift off to sleep, I was thinking to myself that this happens to me all the time. As I was drifting off to sleep, it suddenly happened! I felt like I was rolling off the right side of the bed and decided to allow it to happen. A few seconds later, I felt hands grabbing at my body and felt like my body was turning in a clockwise fashion, faster and faster. When I tried to snap out of it, I couldn't so I panicked and finally woke up."

"Told you," I quipped, not without some feeling of satisfaction, I might add.

This feeling of falling or sinking while drifting off to sleep was my first hint that OOBE occurs at the threshold of Sleep Paralysis. In addition to this, the "echo" of the sensation of owning a body trails behind consciousness as it enters the sleep cycle with awareness intact. For some people, this **NREM** form of OOBE doesn't really pack the punch that **REM** induced OOBE does. Still, it suffices to convince most people that there's more to this Astral Projection thing than meets the eye.

So, the basic feeling of owning a body, coupled with visceral sensations that contrast with where one's body is oriented in space—namely, lying in bed—is what induces OOBE. Put simply, if you're lying supine on your mattress, but you create the visceral feelings associated with, say, skydiving, swinging or floating in water, as long as you can carry these sensations over the Sleep Paralysis threshold, you'll induce an OOBE. Later, we'll explore various methods for doing just that. For now, though, go ahead and experiment on your own and see what you can come up with.

Bear in mind that, just as OOBE depends upon the Parietal Lobe, powerful Lucid Dreaming depends upon the Limbic System. That is, the biological seat of the emotions are needed if your Lucid Dreams are going to be worth recalling. Because the Dream Body is really the Emotional Body carried into the **REM** phase of sleep, the most memorable Lucid Dreams tend to be those that really light up the emotional centers of the brain. Consequently, it behooves the *SCT* student to learn how to cultivate her emotional intelligence. I find that music helps tremendously in this regard. Listening to evocative music while meditating or while falling asleep is one great way to train this. One of my favorite hobbies is sitting or lying motionless while listening to emotionally evocative music (usually without lyrics). I'll put together a playlist that tells a story, as it were, and then I'll meditate on each song, getting all of my senses involved in a visualization. Imagine a stage play or movie in your head, but a lifelike one…a virtual reality. That's a very powerful way to educate your Dream Body to become more emotionally intelligent. Try it tonight!

(3)
Is Out of Body Experience Dependent Upon the Body?

It's a strange question, I know. After all, if you're having an Out of Body Experience, what does that have to do with what's going on inside your body? But the truth is that the two are inextricably and undeniably linked, and in this section I'm going to explain how this is so. Of course, and as always, I'm going to do this with an eye toward how you can apply it to your own attempts at OOBE.

Recall that the Gross, Subtle and Causal bodies correspond to the three broad states of Waking, Dreaming, and deep Dreamless Sleep. The OOBE phenomena is one which engages the Subtle and Causal bodies. It's important to understand that although these three Bodies possess qualities unique to the architecture of their respective Worlds, they're actually limbs of one unified bodymind.

But to what extent are they dependent upon one another?

One of the things which baffles many scientists about the phenomenon known as Near Death Experience (NDE) is the fact that people who recall having them describe a *conscious* experience while they were either clinically dead or very close to it. Putting aside for the moment whether these people were experiencing the afterlife, or perhaps just a Lucid Dream *peri-mortem,* the fact that these persons were conscious at all during such an event is astonishing! More to the point, their being lucid didn't seem to depend upon a healthy body or brain. What makes this so fascinating to me is that most of these people don't have any prior training which might prepare them for such an event. There are, for example, many spiritual systems which aim at immortality of the soul by way of accumulation of Etheric force. I have practiced one such system for many years: Xi'an Taoism.

Like the Milam Sect of Tibetan Buddhism, Xi'an Taoism aims at mastering the continuity of consciousness throughout the three broad states of Waking, Dreaming and Dreamless Sleep. These two schools go about this in their own unique way, but the goal is the same: cultivate your awareness to such a high degree that neither sleep nor death can snuff it out. In Taoism, this is called raising your *Shen,* and this goal is very dependent upon the health of the bodymind. One of the fundamental tenets of the training is to preserve your natural energy (*Qi*) to fuel this endeavor. Furthermore, absolute physical and psychological health are required to see this through. A sick body will die before the spirit has been sufficiently cultivated, and an imbalanced mind won't have the lucidity or stamina to commit to the job.

But if the strength of the spirit is dependent upon the health of the body how can the spirit survive the clearly unhealthy event called death? To put it another way, if the Gross, Subtle and Causal bodies rely on healthy and abundant Etheric and physical energy, how can they survive when that energy is obviously shutting down? And when you consider the fact that most NDEs occur in hospitals where the dying person is either put to sleep on the operating table or else pumped full of morphine to ease the pain of death, one wonders:

What energy source is this dying brain feeding on to remain Lucid?

It could be argued that one can cultivate and use healthy and abundant physio-etheric energy to raise consciousness to the point where it's introduced to an inexhaustible energy source separate from the Gross, Subtle and Causal bodies (Nonduality). However, most NDE survivors have had no such training. My theory is that at the moment of death, when the pineal gland in the brain releases the highly psychedelic compound called DMT (Dimethyltryptamine), the consciousness is given a boost, not only due to the highly perplexing and compelling nature of the psychedelic experience, but also due to the adrenaline it produces—not to mention the actual shots of adrenaline and electricity routinely applied by the doctor to the dying patient to stimulate and revive the body.

Health, Energy and the Three Stages of Lucidity

In my system of Conscious Sleep, I divide Lucidity into three broad stages. Before we delve into these, I'd like to reaffirm that deep stage Lucid Dreaming *is* a form of OOBE. It may not be exactly the same as Astral Projection or NDE, but it *is* a form of the OOBE phenomenon. I realize that many OOBE aficionados debate this point of view, but it's been such a consistent and obvious detail of my own experience that I simply can't ignore it. Regardless what your stance is on this issue, one thing is certain:

Lucid Dreaming, Pellucid Dreaming and Astral Projection depend upon high level Lucidity. I'll only briefly describe the three stages of Lucidity here. For a full discussion of them, consult *Behind the Veil*.

The three stages of Lucidity are:

- **LD-1**
- **LD-2**
- **LD-3**

LD-1 and **LD-2** occupy the first 30–90 minutes of the sleep cycle. In **LD-1,** we experience hypnagogic imagery, slight changes in bodily perception, mild dream scenarios and psychedelic color patterns behind our closed eyes. It's the lightest phase of Lucidity. In **LD-2,** however, the *Veil of Dreams* lifts a little more. Although we're typically aware of our physical environment, the dream world is beginning to take center stage. We might experience sensations of falling or floating. Hypnic jerks and sometimes a brief cessation of breathing can occur at this stage. Without getting too technical, the appearance of K-complexes and Sleep-spindles appear on the electroencephalograph (EEG) at this time. These are thought to serve the dual purpose of releasing stress and sedating the mind for a smooth and uninterrupted transition into sleep. Although most of this phase of the sleep cycle is occupied by **NREM** (Non-Rapid Eye Movement) sleep, and is generally devoid of profound dreams, microbursts of dreaming can and do occur during this time. With special training one can learn to latch on, as it were, to these micro-dreams and ride them like a magic carpet into the underworld of sleep. But the point I'd like you to make note of is that **LD-1** and **LD-2** don't require a raised *Shen* (heightened awareness) to be enjoyed. However, if one wishes to consciously transition into or awaken during **LD-3** (deep-phase Lucidity), then a powerful, healthy and cultivated awareness is an absolute necessity.

LD-3 is arguably the deepest stage of Lucid Dreaming and OOBE. Between **LD-2** and **LD-3** is also where we find almost every conceivable expression of the OOBE phenomenon. How one experiences **LD-3** depends upon several factors, such as how and why it's being experienced in the first place. Is **LD-3** the result of deliberate training? Is it the product of ingesting a psychotropic drug? A concussion? A Near

Death Experience? Also, was **LD-3** entered consciously, as a transition from **LD-2** into deep-phase Lucidity? This last is especially significant because the various sensations and nuances which accompany these transitions aren't available to someone who simply awakens in the middle of a dream.

Accurately describing what **LD-3** feels like is exceptionally difficult. One can employ and exhaust the bottomless well of poetry and still not quite capture what happens behind the veil. In many instances OOBE feels exactly like waking consciousness, only without the laws of physics. In other cases, it can have a very soap bubble-like feeling to it, as if you're living in a world of reflections or holograms. At other times OOBE feels more real than the so-called real world! Awareness of your physical organism diminishes and is literally felt to be separate or separating from your root consciousness. Suddenly you're immersed in and surrounded by a world both familiar and strange, beautiful and terrifying. However you experience **LD-3,** it can't be denied that sustaining it requires a unique anatomy—one which is healthy enough to be relaxed and energized enough to be focused.

Is Conscious Sleep a Type of Qigong?

In the religious school of Taoist *Qigong,* OOBE is a product of the cognitive transition between *Yin* and *Yang.* It takes a little skill to learn how to balance *Yang* and *Yin* so that Lucidity can be sustained. For example, one of the most popular methods of Conscious Sleep is known as the *Wake Back to Bed* method (WBTB). I simply call it "The 4:00 am Method". According to Taoism, the Etheric body (*Qi* Body) begins to transition from *Yin* to *Yang* at around midnight. Translated in terms of physiology, early morning is when the body is well rested, and the brain is beginning to secrete the "wake up" chemicals serotonin and adrenaline, to name a few. Still, the bodymind is relaxed enough to sleep, and one's sleep cycle has already gone through at least three or four rounds. **REM** sleep (dreaming) becomes longer and deeper with each round of the sleep cycle, and by 4:00 am your dreams are as deep and meaningful as they're going to be. Because you're straddling the fine line between sleep (*Yin*) and awake (*Yang*), 4:00– 5:00 am represents a window of opportunity for OOBE. But to remain Lucid in moments when *Yang* is transitioning into *Yin* is incredibly difficult, and many aspiring Veilers give up because they only train at bedtime. At night, your brain is secreting the "go to sleep" hormone, melatonin. You're tired and unfocused. It takes years of dedicated practice to remain Lucid during this time.

Death is another event in which *Yang* is turning to *Yin*. Death is, after all, the ultimate state of sleep! Everything is working against Lucidity at this time. To die is the cessation of Lucidity as we know it. But according to Taoism and Tibetan Buddhism, the individual who masters OOBE while alive doesn't lose Lucidity at the moment of death, but enters the afterlife with full alertness. This, as I've said, presupposes an energy source other than physical or Etheric bodies.

The biggest reason that many people fail at Conscious Sleep is that they don't know where and when to look. You first must know the right timing, when *Yin* is becoming *Yang,* and you then need to learn how to investigate your psyche in such a way that *Yang* and *Yin* stay balanced. Too much or too little of either and you'll end up waking up or falling asleep. After a while, you'll be able to play with this in ever more refined ways. For example, there are advanced Yogis who can ingest LSD or Salvia Divinorum and remain totally unaffected by them. That's not to say that the psychedelic isn't felt to be working, but the Adept remains centered and calm. This is using *Yin* to counter excessive *Yang.* The ultimate test is, of course, the moment of death. Do you believe in life after death? Or is consciousness 100% dependent upon the physical body? Since the Gross, Subtle and Causal bodies are simply the limbs of one bodymind, can consciousness exist separate from either of them? Or when we die will we as Veilers still be sucked down into the abyss, our candles snuffed out for all eternity? Or is death and life simply one great big Lucid Dream?

Or maybe, just maybe…we're each of us limbs of a unified body, sharing an eternal dream…

(4)

Two Functions of the Same Mechanism?

The technique known as **WILD** (Wake Induced Lucid Dream) and the experience called Astral Projection, are perfect examples of the same *mechanism* being employed for different ends. As far as I can tell, both deep-phase Lucid Dreaming and full-blown Astral Projection are equally *out of body* experiences. Of course, when most people think of OOBE, they think of the immortal soul leaving the mortal physical body. But when we say "out of body," we could easily ask, "Which *body* are we stepping out of?" When we fall asleep at night, we're essentially leaving our Gross Body and entering our Subtle Body (which has at least four subsets). We've also seen that, with practice, we can enter these specific aspects of the Subtle Body even while we're awake. Similarly, every time we leave the Dreaming state and enter deep Dreamless Sleep, we're leaving the Subtle Body and entering the Causal Body. We also do this every time we practice formless meditations, such as *Nirvikalpa Samadhi, Yoga Nidra,* the *Cloud of Unknowing,* and so forth, which is to access the Causal Body in a *conscious* fashion (Pellucidity).

I'd argue that OOBE, in the truest sense, doesn't occur until the total annihilation of the physical organism—that is to say, when you no longer feel any disconnection between your individual self and the creative Source of life. Different cultures call this by many different names, but the general idea is that of a unification (or identity) of one's individual consciousness with that of the universal consciousness, and this experience is carried throughout Waking, Dreaming and Dreamless Sleep. The Tibetans, for example, believe that once you've attained continuity of awareness into the deep-sleep state, your soul will also be able to survive the death of your physical body. Of course, whether OOBE ends in spiritual immortality or a confrontation with the Lord of the Universe remains the parlance of those saints and sages who've persisted after the demise of their physical bodies. Since their voices go silent once their hearts do, we don't have any record of the truth or falsity of this claim. For our purposes, we need only note that there are at least three qualifiable forms of OOBE, and all of them are subjective experiences with biological correlates. Not only that, but each of these experiences will be interpreted according to an individual's relationship with his culture and how he interprets its religious and scientific presuppositions.

That interpretive dimension is *very* important. So is the biological examination of such experiences. Both should be used together by an *SCT* student with an eye toward establishing an unbiased and Integral map of attainment. The *behavioristic* examination of a subjective experience doesn't (or shouldn't) equal the denigration of a person's interpretation of her experiences. Just because a vision of Christ or Krishna has a neurological and biochemical component, that doesn't mean that you didn't have an authentic vision of Christ or Krishna! It simply means that we can now measure and qualify that vision by scientific means. The following diagram gives a fairly good idea of how each Body fits into the entire *bodymind*.

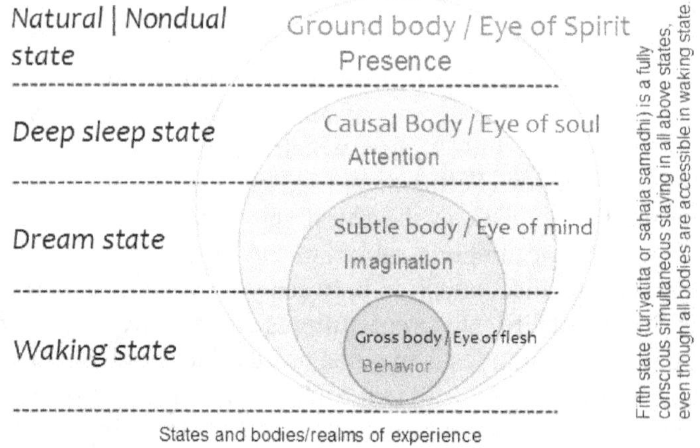

States and bodies/realms of experience

I'd only add that the Subtle Body has at least four subsets which, in some systems, are viewed as "bodies" in their own right. They are *mental*, *emotional*, *etheric* and *astral* bodies, and they tend to be the result of hybrid states resulting from a conscious blending of the Gross, Subtle and Causal bodies. These embodiment zones aren't linear or hierarchical (although they do evolve). Rather, they grade and shade into each other. When these hybrid states are accessed consciously then we have access to some of the rarified experiences upon which *SCT* is based.

As the above diagram illustrates, each Body perceives its environment with an "eye" unique to its own anatomy. The Gross Body sees with the *Eye of Flesh*; the Subtle Body sees with the *Eye of Mind* (and emotion); the Causal Body sees with the *Eye of Soul* (the "I" of the soul); and, lastly, the Nondual Body sees with the *Eye of Nonduality*. Each time you "project" out of one Body and into another, you're basically closing the Eye ("I") of one Body and opening the Eye of another. The factor which separates a *vision* from a *projection* is whether the Body (embodiment zone) being occupied is experienced in a full-sensory manner.

To give one example, if I'm practicing *Qigong* in a relaxed-but-awake state I might be able to feel the Etheric Body's energy channels (*Qi* meridians); but if I then go to sleep and have a deep-phase Lucid Dream (**LD-3**), then I'm now fully occupying my Etheric Body rather than merely observing it. After all, dreams are largely the sensory reflections of what's experienced in the Gross Body. There's more to dreams than that, of course, but there's a very real sense in saying that dreams are sensory and emotional reflections of bioelectrical and biochemical processes in the nervous system. Furthermore, if I can manage to expand those waves outward and travel with them beyond my physical organism, then I've just achieved Astral Projection. So, in this way, the Astral "body" may be a unique trick of the nervous system. Bioelectrical waves are sent forth into the environment and, forming a sort of feedback loop with the nervous system, impressions are received and sent back to the brain to be decoded in sensory language. These experiences are then interpreted according to whatever philosophical framework we're partial to.

Speaking of experiences and their interpretations, let's take a look at the various "symptoms" associated with OOBE and see if we can find a plausible explanation for them.

(5)

The Infamous Vibrational State Explained

Many misunderstand the so-called *vibrational state* associated with Astral Projection. The common notion is that the sensation of vibrations permeating the body (Etheric Body) is a sure sign that OOBE is about to occur. Although this idea isn't totally wrong, it's one-sided and leaves out two very important elements: First, the vibrational state isn't just a sign that Astral Projection is about to occur, it's also a sign that you're waking up! Remember, Conscious Sleep is a *hybrid* state, and this goes for all aspects of Conscious Sleep. It's a hybrid interaction of the Gross, Subtle and Causal bodies (and everything in between). It's also a hybrid interaction of the *five basic brainwaves*: *Beta, Alpha, Theta, Delta* and *Gamma,* and these, in turn, are manifestations of the different wave-states and currents of bio-electricity (*Qi,* Prana, Orgone) circulating in and around the Etheric meridians and Gross Body nervous system.

How this works in practice can be grasped by analogy to the art of making music. Most of us are accustomed to thinking of music as a form of harmonic resonance. But this rather Epicurean way of looking at what music is an illusion of preference. Most of us are aware of what resonance is, though we may not have known what to call it. Resonance occurs when an object is struck, scratched, plucked or billowed, causing it to vibrate at a certain frequency. The consequence of this is that anything else near that vibrating object will also vibrate in response. So, if I'm in a musical Conservatory filled with musical instruments, and I then press the piano key of G-Major, then every guitar, cello, violin or crystal wine-glass in that room will find itself vibrating also at G-Major.

But what looks like resonance at one end is *dissonance* on the other. These musical vibrations which tickle our eardrums are, at their root, little earthquakes. You see, to us they sound pleasant, but to a smaller creature, say, an ant, these vibrations are nothing short of apocalyptic! Furthermore, these vibrations begin with a somewhat violent act on the part of the musician. From the outside, a concert pianist is elegantly pressing the keys to make enjoyable music, but on the inside of the piano are little hammers banging away on strings which have been tightened at varying degrees so that they cooperate while being struck. We hear that cooperation as music. But what's music on one side is chaos on the other, and which one it ends up being will depend upon the perspective of the creature experiencing it.

A similar phenomenon occurs on the level of rational thought. If seven people are sitting in a room discussing politics, and none of them can agree on the issues at hand, then we might call this "social cognitive dissonance," to coin a phrase. We experience this inwardly as a peculiar species of discomfort, as the strings of cherished ideologies are violently plucked by another with an opposing standpoint. But if these seven can acknowledge that their apparent differences are, at their root, just seven different valid perspectives on the same exact issue, then they will discover that their so-called differences may be seven different octaves of the same musical scale of the same song.

Similar is the case with the vibrational state of Astral Projection. The five basic brainwaves, for example, are simply the bioelectrical manifestation of the three broad states of Waking, Dreaming and Deep Dreamless Sleep. As you acclimate yourself to the in-between phases of these bioelectrical currents, and the mind-states they correspond to, you'll become aware that they temporarily overlap in very much the same way that fresh river water, when flowing into the sea, overlaps with the salt water waves.

The presence of your wakeful mind during Astral Projection or Lucid Dreaming causes a sort of dissonance with the sleeping state, but, as we've just seen, what's dissonance on one end is resonance on the other. The music is made by making sure that the strings of your Gross, Subtle and Causal bodies are tuned to exactly the right frequency for the phenomena associated with Conscious Sleep to occur. If the strings are too loose, you'll fall asleep; if they're too tight, you'll wake up. That's the whole art of being a Veiler in a nutshell!

(6)
The Restlessness Method and the Astral Dream Technique

When attempting Astral Projection, it's very important to resist the urge to move your physical body in any way—whether it's changing sleeping postures, scratching an itch, stretching, swallowing, or otherwise fidgeting. You want to remain physically motionless. This will typically create an uncomfortable feeling of restlessness and a strong desire to move. This is the crucial moment for Astral Projection! You want to take this urge to move your Gross Body and use it to move your Astral Body instead. For example, if you're lying on your back, and you feel a strong desire to change to a fetal posture, move your Astral Body in the direction you desire. Of course, this demands that you know how to move your Astral Body. In *Behind the Veil* I offered a series of basic methods designed to train this ability. Here I'm going to teach you some advanced methods of training (and unifying) your Gross, Etheric, Astral and Causal bodies.

We'll start with something I call *The Restlessness Method.*

One of the most powerful and direct ways to induce an OOBE is to use the restlessness and discomfort of the physical body as a springboard. However, the discomfort can't be so great that it has the opposite effect and keeps you locked in your Gross Body, thereby chaining you to the *Veil of Tears*. Here's how it works:

If you're familiar with *The 4:00 am Method* from *Behind the Veil,* then you already know the first half of this technique. More popularly known as the *Wake Back to Bed* technique (WBTB), this approach has received the most attention from mainstream science.

The power behind this technique is its timing. Generally speaking, because the period of time between (roughly) 4:00 am–6:00 am presents a nice balance of Sleepiness and Wakefulness, this is fertile ground for all aspects of Conscious Sleep. For this reason, I always recommend that beginners practice at this time. The Hindus refer to this twilight period as the *Bramamuhurt*—when the soul of God communes with a person's soul.

So, the first thing you must do is set your alarm for 4:00 am. It's best to use an alarm that features an adjustable volume which slowly increases rather than jolts you awake. Being jolted awake is bad for your nerves and *Qi* meridians, and if you wake up too much, you'll disrupt the balance of *Yin* and *Yang* upon which this method depends. You don't want to wake up totally, but only enough to consciously control the experience.

For at least one week, simply get into the habit of waking up at 4:00 am. If you'd like to practice other methods of Conscious Sleep during this time, feel free to do so, but the main point is to learn to wake up every morning at 4:00 am without the need for an alarm. The next step in the technique will explain why. This step also marks the beginning of *The Restlessness Method.*

The next step is to remain completely motionless. And when I say "completely motionless" I mean *don't move a muscle*! By far the most common cause of all failed attempts at early-morning Conscious Sleep has to do with readjusting the physical body for comfort. Don't do that!

Instead, remain exactly as you find yourself upon waking. If you don't already feel a strong urge to change positions, you soon will. And when you do feel it, simply move your Subtle Body in the direction you'd like your Gross Body to go. Even if your desire is to move only one limb, say, your arm, then move your Astral arm in the desired direction while keeping your physical arm exactly where it is.

Remember these simple guidelines:

- Movement experienced in the Gross Body is controlled by the physical nervous system.
- Movement experienced in the Subtle Body is controlled by the Etheric nervous system.
- Movement experienced in the Causal Body is controlled by the Astral nervous system.

These qualifications aren't simply my attempt at New Age metaphysical nonsense. Far from it! They're simply a convenient way to explain how these things are experienced by most people. Another way to put it would be to say that basic physical movement in the waking state is governed by nerve-impulses that are largely unconscious. For example, if there's an apple on my coffee table, and I want to eat it, I simply grab the apple and take a bite. The entire conscious process is really just a two-step procedure of reaching for the apple and putting it to my lips. The physical motions in between these two steps are typically ignored. This is why Subtle Body arts—such as *Tai Chi Chuan* or *Feldenkrais*—which utilize physical movement, are performed very deliberately, slowly and in a highly relaxed but alert state of mind. The goal of these arts is to gradually reduce sole reliance on the physical muscles and replace them with Subtle Body movements. In other words, the goal is to move from Physical muscles, to Etheric muscles, to Astral muscles.

So when I use terms like "etheric", or "astral", or "causal" in this context, what I'm actually saying is that movement, and the consciousness behind that movement, are experienced in radically different ways depending upon one's state of consciousness and the feeling of embodiment (or disembodiment) it generates. When I'm practicing *Qigong*—say, the *Microcosmic Orbit* meditation—I first experience micro-movements on a physical level traveling up my spine and down the front of my body. As I approach mastery, however, even these micro-movements disappear and are gradually replaced by the movement of *Qi*. To be sure, there's an in-between stage where, being at an intermediate level of skill, I can't tell the difference between physical micro-movement and the circulation of *Qi*; but time and consistent practice will soon teach me to spot the difference between them.

As I've said: In the *Veil of Tears,* your muscles move. In the *Veil of Breath,* your lifeforce moves. In the *Veil of Dreams,* your emotions move. In the *Veil of Ghosts,* your consciousness moves. And in the *Veil of Bliss,* all movement ceases until you decide where, when and with what Body to move.

Exercise: The Astral Dream Technique

Now let's expand on *The Restlessness Method* and see where it takes us. The following method was one that I created on the spot, as my own skill at Astral Projection was developing. I call it *The Astral Dream Technique.* It dawned on me as a natural development of my own experimentation, which is how everything develops really.

So here's what to do! Follow the same procedure as *The Restlessness Method* outlined above but add the following steps:

As soon as you awaken in the early morning with a strong desire to move your body, gently tune your mind into the dream scenarios you were just having *and* begin moving your Astral Body. This is a delicate operation, and it takes practice to catch the right balance between Asleep and Awake. You want to move your Astral Body right away because otherwise you'll fall back into sleep paralysis and unconsciousness. Also, you want to become aware of your dreams at this time because you're going to induce an Astral Dream. In the beginning phase of this method, you'll probably only access the **LD-2** phase of Lucidity. That's what you want! Soon, you'll be in full-blown **LD-3**, but only for a moment. You're just passing through the *Veil of Dreams* to get to the *Veil of Ghosts.*

If you've succeeded in following the steps so far, you should now be straddling the Astral and Dream planes. Next, try to spot a dream image and latch onto it with your mind. Once you have it firmly in sight, reach up or into the dream image with your Astral arms. At this phase, it's very likely that you'll actually see your Astral arms reaching for the image. Don't be alarmed; otherwise the excitement will wake you up. (Incidentally, this action of reaching up and into a dream image with your arms is known in Western Hermeticism as *The Sign of the Enterer* and is featured in many banishing and invoking rituals.)

By this time, you should be firmly rooted in the *Veil of Dreams* but in your Astral Body! As such, you are in a unique position. Not only can you more directly interact with dream characters, you'll also be able to transcend the Dream World altogether and roam about behind the *Veil of Ghosts* (the so-called Astral Plane) and the *Veil of Tears.*

Besides the precariousness of either falling asleep or waking up, there's another potentially distracting element with the power to abort *The Astral Dream Method.* It has to do with your Etheric *Qi* system and how it operates. Eventually, you'll be able to override this system, effectively using it to your advantage, but in the beginning it can be quite bothersome. For example, because the early morning hours find the bodymind becoming increasingly more *Yang* (awake), any movement of the Astral Body in a *Yang* direction will wake the physical body up. If, for instance, you try to perform the "forward rolling" technique at this time (see the *120-Days Curriculum* in *Behind the Veil),* or even if you try to sit up in your Astral Body, you might overly stimulate your Etheric Body and wake up completely. Why? Because these are *Yang* movements! That is to say, you're moving your Astral Body in the direction of a *Yang* meridian in your Etheric *Qi* Body. In this case, what typically happens is that the "vibrational stage" of the Astral exit becomes far too pronounced, and your physical muscles and mind become energized to the point where you end up in your Gross Body. This would work to your advantage were you to practice at bedtime when the body is becoming more *Yin,* but during the morning hours, too much of a *Yang* movement in a Yang direction can cause you to awaken.

Furthermore, and this applies especially to men, this early-morning movement of the Astral Body can also cause hyper-sexual arousal. Obviously, too much sexual arousal will serve as a distraction and get in the way of full OOBE. Ironically, this excess sexual energy can also fuel the Astral exit—but only if your mind has been sufficiently trained to do so. The key to avoiding these pitfalls is twofold:

1. You must learn to first reach up with only your Astral arms. If you can manage to first move only your Astral extremities and avoid moving your torso, you should be fine. The rest of your Astral Body will follow automatically once sleep paralysis takes over. Not always, but most of the time.
2. Develop your willpower! If you have poor impulse-control, sexual arousal (or any strong sensation) will pull you back into your Gross Body.

As always, the keys to success are perseverance, good timing, viable methods, and a strong willpower.

(7)
Astral Blindness: Seeing on the Astral Plane

It's not uncommon for beginners to experience difficulty seeing during an OOBE. When not completely blind, a beginner will typically suffer from blurred vision. At times it may seem as though the Astral Plane is shrouded in an eternal twilight, and all you can make out is your hands or feet. I also experience this blindness from time to time. Over the years I've developed methods for countering this problem and I'm happy to share these with you here. Try this:

• With eyes half open, gently gaze at the tip of your nose. Don't strain or go cross-eyed! Simply allow your eyes to rest downward to the tip of your nose. If you do this correctly, your nose will seem to disappear. This does three things: One, it stops your eyes from moving. Because your eyes are trained to move constantly, the energy will fall backwards and switch on your inner-sight. Two, because your eyes move to follow thought, thought will cease when your eyes stop moving. And three, it keeps your energy close to your body, which is what activates the vibrations.

• After a few moments, close your eyes but continue to look as though you're still staring at the tip of your nose. At the same time, become aware of the ringing in your ears. Wearing earplugs is a plus. Simply focus on these two things without straining or turning it into too much of a task; otherwise you'll stay locked in the **BETA** state.

• As you enter the sleep cycle, one or both of the following will happen: You'll either see a light emanating from behind your eyes *or* you'll see the room you're in from behind your closed eyes. Once you do, you can confirm that this is Astral sight by waving your hands in front of your face. They'll appear very clear. (This might surprise you at first. It certainly surprised me when it first happened!)

The yogic practice called *Suriya Shabda* is a very effective **WILD** (Wake Induced Lucid Dreaming) technique which begins by meditating on the subtle tones and ringing sounds in your ears. Awareness of these inner sounds during the onset of **REM** (the pre-**REM** period) sleep has proven to increase the presence a unique form of brainwave, called *K-complexes.* As we've seen, these have a sedative effect on awareness and function as a preserver of unconsciousness (along with slow-wave spindles). *K-complexes* can be evoked by way of acoustic stimulation, which may account for the success of *Binaural Beats* technology in certain forms of Causal meditation. This may also account for the efficacy of *Suriya Shabda* for consciously sidestepping the *K-complexes'* sedative power. This is especially true during the pre-**REM** state when *PGO-waves* occur. These appear immediately before the onset of **REM** sleep and are dormant during **NREM.** *PGO-waves,* also called *P-Waves,* have been proven to increase the strength and duration of the dreaming phase of sleep. This becomes important when we consider the fact that **REM** has been proven to be largely the brain's way of forming new neural pathways to process and consolidate new skills and memories. If *K-complexes* respond best to acoustic and vestibular stimulation, *PGO-waves* respond best to visual stimulation. Combining the practices of *Suriya Shabda, Phasing* (malleable proprioception), and *Dharana* (visual concentration) is an incredibly potent recipe for Conscious Sleep. Lastly, an increase in Nitric Oxide and Acetylcholine production, a minimization of GABA production, alongside an awareness of the root of thought-impulse at the brainstem, and a relaxed focus on the "inner tones" is a powerful combination for the induction of OOBE in particular. As a side note, consider that **NREM** sleep is called "synchronized sleep" because during this time neuronal activity, respiration and brainwave activity are in complete harmony. Therefore, I point out that the practice of Pellucid Sleep is identical to most forms of meditation, especially those that focus on the body's healing potential and the storing and circulating of Etheric force (*Qi*). **REM** sleep, on the other hand, is also called "paradoxical sleep" due to its similarities with the brain's activity during the waking state. The body, however, is asleep. Muscle tone is gone (**REM** atonia), and serotonin is suppressed. For this reason, I associate all contemplative practices with the conscious employment of this state (e.g., Contemplative Prayer, Astral Projection, OOBE, Vision Quests, and even certain entheogens).

CHAPTER FOUR

PELLUCID SLEEP AND DREAMING

(1)
Pellucid Sleep and Dreaming:
Meditation Carried into the Sleep Cycle

Since its validation by mainstream science, the popularity of the phenomenon called Lucid Dreaming has grown rapidly. Arguably the coolest kid in school, Lucid Dreaming is unique in that it represents an actual bridge between science, the New Age movement, and the ancient mystical traditions of the world. Joining the ranks of other well-known rock stars such as Astral Projection, Near Death Experience (NDE), Remote Viewing, and Psychedelia, Lucid Dreaming has opened the lines of communication between the occult and the obvious.

I've been a Lucid Dreamer for over twenty years. My journey began as a child of only nine summers, a journey that would eventually lead me to create the system I call *Subliminal Cognition Training (SCT)*. The spiritual and psychological disciplines that went into the construction of *SCT* have taught me not only how to actively participate in Lucid Dreaming, but also how to spot, engage, and strengthen the other "muscles" involved in Conscious Sleep. One of the most important of these "muscles," the stabilizer muscles, if you will, belong to the Causal Body. (We encountered the Causal Body in Chapter Two when we learned the skill of Trance and applied it to the practice of Embryonic Breathing meditation.)

The ability to remain alert and, in a word, *unaffected,* during specific or all phases of the sleep cycle, is called *Pellucidity.*

We learned in *Behind the Veil* that the sleep cycle is composed mostly of **NREM** (non-dreaming) sleep. Although bursts of dreaming can occur during **NREM**, they're usually less colorful and dramatic as dreams in **REM**. Whenever you're meditating and see dream scenarios dancing behind your closed eyes, that's a light form of Pellucid Dreaming.

In this Chapter, we'll explore the topic of Pellucidity. We'll see how differs from Lucid Dreaming, how to deepen our experience of it, and what benefits and dangers this might involve. It helps to know that *Pellucidity is really just meditation carried into the sleep cycle.* Just as we actively avoid getting lost in thoughts and emotions during sitting meditation, so too do we avoid getting lost in dreams while practicing Pellucidity. In both of these events, we rest in pure Being, like a candle flame in a windless room.

Meditation: Another Name for Conscious Sleep

After many years of Lucid Dreaming and other forms of Out of Body Experiences, on top of many years of practicing various forms of meditation to gain control over those experiences, I began to see that these two seemingly discreet areas of psychic activity are, in fact, just different names given to specific manifestations of the same phenomenon.

Perhaps a few examples would shed some light on this claim:

- In the ancient Hebrew mystical tradition, the post-rabbinical texts known as *Hekaloth* and *Merkabah* describe the methods and planes of "spiritual ascent" through Lucid Dreaming and Astral Projection. Of course, then, as well as today, these two psychic capacities are rarely teased apart in the texts.
- The Huichol Indians of Mexico induce Lucid Dreaming states by ingesting plants to enhance the vividness of dreams. At other times they ingest peyote, a powerful psychedelic, to induce vision-quests and OOBE.
- In the Tantric branch of Tibetan yoga, the *Milam* method of attaining spiritual enlightenment through Lucid and Pellucid Dreaming is one of the oldest in the world. In this approach, the adept uses advanced meditation to enter into the sleep cycle with full awareness.
- Vedanta yoga, arguably the most comprehensive systems of psychic mastery known to man, claims that human beings possess a Gross, Subtle, Causal and Nondual "body", corresponding to the three broad states of Waking, Dreaming and Dreamless Sleep, respectively, with the Nondual Body being the conscious experiencing of all three Bodies simultaneously and at all times. The Vedantist "athlete" achieves this through specific meditation practices.

As you can see, there truly is no separating meditation and Conscious Sleep. In the final analysis, they are one and the same thing. Granted, each of the aforementioned capacities and experiences demand a unique approach, which is why the word "meditation" has come to mean so many contradictory things. If you take, for example, the Lucid Dream induction technique popularly known as Guided Meditation, and you put it side-by-side with the "no-thought" meditation of Zen Buddhism, these two methods of meditation clearly have little in common! But then again, neither does the non-dreaming phase of sleep have anything in common with the dreaming phase. And yet they're inseparable from each other! Dreaming (**REM**) and non-dreaming (**NREM**) are the two poles of a single phenomenon called *Sleep.*

(2)
My Initiation into Pellucidity

It was a hot August afternoon. The year was 1998. Having just arrived home from a brutal thirteen-hour workday of hanging sheetrock, I was looking forward to my first lesson with Dr. John Mumford (Swami Anandakapila Saraswati). I was looking forward to it because I was going to be taught the true purpose of the *Savasana* pose of Hatha Yoga, called *Yoga Nidra* (Conscious Sleep). Sleep, conscious or not, was most welcome as far as I was concerned! Little did I know that I was about to have my mind blown wide open.

Dr. Mumford begins with the typical instructions for *Progressive Relaxation.* Starting from the feet and slowly progressing up the body, you gently lead your awareness into each zone of the body (called "marmasthanani") and relax the area fully before moving on to the next zone. It's important to stay alert and keep the mind engaged in the exercise, otherwise you'll likely fall asleep. This combination of deep relaxation and concentration results in a gradual descent into Conscious Sleep.

I should point out that, at that time, I had no knowledge of the different phases of the sleep cycle. I simply performed the technique as instructed, step by step, and had no idea of what to expect. It would take several years of practice before I'd come to see the importance of this exercise.

After about half an hour into my practice of *Savasana,* I noticed I was having considerable difficulty maintaining awareness of my body. My mind, too, was wobbling and wavering between following the instructions, on the one hand, and getting lost in absurd dream-scenarios and internal dialogue, on the other. My breathing would suddenly seem to stop, and I'd briefly come back to awareness with a gasp. Still, I persisted in following the exercise through to the end. Once the progressive relaxation had reached the top of my head, there began the second phase of *Yoga Nidra.* At that point in the exercise, my awareness of myself as Daniel Kelley wasn't something I could easily define if asked to do so. Rather, I just *was.* That is to say, I was consciousness without a body, without reference or content. Years later, I'd learn that this was simply the first phase of the sleep cycle, and I was experiencing it *consciously.*

The second phase of Dr. Mumford's instructions for *Yoga Nidra* involves rotating your awareness counterclockwise, in ever expanding circles around the body. These sweeping spirals of awareness are gradually led upward and away from the body. It was precisely here, as I lay supine on the floor, that my breakthrough occurred. As I spiraled my awareness in ever-expanding circles, I suddenly became aware of my body again. Only this wasn't my *physical* body! I felt strange electrical currents coursing through me, and it felt as though the entire universe was rocking and waving in a circular motion.

Then it hit me…

I had experienced this before! In all my years of spontaneous Lucid Dreaming and OOBE, there were moments when I felt these exact same sensations. The act of gradually entering the sleep cycle through the practice of *Yoga Nidra* had allowed me to consciously glimpse the liminal phases of Conscious Sleep. Moreover, this practice had shown me the location of the sleep cycle where resides the beginning phases of OOBE and Pellucid Sleep and Dreaming. Today, *Yoga Nidra* is one of many methods for inducing what has come to be called Wake Induced Lucid Dreaming (**WILD**).

I went on to practice *Yoga Nidra* for the next twenty years, adding to it and refining it as new experiences occurred. But the essence of *Yoga Nidra* lies in its power to produce what's been called the *Causal* state of consciousness. Generally speaking, the Causal state is just that: the cause of all other states of awareness. Think of it as the root of self-awareness. The Causal state is the aim of such disciplines as Zen meditation, the *"Cloud of Unknowing"* of the Gnostics, and the *"Clear Light"* meditation of Tibetan Buddhism. It's also the essence of Pellucid Sleep and Dreaming.

The term "Pellucid Dreaming" was first introduced by the philosopher, Ken Wilber, in his book *One Taste* (Shambhala Publications, 2000). Sometimes called *Translucid* Dreaming, Pellucidity is the less popular sibling of Lucid Dreaming. This is unfortunate. For one thing, Pellucidity is the very root of all other forms of Conscious Sleep. Without strong Pellucidity, you wouldn't be able to sustain consistent Lucid Dreaming. This is one of the most common reasons why many people experience Lucid Dreams only once in a while, randomly and seemingly without any rhyme or reason.

Pellucid Sleep and Pellucid Dreaming are different in that the latter occurs during the **REM** (dreaming) phase of the sleep cycle, whereas the former occurs during the **NREM** (dreamless) phase. Unlike *Lucid* Dreaming, which involves an active participation with the dream narrative (to a greater or lesser degree), Pellucid Dreaming is a passive witnessing of the dream state, and tends to find the sleeper unwilling (but not unable) to interfere with the dream.

Does this sound familiar? It should!

That's just another way of describing the aim of mindfulness meditation. So it follows that Conscious Sleep can't be reduced to Lucid Dreaming alone. Conscious Sleep is a multifaceted tapestry that contains Lucid Dreaming, OOBE, Meditation, Mindfulness, Astral Projection, NDE, Vision-quests, Soul-retrieval, and so much more. Lucid Dreaming may be the coolest kid in class right now, but her popularity comes on the heels of Pellucid Sleep and Dreaming.

(3)
Pellucidity and the Skill of Trance:
The Four Stages of Pellucidity

In *Behind the Veil* I stressed the importance of learning the skill of Trance. In this section, I'll elaborate on this theme, but the focus will be on the *why* more than on the *how*. This fundamental skill is of the utmost importance, as it's the key to the relationship between meditation and the four stages of Pellucidity. The four stages are:

- **PS-1**
- **PS-2**
- **PD-3**
- **PD-4**

NOTE: PS-1 and **PS-2** are referred to as Pellucid *Sleep* rather than Pellucid *Dreaming* because you're not really dreaming during **NREM**. There may be microbursts of dreaming, sure, but elaborate and profound dreams don't begin until the onset of **REM.**

The skill of entering Trance is really no more than the conscious induction of the initial phases of sleep. In sitting meditation, such as Embryonic Breathing and Microcosmic Orbit meditation, as in light **PS-1** presents itself as total cessation of abstract thinking and mental chatter, deep relaxation of the physical body and subjective warming of the hands and feet. **PS-2** presents itself in sitting meditation as total loss of bodily awareness, "nodding off," occasional snoring, and sensory withdrawal. This is the most regenerative stage of sleep, when the **DELTA** brainwave predominates, and it's for this reason that the practice of Embryonic Breathing targets this stage of Pellucidity. Remember, the main purpose of Embryonic Breathing is to store abundant *Qi* in the Lower Dantian to fuel the regeneration process.

The third and fourth stages of Pellucid Sleep represent Pellucid Dreaming proper:

PD-3 is achieved the moment you can sustain awareness through hypnagogia, microbursts of dreaming, and the sedative *K-Complexes* without getting lost in them or falling asleep. This is harder than it sounds. Unlike the Pellucidity achieved during sitting meditation, the capacity to remain alert during this phase of sleep *while lying down* is exceptionally difficult, which is one reason why most meditation methods are practiced in a sitting posture. The habit of falling asleep while lying down is very deeply ingrained, and it's a habit that must be kicked with both feet while learning Conscious Sleep.

PD-4 is the most profound level of Pellucid Dreaming. It's been achieved the moment you can sustain awareness into **REM** sleep without getting lost in Vivid or Lucid dreams. It's difficult to describe what this feels like. The most that can be said is that it's like being in the womb of the universe itself, silent and peaceful, but very much aware of the distant parade called *life*. Dreams come and go. Feelings come and go. Indeed, most things that arise are happily disregarded in favor of the profound bliss of pure being. The only thing that tends to jolt most people out of the immovable calm of **PD-4** is the shock of Astral Projection exit-symptoms.

Unlike Vivid and Lucid Dreaming, which are best accessed in the **REM** stage of sleep, Pellucid Dreaming is best learned during **NREM** stages of sleep, at least initially. This is great news since **NREM** sleep makes up roughly 75% of the sleep cycle! That means that there are more opportunities for Pellucid Dreaming than there are for Vivid and Lucid Dreaming. Indeed, some people learn Lucid Dreaming spontaneously by learning Pellucid Dreaming first, and I believe that's how Tibetan Dream Yoga was developed. Skilled meditators, capable of carrying their meditation through the entire sleep cycle, eventually discovered that they could choose to either engage or passively witness their dreams. After all, Lucid Dreaming is impossible without at least some degree of Causal Body (Pellucid) development.

The goal of learning Pellucid Sleep is the ability to sustain it into and past **REM** sleep. I should point out that it's notoriously difficult to maintain stable Pellucidity during the transition from **NREM** to **REM**. It's not unlike being given a powerful psychedelic while attempting to meditate. Imagine trying to remain psychologically centered and calm after taking LSD or DMT! Naturally, this requires patience, regular practice, and a certain amount of time to accomplish.

(4)
Bend To The Light: Conscious Sleep as a Training for Death

The similarities between Conscious Sleep and the timeless myth called *The Hero's Descent* are undeniable. We find this theme in virtually every known culture of the world, from the caves of the Himalayas to the jungles of Africa to the plains of the Western Americas. Briefly, *The Hero's Descent* involves a dramatic encounter with the Hero's own fears, bringing them into sharp focus, with the probability of his own demise being the worst of the Hero's terrors.

The most perennial example of *The Hero's Descent* belongs to the Shamanic traditions of the world, and this includes the famous *Bardo Thodol* (Tibetan Book of the Dead). Death and rebirth rituals of Shamanic cultures are practiced to this very day, and typically involve a "vision-quest" or "soul-retrieval" experience. These can be quite profound—traumatic even—and are produced in a number of different ways. I'd like to discuss what soul-retrieval is and why it's performed.

If you think of soul-retrieval as a magical-minded expression of the *Individuation Process,* then you're on the right track. Created by psychologist, Carl Gustav Jung, the Individuation Process involves uniting the Conscious and Unconscious regions of a person's psyche. It's assumed that a large percentage of what's called "mental illness" can be healed by becoming, as it were, a whole person. You see, most of us live in a small portion of our total selves (small "I"). Consequently, we become imprisoned within the walls of our own minds and the rest of what makes us individuals becomes split off from the total Self (big

"I"). The result of this psychic divorce is neurosis, existential meaninglessness, anxiety, and a nagging sense that something's missing.

Soul-retrieval is a quest, the aim of which is to reclaim those alienated parts of the psyche…

The end result of this is holistic integration of the little "I" with the big "I" is a more balanced, sane, healthy, courageous, insightful and relaxed person. But the road is long and the obstacles great. Those exiled elements of the Self are coveted and guarded by fearsome dragons of the Pit, and to win the day the Fool must become a Knight. Only, the Fool doesn't become a Knight *first* and then slay the Dragons; rather, the Fool becomes Knighted in the very act of facing his fears *as a Fool!*

That last part is very important to understand, because if you wait until you're brave enough to make *The Descent*, you'll never do it.

I equate *The Hero's Descent* with the plight of the dedicated Veiler. Sadly, many Lucid Dreamers never encounter the death/rebirth process in their nightly jaunts because their training plateaus at the "psychic video game" phase. Consequently, many Oneironauts only superficially engage the spiritual facets of Conscious Sleep. I've coined the term "Veiler", to distinguish between those people who are aiming higher and those who are just having fun.

As I hope you know by now, *SCT* aims at the attainment of the continuity of consciousness throughout the three broad states of Waking, Dreaming and deep Dreamless Sleep. One of the primary elements of this system involves *The Hero's Descent* and an encounter with egoic annihilation.

The simple truth is that we go through this mini-death every night, only we're not present when it happens. We're drooling on our pillows. That said, you'll logically ask, "Why would anyone want to experience self-annihilation?!" The answer to this question is a little complicated, but the skinny answer is that it frees you from your restricted identity to only one expression of your total consciousness, namely that of the *Waking* state, so that you're now free to explore the hidden treasures of consciousness and, frankly speaking, to hear what the rest of you has to say.

Perhaps some examples will clarify the importance of this aspect of Conscious Sleep:

Have you ever been addicted to anything? Well, I was! I smoked cigarettes for twelve years, beginning at the tender age of twelve and quitting at twenty-four. It wasn't easy! I tried everything: the nicotine patch, the pills that make cigarettes taste bad, cigarettes that gradually decrease nicotine content until you've "weaned" off of them entirely. Nothing worked…

Eventually, the only thing that did the trick was quitting, as they say, "cold-turkey," and clawing my way through the withdrawals. One thing I discovered was that my craving completely vanished whenever I was asleep and Lucid Dreaming. This may sound like an anticlimax, but the effect it had upon me was profound. I noticed that, even though I was fully conscious in my dreams, I had absolutely no desire to smoke cigarettes! What changed?

Well, the only conclusion I could draw was that I was either tapping into a part of my nervous-system that was beyond the reach of addiction, or I was accessing a different "body" entirely. Whichever it was, one thing was certain: I was experiencing a world and a life in which I was freed from addiction.

I also utilized this unique function of Conscious Sleep when I had a terrible toothache. I noticed that the pain completely vanished when I entered Pellucid and Lucid Dreaming. At one point, I was at a dentist appointment and met a soldier in the Marines. She was a woman of about thirty, and had just undergone root canal surgery without anesthesia. I asked her how she accomplished such a feat and she said, "I put myself into an in-between state of sleep and awake. I know the pain is there, but it's somewhere on the fringe of my awareness."

Five years later, I accomplished the same thing when I had my wisdom teeth removed. In its essence, this is really just a form of self-hypnosis, as hypnosis is also a creative use of Conscious Sleep.

So what does all this have to do with the proverbial descent into the Underworld of the psyche?

I can think of no better answer to this question than this saying of a famous Zen master:

"You suffer because 99.9% of your problems are about yourself, and there isn't one."

This is not saying that you don't exist. Rather, it's saying that there's more to you than the self you so desperately cling to. And to truly encounter these deeper fathoms of your consciousness, you must loosen that chronic grip you have on your soul. The systems of Conscious Sleep are designed to teach you how to do just that.

The fundamental skill to learn during this training is *surrender of your need for control.* Anyone who's ever ingested a powerful psychedelic will attest to this basic tenet, and Conscious Sleep *is* a psychedelic experience. Besides the actual transition from Awake to Asleep, there's a specific point during the sleep-cycle when you actually die as a conscious being. I call this threshold *The Veil,* and it truly is an experience of annihilation on all levels of being and knowing. In fact, it feels as if the entire universe is being swallowed up in an eternal grave. But if you can persevere past this point, you'll discover that, far from being the end of the world, you've just encountered the beginning of a new one. And isn't that what *life* is all about?

(5)
The Oversoul: Lord of the Pellucid State

"We shall not cease from exploration, and the end of all our exploring will be to arrive where we started and know the place for the first time."
— T.S. Eliot

It was a variety of specific experiences and revelations that led me to understand the above quote. It began in early childhood. I stumbled upon, or was perhaps guided by, some unseen hand to a *center* within my consciousness free from the drama and agonies of life. I still recall with fondness those blissful moments spent in that spiritual center, soaking in Eternity. Usually in the early morning hours, as I lay in bed, with my consciousness floating on the threshold between my dreams and the sounds of the awakening world, I'd enjoy this secret heaven. Sometimes I could feel my physical body against the mattress; at other times I couldn't feel it at all. I felt instead as though I were at the center of all creation, a great spectator of all that is or ever was. Astral Travel was also common in those days while I was in the Pellucid state.

Such are the treasures of Pellucidity.

As I grew older, I could see in people who were sick, depressed or dying an unconscious desire to go back to this spiritual center. This inner pagoda is like an invisible Eye watching the theatrics of our individual lives; it knows the secret to our stories. It usually doesn't gift us with the knowledge of this secret, and I think I know why.

We need to forget that we're playing a role in order to fully believe it. And we need to believe the story in order to throw ourselves fully into it!

Moreover, we need to fully believe in our "fictional" self and its myriad roles in order to exhaust the energies (karma) bound up in those roles. In short, we need to forget that we're playing a role, that we're dreaming while awake. Plato referred to this forgetting as "metensomatosis", and the act of recalling that our lives are just *functional fictions* as "anamnesis". And this recalling of the self to its spiritual Center seems to strike only certain people. Why? I don't yet know. Maybe I never will. But I'm one such person…

My experiences with this inner Eye have left me wondering whether rediscovering it is intended to be a blessing or curse. Or is it even "intended" at all? And, if so, then by what? Whom? One's own Holy Guardian Angel? God? Goddess? Or is it all a strange accident?

The famous American essayist, Ralph Waldo Emerson, referred to this transcendent Center as the *Oversoul*. In his masterpiece bearing the same name, Emerson writes:

> "We live in succession, in division, in parts and particles. Meantime, within man, is the soul of the whole; the wise silence; the universal beauty to which every part and particle is equally related; the eternal One."

Emerson is saying that our individual identities are mere actors on the world stage. Behind the face we show to the world there lies our soul (true self), which is but an envoy for the greater Oversoul which transcends, but includes, the individual souls of mankind. Your individual ego may or may not be a faithful representative of your true soul and self. If it is, then you ally yourself to the Oversoul which has its own intelligence and Will.

My own experience with the Oversoul convinces me that Emerson was on to something. And almost all of my experiences with the Oversoul have been had during Pellucid Dreaming. It appears that the human soul, when not resting in the Void as a "consciousness without consciousness," concerns itself only with taking stock of those aspects of our lives that hold profound meaning or purpose. The fleeting anxieties and urges of the ego seem to hold no appeal for the soul within man.

That the Oversoul is most easily accessed through Pellucidity shouldn't come as a surprise. After all, the Causal Body is the direct link between your ego and your soul. It carries the "karmic script" that you must play out in the fictional roles you identify with in daily life.

When I first began experiencing the Oversoul in the Pellucid state, I experienced it as a sort of internal Eye, or perhaps a camera, that was taking stock of the essences of the various milestones of my lifetime. For example, have you ever heard the theory that a person's life "flashes before his eyes" at the moment of death? This holds that the major themes of your life will replay before your mind's eye in the moments preceding your death, like an inner movie. In my opinion, this experience holds the deeper meaning behind T.S. Eliot's quote.

A typical encounter with the Oversoul during Pellucid Dreaming goes something like this:

Usually during the second or third round of **REM**, when dreaming is especially vivid and prolonged, it's possible to catch a glimpse of the workings of the Oversoul. Spontaneously, or through willful practice, you might root yourself in your Causal Body and observe, as if through a window, the theater of your dreams. I find the hours from 3:00 am to 5:00 am to be particularly potent times for Pellucid Dreaming of this magnitude.

At first, you may find yourself awoken by a strange emotional sensation, a psychological mood with a distinctly nostalgic tone. Sometimes this is a pleasant experience, sometimes not. What makes it pleasant or unpleasant often depends upon your attitude toward change, aging and especially death. Remember that the priorities of your soul are often different from those of your ego. Thus, when you glimpse your soul's "thoughts," you'll find them centered on major life themes rather than the quotidian details of your life. The signature mood of an Oversoul encounter is one of a bird's eye view of the quintessential thematic tone of your entire incarnation. So, if throughout the years you've experienced many changes in your identity, your soul takes a snapshot of those changes. Everything else falls by the wayside and is of no concern to your soul. An "existential crisis," for example, is something your soul will take note of. Your favorite singer, on the other hand, will most likely be cast aside.

The dramatic shift in perspective offered by the Oversoul is always quite sobering. Most human beings are a loose collection of sub-personalities, each taking center stage at any given time. Not only that, but the very locus of your overall personality changes as you get older. Consequently, it's easy to forget at forty the way you saw the world when you were a teenager or small child. But your soul remembers!

Your individual soul is like a small tendril extending from the Oversoul. You might think of it as a finger on the Oversoul's hand. Some souls are like the pinky of that hand, others are the index-finger or thumb. No matter what activities any of those fingers do throughout a lifetime, nothing will change the fact that a pinky is a pinky and a thumb is a thumb. We each have a nature, and an encounter with the Oversoul always silences our sub-personalities and recalls us to our true nature.

It's very common for the personality to align itself with the soul during middle age. This is the Autumn of a lifetime, and by this time we've lived through enough seasonal transitions to begin to intuit that which remains relatively unchanging in the midst of them. It's also not uncommon to have more Pellucid encounters with the Oversoul during this period in life. My own encounters with the Oversoul began roughly around the age of thirty-five. I began to spot a pattern of increasing Pellucid Dreams that featured the aforementioned "nostalgic" mood, especially during the Autumn and Winter months.

My experiences were such that I'd sometimes wake up crying. At some point during the night, often in the middle of a Lucid Dream, I'd suddenly become rooted in my Causal Body. My mind became like an invisible camera that would first project a nostalgic dream and then take snapshots of it. Many times, in fact, my dream would suddenly "black out," as though my Third Eye had just blinked. This would be accompanied by the clicking sound of a camera shutter! There was also an unpleasant awareness of the vast amount of time that had elapsed since the biographical period portrayed by the dream and my current age. In other words, I felt *older,* and I silently marveled at how stealthily and silently the years were killing me. This morbid insight led me to scour my lifetimes, past and present, for those salient features and values that I'd all too often neglected to cultivate. In short, these encounters with the Oversoul compelled me to reevaluate my priorities in a sincere way.

So how can you practice aligning yourself with your soul, which is part of the greater Oversoul? Well, the most obvious method is to practice Pellucid Sleep and Dreaming; but is there anything you might practice during the waking hours?

One thing you can do is write an autobiography. This can be as profound or simple a project as you wish, but the key is to divide your life into at least three epochs. The most obvious scheme would be Childhood, Adolescence and Adulthood, but you can arrange it according to your own age and preferences. Regardless of how you choose to proceed, the point is to begin contemplating and articulating the major milestones in your own life. Ask yourself:

- What have I valued most in my life? And how has it changed throughout the years? Has it changed? If so, why? If not, why?
- Have I loved deeply in my life? Have I allowed myself to be loved by myself and others?
- What have been my primary interests in life? And who, other than myself, has been involved in those interests with me?
- Am I afraid of death?
- Have I been open and honest with myself and others, especially about the unwanted aspects of my personality?
- What has been my attitude toward family and friends and community? Have I ever felt like I belonged?

I'm sure you can think of many more questions to ask yourself. The point is to distinguish between the trivial and the significant, and then give your complete attention to what's significant! This is usually a shift of focus that's not without its challenges. To begin with, most of us will resist this perspectival shift in subtle ways. Some habits must be kicked with both feet, foremost among them being the habit of distraction from what's truly important to the soul within us.

Once you discover what your soul needs to work through, what it values, and what it takes note of, the wise thing to do is to live in such a way that honors that True Will. If you don't, and if you decide to lie to yourself, then you may become sick. The illness can be psychological, physical, spiritual or all of the above. But the blunt truth is this:

There exists within you an Eye. It's always watching and taking stock of your life. You can either honor or ignore the facts as this Eye perceives them. The choice is yours. If you honor it then you've found the surest pathway to avoiding nihilism. But if you choose to ignore the needs of your soul, then you may be shocked and mortified one day—perhaps on your death bed—by what it knows.

CHAPTER FIVE

LUCID DREAMING: WHY, WHAT, WHEN AND HOW

(1)
What is Lucidity?

This may seem like a rhetorical question, but it's not. You see, the type of awareness employed during a Lucid Dream is, in many important ways, qualitatively different from the awareness of the typical waking state (and in many ways similar). However, just as you lose yourself in the daily tasks of life while you're awake, so too do you lose yourself in your dreams while you're asleep.

According to the "LuCID Scale" (Voss, 2013), science has concluded that the primary factor which distinguishes a Lucid from a non-Lucid dream is the quality of *Insight*. In other words, a Lucid Dreamer isn't duped by the bizarre logic of the dream world. So the next time you wake up naked next to your celebrity crush, pinch yourself: you're probably just dreaming! But that's not what most people do. They simply take the dream at face value. Consequently, they remain unconscious and Lucidity doesn't occur.

And why should it? Our dreaming minds simply mimic how we use our wakeful minds. That is, we tend to react to life instead of responding consciously to the events of our daily lives. We go on auto-pilot until some irregularity in our routine shocks us into Lucidity.

The practice known as *mindfulness* is just one of the ways by which we can wake up from the dreams of our daily lives. The essence of mindfulness is *self-reflective awareness.* Not the hyper-vigilant awareness of being overly self-conscious (although they share certain characteristics), but rather the relaxed yet alert centeredness of consciousness within your very being. This mindful awareness has been likened to a floodlight, which shines equally upon everything, as opposed to the spotlight-type of awareness called *concentration* which focuses on one thing to the exclusion of all else. Translated into terms of the five brainwaves of an EEG, every time you approach something like it's a task to be completed you remain stuck in the **BETA** wave state (waking consciousness). The moment you relax this work-oriented mindset and just remain with things as they are, you fall into the **ALPHA** wave state. We're all familiar with this state of mind. Whenever you passively listen to the rustling of leaves on an autumn evening, or to the sound of the rain falling upon the roof of your house like a bedtime story lulling you to sleep, you're entering an **ALPHA** state. **ALPHA** is a useful and enjoyable state, but it's also a transitional state between normal waking consciousness and Lucidity.

Many people don't understand that *Lucidity* is a synonym for *Mindfulness.* They're the same exact thing! Just as you can get lost in a fantasy about something that happened in your past or might happen in your future, so too can you get lost in a dream about a flying kangaroo. The important thing to understand is that you can become mindful in both of those situations. In fact, the very awareness that allows you to get lost in fantasy is Lucidity! In the same way, to consciously move from **BETA** to **ALPHA** to **THETA** (dreaming), you need to know that anything you *do* will keep you locked into the **BETA** wave state. Therefore, the only thing you can do is *be* and *watch,* which isn't a "doing" in the typical sense, but has a movement all its own. If you can carry this mindfulness past **ALPHA**, **THETA** and **DELTA** (dreamless sleep), then you enter the **GAMMA** wave state, which is Lucid Dreaming proper. From there, you can choose to get involved in the dream (Lucidity), passively watch the dream (Pellucidity), or even Astral Project (OOBE).

Is Lucid Dreaming the Same as Astral Projection?

At the risk of beating what is by now certainly a dead horse, the answer is: *Yes and No.* Astral Projection is Lucid Dreaming-PLUS. What that "something extra" might be hard to pin down technically, but practically the rules are simple.

Lucid Dreaming is an Astral Body *lubricator,* as it were, and gradually teaches you that your self-awareness has the potential to *move.* That is to say, your consciousness is malleable. The problem that many aspiring Veilers face is they get lost in too many methods, and forget to dissect them to their common essence. Practicing at bedtime is fine at intermediate to advanced levels of skill, but not during the neophyte stage. That's the first thing. The second thing is that there's a *Yin* and *Yang* aspect to the essence of these skills. For example, practicing mindfulness at every moment is the *Yin* aspect of training. Once the mind is silent and attentive, you must then play with your perception in novel ways (e.g., reality checks). That's the *Yang* side of training. Remember, the only way to learn Lucid Dreaming or Astral Projection is to Lucid Dream and Astral Project! You can't accomplish these things through force. It doesn't work that way. You'll lose consciousness every time. That means you must train during the day, not just at night. Remember, the goal is to become capable of sustaining awareness *at all times.* This isn't easy, but it's truly the heart of the matter. In a very real sense, becoming mindful during everyday life *is* Lucid Dreaming! Well, it's actually Pellucid Dreaming. It becomes Lucid Dreaming when you begin to manipulate your mindful perceptions.

The essence of manipulating perception is twofold:

1. Become mindful.
2. Ponder the mystery and wonder of the cosmos and interact with that mystery in creative and novel ways.

What does it mean to be mindful? It means that when you catch yourself chattering in your head, running the same old tired scripts that keep you sleepwalking through life, you notice it and the noticing *is* the mindful state. At first it lasts only a moment and you're right back to daydreaming. But it can be deepened with practice. One such practice is the "reality check" method in which you see life as a dream. But the Reality Check method isn't just about seeing life as a dream; rather it is becoming aware of yourself as the dreamer. From that launching pad you can then begin to manipulate the Dreamer's perception. One example of how to do this is to go for a walk or a drive. Look at the scenery rushing by you, and ponder the fact that you live on a gigantic globe called a planet, and that you may in fact be upside down at this moment. Sure, it may look like those Autumn leaves are falling *down* toward the Earth, but they may actually be falling up! In fact, they're falling *inward* toward the Earth due to gravity. You might then contemplate gravity and how it affects everything, including consciousness. A favorite method of mine is to imagine that gravity is reversed and the sky is actually the floor. I'll then cultivate a feeling of insecurity, as if I might fall toward the floor of the sky at any moment. Or I'll try to manipulate my awareness directly and flip my awareness in a slow or fast somersault, forward and backward. Or I'll close my eyes and conjure up the vivid feeling of swimming through water against a current.

It's important to understand that dreams are mostly the consolidation of new data. If you can make the new data take the form of malleable consciousness, then your subconscious will respond accordingly. It will literally build the muscles needed for the job (neuroplasticity). This then opens the door for Lucid Dreaming and Astral Projection.

Bear in mind that Astral Projection can occur at any time during the three phases of Lucidity. It's not unlike a thunderstorm in which a tornado can occur at any time. All the required conditions are there, all it takes is for the wind to blow in a certain direction and *wham!* Lucid Dreaming is now full-blown Astral Projection. After all, the *Veil of Dreams* is but a step away from the *Veil of Ghosts,* and Lucid Dreaming is the Astral Body soaring through the *Veil of Dreams.*

Lucid Dreaming, and many other forms of OOBE, work by tapping into your brain's attempt at consolidating new information and experiences by forming new neural connections—only you're doing this in a full-sensory and conscious fashion. This is why Lucid Dreams and OOBE are known to occur spontaneously whenever you fall asleep in a new place. It's the *newness* of it. So, if you've just learned how to skydive, for example, then you're at an advantage during that time to Lucid Dream about, say, flying or free-falling. Later on, if you continue to skydive and your brain fully digests the new skill, then your brain will begin using the experience (sensations) associated with skydiving in dreams as a metaphor for something else. For example, if you're feeling emotionally suffocated in a romantic relationship, then your subconscious may begin sending you dreams about skydiving. Such a dream may be a clarion call to get out of the constricting relationship. Conversely, a dream about skydiving may come to symbolize your happiness or excitement about a new phase in your life.

A key to unlocking access to consistent Lucid Dreaming and OOBE is *novelty*—that is, a willingness and desire to learn new things. This newness functions like an electric outlet for Conscious Sleep. For instance, let's say you've never been on a rollercoaster before. Then you do. That night, you cycle through some methods for inducing OOBE or Lucid Dreaming, and suddenly find yourself travelling through spacetime at a rapid pace. That experience is due to your brain wiring your rollercoaster experience to its neurological hard drive. I've even induced OOBE by recreating the sensation of swinging on a swing-set at my local park! This is another reason why Conscious Sleep is such a powerful way to polish new and old skills. But the point I want to you remember is this:

If you want to make Conscious Sleep a regular part of your life, then you must continue to learn and experience new things.

That's one half of the formula. The second half is to learn to bring mindfulness (meditation) into the sleep cycle. What many allopathic doctors fail to realize about many "sleep disorders" is that they're often blessings in disguise. Just think: most of the "onset" of sleep disorders like "exploding head syndrome," dissociative disorders, night-terrors, and so on, flare up during times of sudden change and upheaval in the life of the "sufferer." But this is simply a brain forming new neural pathways! The difference is that Veilers experience these neurological transformations *consciously*. This can be quite alarming if you don't understand what's happening to you.

One man's terror is another man's treasure!

(2)
Descent into the Underworld.
How To Remain Conscious While Falling Asleep

"There's an in-between state where the part of your brain capable of intention becomes "drugged," literally, and completely forgets why it came to work! We see this stage of the Hero's Journey in the myriad tales of the Hero's descent into the underworld. He or she is distracted by beguiling Sirens and seductions. The wise hero becomes immune to snake venom before venturing into the pit. This is accomplished by repeated confrontations with this delirious state. Gradually, one becomes familiar with this sleep-intoxication and can remain aware while crossing over."

— *The Hero's Journey* (Daniel Allen Kelley, 2018)

In the classical mythological tale called *The Aeneid,* the hero Aeneas descends into the underworld and encounters several demons, one of whom is the demon called *Sleep.* In the story of *The Wizard of Oz,* Dorothy and her companions are thwarted on their journey to Emerald City by the Wicked Witch of the West, her weapon of choice being a spell of sleep induced by a field of opium poppies. And in the book by Michael Ende, *The NeverEnding Story,* Atreyu and his horse, Artax, are almost overcome in the Swamp of Sadness by a death-like sleep as their home—the dreamworld of Fantasia—is being swallowed up by a pernicious and mysterious force called *The Nothing.*

The technical term for this perennial descent into the underworld is *Katabasis,* the coming back from which is termed *Anabasis.* As you've probably guessed, these mythological themes are perfect metaphors for the act of Conscious Sleep and its nemesis, *unconsciousness.* The act of falling asleep and waking up consciously is a death/rebirth process in which the oneironaut plays the hero/heroine. The process of becoming a Veiler is the enactment of our personal myth, and like all myths we can expect to encounter forces and characters both familiar and strange. We'll encounter guides and trials, adventures and monsters, challenges and the magic to overcome them. And it all begins with our acceptance of the Hero's Call, followed by the famed descent into the underworld. The underworld of sleep and dreams…

In this underworld of our subconscious and collective unconscious minds we'll encounter angels and demons alike. We'll encounter the hopes and fears, not only of our own psyche and the egregore of our particular culture, but of consciousness as such. It's important to understand that, just as Dorothy Gale with her Ruby slippers, Atreyu with his Auryn talisman, or Merlin with his magical staff, our totem (power-object) during this descent into the underworld of sleep is CONSCIOUSNESS! For a truly successful Katabasis/Anabasis we need to be able to withstand the intoxicating spell of what I call the *Sleep Serpent*. When it comes to getting a healthy night's sleep, the sleep serpent is your best friend, but in your quest to become a Veiler that snake is your arch-enemy!

Becoming Immune to the Venom of the Sleep Serpent

Anyone who's practiced sitting meditation after a long day's work is all too familiar with the seductions of the sleep serpent. You start out strong. Your posture is perfect, your breathing is regulated, you're relaxed but focused, and then it happens:

You wake up an hour later drooling on your meditation cushion because you nodded off again!

Some hero you turned out to be, aye?

Well, I'm here to tell you that you're not alone. This happens even to seasoned meditators, to say nothing of Lucid Dreamers. I've developed a method by which you can gradually become immune to the venom of unconsciousness. I'm presently going to share this method with you, but first let's start by addressing a common concern I often encounter among students who practice this technique.

If I become proficient at bypassing unconscious sleep, won't I be inadvertently training myself to become an insomniac?

This is actually a very significant question, and I've seen it asked many times on Internet forums only to provoke laughter and scorn from many oneironauts. But the simple truth is that the answer is: Yes, sometimes it happens that a period of insomnia results from this practice. I'd be lying if I told you otherwise. The reason for this is that your brain isn't accustomed to the request to remain conscious during the sleep cycle, especially when everything else in your bodymind is sending chemical signals to go to sleep. That said, I've highlighted several important and time-tested tips designed to sidestep this problem:

- Practice While Sitting Up!
- Practice In the Morning and/or Afternoon!
- Gradually Practice on Increasing Degrees of Reclining Posture!
- Allow Time to Develop the Proper Neuronet for Conscious Sleep!

I've used these methods for many years and my students also use them to great effect. Let's take these helpful tips in the order in which I've listed them:

Practice While Sitting Up

This is a no-brainer. Most meditation is practiced in a sitting position because do so promotes mental alertness. The human nervous system has been trained for millennia to remain alert while the body is erect, to relax while reclining, and to sleep while lying down. As always, we want to ride the wave of these evolutionary developments and use them to our advantage whenever we can. You can think of it as the Tao of Conscious Sleep.

Practice in the Morning and/or Afternoon

This works along the same lines as the above recommendation. I always tell beginner-level students who desire to experience Lucid Dreaming that they should first establish a Circadian Rhythm, then purchase an alarm with adjustable volume settings, set their alarm for 4:00 am, and then (without getting out of bed) begin a Lucid Dreaming technique. This approach yields such consistent results that it has become a staple of most systems of teaching Lucid Dreaming. The reason for its remarkable success is that this method utilizes the natural rhythm of human biochemistry. If you practice only when you go to bed at night then you're actually swimming against the tide of nature, which includes your own biorhythms. At night, you're probably pretty tired from the day! Add to this the fact that the pineal gland in your brain is beginning to flood your body with the sleep hormone called melatonin, a process which starts as soon as the sun begins to descend over the horizon. With this in mind you can see how difficult and counterproductive it can often be to practice Conscious Sleep at bedtime. Of course, this doesn't mean that you *shouldn't* practice at this time, but it shouldn't be the *only* time you practice, especially if you're expecting to see quick results.

Gradually Practice on Increasing Degrees of Reclining Posture

This is the method I used to train myself to remain alert during my own frequent descent into the underworld, and is one of the unique contributions of *SCT* to the contemporary study of Conscious Sleep. Considering what we've discussed thus far it should be obvious how and why this tip works. What we're trying to do is gradually retrain the bodymind to remain alert in all three of these basic postures (neuroplasticity). This is nothing new, and the Yoga traditions have known this for thousands of years (Asana).

Allow Time to Develop the Proper Neuronet for Conscious Sleep

Like any newly acquired skill, Conscious Sleep requires a specific anatomy to become a stable and consistent trait of your experience. Whether learning to walk as a toddler, learning to run as an Olympic track star, or learning to play the violin, we must develop the proper neuronet to house the desired talent. Some people have a little more natural talent than others, which is why we all learn at a different pace, but regardless of who you are, you're still going to have to pass through the learning-curve just like everyone else. The important thing is to make the firm decision to do it and stick with it to the end.

Want to Try It Out?

The only thing left to do is put everything we've learned into practice! After all, if we don't answer the Hero's call to battle than we'll never have the adventure we long for. So how do we begin our descent into the underworld? How do we become immune to the sleep serpent's venom? Well, first, we must go it alone. I mean, really, you can't even have a thought to keep you company.

In *Behind the Veil,* I prefaced the *120-Days Curriculum* with the fundamental practice of Trance. Without first acquiring the skill of entering Trance and sustaining it for at least thirty minutes, you don't stand a chance against the magic of the sleep serpent! Believe me, you'll lose every time. A famous mystic and poet once admonished, *"Be thou athlete with the Eight Limbs of Yoga, for without it thou art not disciplined for any fight!"*

I couldn't have said it better myself!

The Trance State: The Entrance to the Underworld

In my workshops, both online and in-person, I'm often met with confused looks when I describe the secret key to entering the Trance state. The confusion stems from the paradoxical nature of Trance. The Zen practice called Zazen makes for a perfect example. The traditional instructions for Zazen are pretty simple. You're told to sit with your spine erect but relaxed, with your head gently suspended as though a string were softly pulling your head upward toward the sky, with your eyes either closed or halfway open and staring softly forward and downward, either at the floor or the tip of your nose. A little later you're to include a relaxed but focused attention on the natural rhythm of your breathing, but in the beginning you're told to just sit.

Sounds easy, right?

Okay! I dare you to try it right now. Find somewhere comfortable to sit. Now just sit there. Don't do or think of anything else for the next thirty minutes. Don't worry, I'll wait.

***

Hey, you're back! So how did it go? If you're like me when I first tried this exercise, you couldn't manage even five minutes without getting lost in thought, internal dialogue, or physical restlessness. If this describes you, don't dismay. Entering the state of Trance isn't easy when you first try it. It can take months or years to master it. It took me roughly two years to become proficient at it, and I still haven't exhausted my full capacity to deepen this most basic of psychic talents!

The practice of *Zazen* has been aptly likened to two professional dancers. When you're watching a performance of, say, a waltz demonstrated by two skilled dancers, it's hard to tell who leads and who follows. In much the same way, when you're entering Trance it's hard to say what you did to enter it and what you didn't do to enter it. On the one hand you've made the conscious decision to sit in *Zazen* and enter the Trance state. That looks like a form of *doing,* and yet all you're really "doing" is sitting there and allowing everything to be exactly as it is in that moment! To say "Yes" to the Now without feeling the need to add or subtract anything from the moment is the fastest route to disengaging your present state of consciousness and enter sleep.

This can be put another way…

In terms of bioelectrical brainwaves, if you're in **BETA** (awake/task-oriented), then anything you do while in that state will lock you into that state. In other words, **BETA** is converted into **ALPHA** by the firm decision not to *do* anything. We're all familiar with this state and it has two modes, one productive and the other counterproductive to our quest for Conscious Sleep. Whenever you're reading a book and suddenly realize that you've leafed through four pages without remembering anything you've read, you're in **ALPHA**. Conversely, you're also in **ALPHA** whenever you *do* remember what you've read. In other words, you're processing data without ruminating about it. In the first case you're on autopilot; in the second case you're relaxed but it's a *curious* relaxation. Because if its curiosity it's very fertile, and as you've probably guessed it's this latter expression of **ALPHA** that we're aiming for in our practice of Trance. Just as you can passively but curiously watch your favorite sitcom on TV, you can sit and watch your breathing, emotions and thought-processes with the same detached but curious gaze. Follow this formula long enough and you enter the **THETA** state of consciousness. This marks a pivotal turn-of-events, as the **THETA** state begins your true entry into the under-world of sleep!

Most people are shocked to find that Conscious Sleep is actually a synonym for most forms of meditation, but it really isn't that far of a stretch. Almost everyone has access to the three broad states of Waking, Dreaming and Dreamless Sleep. It logically follows that almost any other state of consciousness that you can conceive of is likely to be a variation of one of those three fundamental states, alone or in combination. So there it is: *Meditation IS Conscious Sleep!*

To successfully perform our descent into the dark underworld of sleep we're going to need a bright lantern. That lantern is our consciousness itself, and just as a lantern can't burn without fuel and without shelter from strong gusts of wind, neither can our awareness burn brightly and stably enough to illuminate the dark cave of **DELTA** sleep without adequate rest, diet and adrenal strength. **DELTA** sleep is the dominant brainwave found in dreamless sleep, babies, and coma patients, so you can imagine how challenging it can be to maintain alertness here. In fact, the very sleep cycle itself can be likened to a vast ocean of **DELTA**, with tiny islets and streams of **THETA** and (more rarely) **GAMMA** waves here and there. **DELTA** sleep is largely the province of **NREM** (non-rapid eye movement) sleep, and accounts for roughly 2/3rds of a sleep cycle. If allowed to complete a full night's rest (eight to twelve hours), then **REM** sleep can transform from a small stream to a large river, which makes it more probable that Lucid Dreaming can occur. It should be pointed out that *conscious* **DELTA** sleep (called Pellucid sleep) is synonymous with deep meditation and is precisely what we need to master if we wish to be successful in our *Katabasis/Anabasis*. Without sufficient training in Pellucid Sleep and dreaming we don't stand a chance at falling asleep consciously. Of course, that doesn't mean that we can't still practice the "4:00 am method" and enjoy Lucid Dreaming. We can! But our experience of it will be limited to the hypnopompic phase of sleep, when what we really want as Veilers is to enjoy the full spectrum of Conscious Sleep, which includes the hypnagogic phase as well.

To begin practicing, find a dark and quiet place to comfortably sit without distractions for at least half an hour. Use earplugs and an eyeshade if necessary. Next, enter the Trance state by *just sitting,* as previously explained. If you have difficulty doing this (and you will!), try this little trick:

Conjure up the conviction that everything you've ever wanted is yours and everything you could ever think of accomplishing has been achieved!

You should notice a brief but sudden feeling of contentment. This can be deepened! More importantly, notice the work that this contentment does for you. Normally we're split into two parts, with one half of our psyche being the watcher or doer and the other being the experience being watched, the idea being thought, or the activity being done. In other words, we're always attempting to see ourselves from the outside, as it were, rather than just being what we are in the moment. This contentment relaxes this tension and allows us for the moment to just *be.* That's why the fastest route to never learning how to successfully meditate is to sit there with eyes closed and repeatedly wonder to yourself, "Am I doing this right?" Rather, just be there with whatsoever arises and say "Yes" to it…and then wait! The moment you start to feel yourself nodding off, gently focus on your breathing. Don't do anything with the breathing rhythm just yet! Simply watch it as you would your favorite TV show. This will serve as an anchor for your alertness. Lastly, resist the urge to lie down and go to sleep. Don't give in to the venom of the sleep serpent! Simply sit there and know that by doing so you're slowly becoming immune to that venom.

For now, we need to get into the habit of practicing Trance on a regular basis. As we've learned, the optimal times to do so are morning and afternoon. At these times the *Yin* energy is fading, and the *Yang* energy is ascending. Of these two times the early morning is most suitable for practicing beginner-level Conscious Sleep. With time and dedication you'll soon be able to fall asleep at bedtime while retaining full awareness of the transition. When that time comes, try this:

Fire Breathing Technique: The Yang Breath

Before you retire to bed for the evening arrange your sleeping space so that it's free of distractions such as loud noises, bright lights, or activity of any kind. Next, you'll need a Memory Foam wedge or recliner of some kind that you can fall asleep on while reclining on your back at roughly a 45° angle. Lie down and relax for a few minutes and enter a light Trance state (**ALPHA**). Next, place the palms of your hands over your navel with your dominant hand on top of your non-dominant hand.

Gently begin *Fire Breathing* by inhaling quickly through your nose and exhaling somewhat forcefully out of your mouth. Do thirty repetitions, gradually increasing the speed of hyperventilation as you go. Once you reach thirty breaths, exhale fully and hold the breath out for as long as you can. Then inhale fully and hold the breath for a slow count of fifteen and begin the process all over again. Repeat four times. You'll notice after the second round that you're able to exhale and hold the breath out for longer and longer periods of time. I've gone up to three minutes without the need for air! This is because you've flooded your body with oxygen during the hyperventilation phase, so your need to inhale is reduced.

Every cell in your body holds on to the oxygen until the carbon dioxide builds up in your lungs as you hold your breath out. When you feel the need to inhale, that's your body telling you that a sufficient quantity of carbon dioxide has built up. When you do so, your cells, which have been holding on to the excess oxygen, relax and flood your body with oxygen rich blood. (This is the breathing technique suggested by some physicians to prevent unconsciousness during a heart attack when one is alone. During a heart attack you often have about ten seconds before you might lose consciousness. This technique could keep you conscious long enough to get to a phone or an emergency room. Imagine what it could do for you as you're falling asleep at night and attempting to do so *consciously!)*

Once you've completed three rounds of fire breathing, relax and breathe naturally. Allow yourself to drift further and further into Trance (Conscious Sleep). You should notice an increase in hypnagogic imagery and a pleasant, natural high. You've essentially balanced the dominant *Yin* energy of night time with the *Yang* energy of the fire breathing. This process of adjusting the *Yin/Yang* balance of the body is known in Taoism as *Kan/Li* (water/fire). With it you effectively stimulate the adrenal glands of your body, which is a secret key of successful Conscious Sleep. Master it and you'll have gained a powerful antidote to the intoxicating venom of the Sleep Serpent.

(3)
The Basic Types of Dreamer

It's unfortunate that many books on Lucid Dreaming operate on the assumption that the reader is of the same dreamer-type as the author. The truth is that there are at least four types of people when it comes to dreams. The way I qualify them is simple. Almost any dream takes place from a first-, second- or third-person perspective. Sometimes a dream contains all of the above—the fourth type of dreamer. That would be an ideal situation, as you can then integrate the energies of each figure you meet in your dreams. After all, just about all of the characters you meet in a dream are projections of some aspect of yourself. The typical situation, though, is that a person is either one type or the other, and rarely all three at once.

It's a rewarding practice to become Lucid (or Pellucid) and feel into the roles you're playing in a given dream, with an eye to uncovering the psychological reason behind that favored perspective. You might also examine your behavior while awake and interacting with others. Do you tend to lose yourself in relationships? If so, then that may be the reason why you always dream in the second-person. Or perhaps you're a very introverted person, and you therefore root yourself in a first-person perspective. That may be why you tend to dream in the first-person as well. Or perhaps you have a job that demands you constantly consider an audience. Actors, writers, politicians, managers, and so on must always bear in mind an audience. Consequently, such persons may dream in the third-person.

Lastly, if you can take all three perspectives interchangeably, you may be a very integral thinker and in the habit of considering all available perspectives. This egalitarian habit may spill over into your dream life. Take a moment to comb through your Dream Journal and try to spot a pattern in first, second or third perspective dreams. At the same time, take note of the emotional quality of these dreams. Are they pleasant? Are they nightmarish? Are they a combination of these? Then take stock of your daily life and try to uncover the reasons why your dreams take on a certain quality when experienced through a given perspective.

(4)

Lucid Days, Lucid Nights: Mindfulness and Conscious Sleep

What's the difference between Observing and Witnessing?

To answer this question let's try a little experiment. As you read these words, become aware of yourself reading. That is to say, cultivate a "double-arrowed" attention that includes you as the Observer *and* the page as the Observed. You see, most of the time we focus on one or the other; rarely do we focus on both at the same time.

Next, close your eyes and focus on your train of thought. Don't focus on any particular thought, but rather on the process of thinking itself. Then, become simultaneously aware of both the Thinker and the process of Thinking. This is the first phase of *Mindfulness* training, which has become quite famous in modern times.

Now comes the pivotal moment. Keep your eyes closed and focus not on the Thinker and the Thinking, but instead focus on the Thinker only. Can you observe the Observer? This takes a little practice for most people, but the answer is *yes you can!* And once you realize that you can focus on that part of you that you normally mistake to be your true self, *observing* stops and *witnessing* begins. This witnessing self is what the Buddha called "right-mindfulness", and it's a powerful tool in training your brain to become conscious during sleep.

The trick is to learn to observe, not with thought, but with consciousness itself. What we usually do instead is we look *with* thought. But the simple truth is that we *are* thought. That is to say, the content of our consciousness *is* our consciousness. The miracle of this realization is that thought comes to a halt once it's truly understood; but it has to be understood, not merely played with intellectually. The best way to do this is to become a witness to your thoughts and, eventually, to the total movement of your bodymind. Having done this to a sufficient degree, you'll eventually begin to see that the part of you that's witnessing thought is consciousness itself. This is a paradox, to be sure, but it happens to be true. The miracle occurs when the illusory bridge between the Observer and Observed vanishes, and only consciousness remains. Unlike thinking, which is fidgety and tense, the act of pure witnessing is still and relaxed. Let that be a criterion for success in the practice of mindfulness:

Observing with thought is tense; witnessing with consciousness is effortless.

You'll know when your mindfulness practice is being done correctly because you'll simply come back to your senses without any real effort. In other words, the realization that you've been lost in thought *is* the beginning of pure mindfulness. No effort needs to be made from that point, other than perhaps an active and curious attention to the vicissitudes of your bodymind and environment while awake and asleep.

(5)

Speak! I'm Listening:
Mindfulness Practice Behind the Veil of Tears

When students ask me what I feel is the best way to begin meditation practice specifically for Conscious Sleep, I usually offer the following advice:

1. Don't TRY to meditate.
2. Don't begin practicing on a meditation cushion, but rather in daily life (Channeling Intensity).

3. After about four weeks of Channeling Intensity training, begin "sitting meditating."
4. Begin by simply sitting in your favorite meditation posture for five to ten minutes at first; then, after a week or two, slowly increase the time to at least one hour.
5. Begin "mindfulness" training.

The importance of Mindfulness in the attaining of the Continuity of Consciousness can't be stressed enough. Whether your goal is Lucid Dreaming, Astral Projection, Pellucidity, Meditation, or what have you, *Mindfulness is the primary ingredient to successful practice.*

In the beginning stage of Mindfulness training, one begins by cultivating a "double-arrowed" type of awareness. That is to say, one includes both the external and internal environments into a single act of steady observation. To this type of attention we give the name "Mindfulness." The consciousness engaged in Mindfulness is referred to as the "Witness."

To understand what the Witness is, imagine a large silver ball with a highly reflective surface. At the same time, imagine this mirror-ball surrounded by innumerable other mirror-balls. Everything reflected in the central ball is also reflected in all the other balls, indefinitely. Such is the nature of the Witness.

When you first discover the Witness, you'll feel as though you're attending from a definite center of consciousness. Everything arising within and around you will feel as though it's somewhere on the periphery of your awareness, but nothing touches *You.* You're just a mirror, or perhaps the sky: all manner of weather arises and passes away, but you remain the untouched and untouchable sky. This is the Causal Body. Mindfulness is a Causal Body practice, and with practice, it can be accessed at any time of the day or night. And you must access it as often as possible, for without it you'll only go so far in your quest for the Continuity of Consciousness.

In this section, I emphasize the process of regulating the mind. This tends to be the most difficult of what the Taoists refer to as *The Five Regulatings* in which a meditator regulates his body, breath, mind, lifeforce and spirit, respectively. For this reason, how to regulate the mind forms a large portion of most meditation systems throughout the world. Each of these systems approaches this topic in their own way.

In *SCT,* we begin with Mindfulness training. The following practice is designed to sharpen your Mindfulness which, as we've seen, is your strongest ally in your quest for constant consciousness.

The Practice

First, find a notebook and a pen. Place the notebook on your lap or a table, and rest the tip of the pen to the page in preparation for taking notes. Now, put the book down and sit quietly for five minutes. Set a timer if you like. Your eyes can be open or closed for this exercise. Breathe naturally. Next, gently direct your attention toward your thoughts. What are you thinking right now? Don't get too complex about the answer, but rather simply take note of the theme that's occupying your mind at this moment. Then, in one or two words, describe this theme and write it down in the notebook.

After you've written down this first theme, keep your attention gently but fixedly on the content of your thoughts. Adopt an attitude of curiosity, one that says, "Speak! I'm Listening." I don't mean that you must say these words aloud. Rather, adopt an attitude of curious inquisitiveness toward your own thoughts as though listening to the confessions of a close friend.

Continuing in this way, simply watch and wait for another "theme" to arise in your mind. When it comes, write it down in your notebook.

Finally, after five minutes have passed, take a look at your notebook and look for patterns. For example, was there one specific theme or train of thought that repeated or dominated the session? What feelings, if any, were associated with these thoughts? Where in your body did you feel these feelings? And so on…

If you practice this simple exercise long enough a few things will start to become apparent. You'll notice that the act of attending as a Witness of thought actually silences thought. And wherever thought doesn't cease or slow down as a result of Witnessing, the way you respond to thoughts changes significantly. The conditions that give rise to knee-jerk reactions are removed when you take the role of Witness rather than Victim of your mind. You see, when you learn to include in one act of observation both your thoughts and your emotional reactions to them, you're occupying your Causal Body. And the Causal Body is the very root of your Ego—that is, *You.*

Speaking of the Ego, what exactly is this thing called "I"?

(6)
The Genealogy of Volition: What Is Egoic Consciousness?

Have you ever seen a Newton's Cradle? It's that nifty contraption that adorns many desks, the one with the three metal balls. One ball strikes the middle, setting the ball on the other side in motion. That ball, in turn, strikes the middle ball setting the other ball in motion. And so on, *ad infinitum.* The middle ball remains stationary all the while, serving only to transfer the force that keeps the metal balls on either side of it in a perpetual game of Tag-You're-It.

Although perhaps a crude analogy, I believe it's one way to illustrate how Egoic Consciousness operates. Just as the forces that propel a Newton's Cradle are very complex when you get down to it, the Newton's Cradle itself is fairly simple; so, too, are the forces of life very complicated while the Ego itself is rather simple.

Andrew Cohen, the Evolutionary Spiritual teacher, once addressed a group of disciples and told them flatly that "ego is a closed loop." This blunt statement by Cohen immediately calls to mind the symbol of the Ouroboros Serpent, the snake that's consuming its own tail. And what Mr. Cohen was trying to tell his students is that we take for granted that we're capable of making individual *choices*. For better or worse, this is not the case. Our ego, like the stationary ball of the Newton's Cradle, is simply a transfer station of powerful and complex forces vying for ascendency. These forces come together and create a trajectory. Unlike the Newton's Cradle, however, our Ego—our "I"— isn't given just one direction in which to swing. Rather, it's given *many* directions in which to do so. These forces come together and generate a panorama. We look in this direction and, depending upon how *conscious* we are of the many ways in which we might swing, we'll more or less "choose" the direction of the most powerful urge. In other words, that metal ball in the middle (i.e., the Ego) has to become more sensitive (responsive) to the other metal balls hammering against it. This, of course, begs the question:

What conditions give rise to the cultivation of greater sensitivity? Or, to put it more Postmodernly: *What is the "Genealogy of Volition"?*

If you look at the myriad versions of the Ouroboros, you can see one thing shared by all of them: they portray a serpent or two nourishing itself on itself. A closed loop…

What this means, generally speaking, is that Egoic Consciousness is a psychic game of Hide-and-Seek, and this polarized dance creates the very energy that fuels the Ego. More to the point, this game of Tag-You're-It generates the illusion of choice. The forces that lie above and beneath the Ego are very complex in that they are, in a manner of speaking, both new and incredibly ancient.

So what is the Genealogy of Volition?

Well, according to my own good light, I can see that the tower of my Ego is composed of bricks that were put in place because, at one time, they served their purpose well. In neurological terms, habits were wired in because they were fired up over and over again in response to certain challenges.

That's all good and well… But what happens when these bricks are faced with a storm for which their mortar is ill-equipped? Well now! This is the genealogy of higher volition! Or, what we would call self-transcendence and Awakening.

Higher Volition occurs when old structures are faced with oppositional forces which they're ill-equipped to handle. Consequently, new structures have to be built so the transference of these forces can begin. Having been successfully accomplished, this heightened and more competent level of sensitivity and integration creates a new closed loop—but a more spacious one.

Some would claim that this awakening proves that the soul exists. Some would even go so far as to say that a soul isn't born with your physical organism. Rather, your soul must be created. Well, I won't speak on the soul; but I will say this: What choice do you have?

(7)

Conscious Sleep and Religion

Conscious Sleep is nothing new. Indeed, one can find examples of Astral Projection, Lucid Dreaming, Vivid Dreaming, and Pellucid Dreaming scattered throughout the religious and mystical art and literature of the world. The only difference is that these spiritual traditions couch these experiences in arcane terminology. To give a few examples: the Western Hermetic tradition doesn't call it "Remote Viewing"; it calls it "Skrying in the Spirit Vision." Ancient Hebrew mysticism doesn't use the term "Astral Body"; rather it is called "Merkabah." Shamanic traditions don't call it "Vivid Dreaming"; they call it "Visions" or "Sky Walking." And so forth…

Another well-known spiritual tradition, Taoism, also couches the various forms of Conscious Sleep in obscure terminology. Take, for example, this passage from a Taoist Classic:

> "If Valley Spirit does not die, you have gained the gate to Xuan Pin. Exit and enter as softly as the Tao exists within. When cultivating Shen to return it to the insubstantial nothingness at midnight, use the river to transport Qi to Kunlun."[4]

"Valley Spirit" is a reference to the cognitive part of the Causal Body, what the Chinese call *Shen,* and is said to reside between the two hemispheres of the brain where the pineal and pituitary glands are located. The Valley Spirit is considered a "post-birth" essence and therefore susceptible to death and illness. However, with special training this Valley Spirit can unite with the spirit of Nature, which is considered "pre-birth," and thereby become immortal. To the ancient Taoists, the Continuity of Consciousness throughout the Waking, Dreaming and Dreamless Sleep states was synonymous with the ability to survive the physical death of the body. The spirit of Nature is called *Xuan Pin,* which basically means the "Mother of Essences." The admonition to return this cultivated *Shen* to the "insubstantial nothingness" at midnight is just another way of saying "remain conscious throughout the sleep cycle." To accomplish this "as softly as the Tao exists within" is an exhortation to do this skillfully and without force. Finally, to "use the river to transport *Qi* to *Kunlun"* refers to the importance of feeding your heightened awareness with bioelectricity. The "river" refers to the *Thrusting Vessel* located along the

---

[4] Translated by Dr. Yang Jwing Ming: *Qigong Meditation: Small Circulation* (YMAA Books, 1994).

spinal cord.[5] *Kunlun* refers to a mountain and is a reference to the brain and the activation of more brain cells via *Qigong* practice.

I could fill volumes with examples from other traditions. This shouldn't come as a surprise, since everyone has access to waking, dreaming and deep dreamless sleep. It makes sense that most rarified forms of consciousness are merely extensions, reflections or combinations of these three natural states of awareness. Take, for instance, the *Jhanas* of Buddhist meditation. The entire process of ascending these states of absorption entails putting to sleep the various aspects of our bodymind until only pure consciousness remains burning like a flame in a windless room. Indeed, you could say that the various *Jhanas* are but the secondary and tertiary Veils of Pellucid sleep and dreaming![6], That would be an accurate way of viewing them.

The same goes for many (some say all) religious epiphanies. The visions, religious conversions, angelic communications, all tend to occur in an altered state of consciousness similar to Lucid Dreaming. I don't mean to say that these experiences are not valid, only that they tend to occur while in a Lucid Dream scenario. Consider the following story by St. Augustine in which a dream figure—that of a young man—confronts Gennadius about his Lucid Dream state:

> " 'Where is your body now?' asks the dream figure.
>
> 'In my bed,' Gennadius answers.
>
> The dream character then asks, 'Do you know that the eyes in this body of yours are now bound and closed, and at rest, and with these eyes you are seeing nothing?'
>
> 'I know it,' Gennadius answers.
>
> 'What then,' the young man replies, 'are the eyes with which you now see me?' Unable to discover an answer to this, Gennadius fell silent."

---

[5] The *Thrusting Vessel* is one of eight *Qi* reservoirs in the Etheric Body and is classified as a *Yin* Vessel. Its location is along the spinal cord between the perineum and brain.

[6] Pellucidity is detached mindful witnessing attention carried into the sleep cycle. In SCT, I qualify four stages of Pellucidity. Pellucidity is unlike Lucid Dreaming in that the latter involves a conscious but active participation in the dream, whereas the former doesn't. When Pellucidity becomes active, it's no longer Pellucidity, but rather, Astral Projection.

Augustine concludes with the following admonition:

> "Every day man wakes and sleeps and thinks. Let him say whence come those thoughts resembling the shapes, the qualities and the motions of bodies yet not composed of corporeal matter. Let him say it, if he can, but, if he cannot, why does he rashly try to form some kind of definitive opinion about these very rare and unusual experiences when he cannot explain the constant and daily ones?"[7]

Oddly, despite the enormous attention placed on sleep and dreams in the Judeo-Christian Bible, the Catholic Church has avoided—and in some cases reviled—anything associated with them. Starting in the Middle Ages, the dominant attitude of the Church toward dreams and visions has been one of suspicion. In many instances, the Church has considered these to be the work of the Devil himself. Be that as it may, dreams, visions and even Astral Projection have all played an undeniable role in the Judeo-Christian faiths.

By far the oldest recorded religious reference to Conscious Sleep is found in the ancient Hindu *Vedas* of India. This ancient source of Conscious Sleep instruction also includes the *Vigyan Bhairav Tantra*. This Indian influence eventually moved to Tibet, resulting in the Milam branch of Tibetan "dream Yoga." Then it migrated to China and merged with Taoism, and finally settled in Japan where it became what's now known as Zen.

In Islam, the prophet Mohammed's *Laylat al-Miraj* is an account of a Lucid Dream that provided him with spiritual initiation. The twelfth century Spanish Sufi *Ib El-Arabi* insisted that mastering Lucid Dreaming is an essential skill for mystical Adepts. Even a hard-nosed philosopher like René Descartes speaks openly about his Lucid Dreams.[8] The Epicurean philosopher Pierre Gassendi also discussed the importance of Consciousness Sleep.[9]

---

[7] St. Augustine, Letter 159 (A.D. 415).
[8] René Descartes, *The Olympica.*
[9] C.B. Brush (1972). *The Selected Works of Pierre Gassendi.* New York: Johnson Reprint Corp and R. DeBecker (1965). *The Understanding of Dreams.* London: Allen and Unwin.

(8)
Mindfulness Practice for Lucid Dreaming

So how do you practice Mindfulness for Conscious Sleep?

To begin with, it's important to know which aspect(s) of Conscious Sleep you wish to train. Because each aspect of Conscious Sleep requires a specific application of Mindfulness, you must first know the aspect you're training and the methods best suited for the attainment of that particular aspect. For example, if you've already achieved relatively stable Lucidity, but your dreams aren't very vivid or memorable, then the Mindfulness methods you require are those that focus on the enhancement of the five senses. Or, if you've achieved a high level of Pellucidity, but your Lucid Dreaming skills are somewhat lacking, you need to apply daily Mindfulness methods with, say, Reality-Check techniques.

As a rule, the best combination for daily maintenance of Conscious Sleep of all varieties is as follows:

1. The "double-arrowed" awareness discussed earlier.
2. As soon as you awaken, consider the possibility that you're still dreaming.
3. Etheric Movement (the secret key to practices like *Tai Chi, Nei Dan Qigong* and Astral Projection).
4. Diet and exercise: avoid excess stimulants, sleeping pills, and cannabis. Avoid overworking and anything else that exhausts your adrenals.

At the heart of all these practices is Mindfulness and your ability to carry it into the sleep cycle—a process that begins when you learn to function as a *consciousness* and not merely an *observer*.

The Practice

Redirect your attention to the *Speak! I'm Listening* exercise in section (5), above. Minus the notebook and pen, you'll be applying this same method as you fall asleep. Furthermore, you're going to practice it immediately upon waking. The following is a combination of the *Wake Back to Bed* (WBTB) and *Meditation Induced Lucid Dream* (MILD) techniques.

STEP ONE: Set an alarm for 4:00 am. As always, be sure to use an alarm with setting options that allow a gradual increase in volume. Alarms that jolt you suddenly from sleep should be avoided.

STEP TWO: Arrange that you'll remain undisturbed for the night. In my own experience, it's best to sleep alone when training Conscious Sleep. This is especially so in the beginning phase of training.

STEP THREE: Lie down in a supine posture on your bed. If you can manage to do so, sleep on a slight incline. This enables you to remain semi-alert while dozing off.

STEP FOUR: Relax your mind by first relaxing your body. If you don't have a favorite technique for doing so, you may use the *Progressive Relaxation* and *Mobile Mental Focus* techniques offered in *Behind the Veil*. For now, simply feel your body melting into your mattress every time you exhale. This should relax you sufficiently for this exercise.

STEP FIVE: Gently turn your awareness to your thinking process. Are there any thoughts present? Take a mental note of any themes that arise in your mind and simply let them go. This is like watching someone "channel surfing" on a television set while you watch them do so.

STEP SIX: At some point, you'll notice that your thinking process becomes, in a word, *absurd*. You may, for example, catch yourself thinking about a purple unicorn or an event that never occurred. It takes a little practice, but soon you'll be able to use these absurd thought-loops as cues, alerting you to the fact that you're dreaming. These dreams, which begin early in your sleep cycle, typically only scale the first two stages of Lucidity or Pellucidity.

STEP SEVEN: Eventually, you'll simply fall asleep. Allow this to happen. Then, once your alarm goes off at 4:00 am, shut the alarm off and lie back down in your initial posture. Repeat steps 1–6.

Successful Conscious Sleep is largely a matter of combining methodologies until you find what works for you. This is that "secret key" I spoke about in the Preface to this book. When combined with proper timing and an understanding of the sleep cycle, you should have little problem discovering your key to becoming a Veiler!

A Little Secret for You

On nights when you're particularly tired, you can enter a **REM** cycle fairly quickly. On such a night of exhaustion, simply follow the aforementioned steps and watch what happens! The plus to this little secret to rapid-onset of **REM** is that you can utilize the remaining *Yang* of daytime to mingle with the rapidly encroaching *Yin* of your bodymind. Although I've personally reached deep-phase Lucidity on many occasions using this method, usually only **LD-1** and **LD-2** are reached. At any rate, you'll enjoy some truly magical closed-eye visuals, insights and practice time.

Oh! Speaking of combining methods, you may also utilize a Reality Check in the previous exercise. To perform a Reality Check, Simply question whether you're awake or asleep as you're drifting off. This makes for a powerful primer for successful practice.

(9)
The Truth about the Reality-Check Method

The problem with the Reality Check method as it's often taught today is that most people don't take it far enough. Until your Reality Checks begin to show up in your dreams, you haven't reached the goal of this ancient method of training Lucidity. This also applies to Pellucidity. The primary difference between Lucidity and Pellucidity Reality Checks is that the former is an exercise in mindfulness and interrupting "normal" perception by questioning the reality of direct experience, whereas the latter is strictly a mindfulness exercise in which you periodically turn away from the dream of life and focus solely upon your own existential awareness. As an example of how Reality Checks can be used to train Lucidity, imagine that you're taking a leisurely stroll through the woods on a lovely Spring afternoon. Majestic pine and maple trees tower above your head, the warm wind plays through your hair, and the dappled sunlight casts a diamond-shaped net across the water of a nearby brook. This may seem like a pleasant experience—and it is—but what if you were to alter your perception of this idyllic paradise? That is, what if you were to make the experience a little more *psychedelic*?

I'm not suggesting that you drop acid. Rather I'm suggesting that you create the psychedelic experience *directly,* using only your imag-

ination. To give but one example (one of my favorites!), let's spice
things up a bit and imagine that you're on the underside of the Earth,
and therefore, upside down. You're walking through the woods on the
underbelly of a planet in the middle of outer space. Isn't that far out?
And it's not enough that you *think* of this awkward but wondrous
situation; you must *feel* it! That's the key to making it work. Involving
your proprioception is also a crucial factor here. Your sense of spatial
orientation is a powerful influencer of your sense of reality, so if you
really feel yourself as upside down then your subconscious mind will
think you're dreaming.

If the above perception-play isn't enough, you can add to it by
contemplating the fact that when something falls to the ground, it's
not really falling *down* to the Earth, but inward toward its center. You
can carry on in this manner indefinitely, pondering and feeling *The
Mystery* for hours if you're so inclined. The point is that you're stepping back from autopilot mode and interrupting it, so to speak. This
disturbance of routine perception is the secret key to leaving an
impression on your subconscious mind. This is crucial, for it's your
subconscious mind that needs to be taught to *want* Lucidity.

To use Reality Checks for Pellucid Dreaming, it helps to remember
that Pellucidity is strictly a mindfulness exercise. Mindfulness is a
form of *self-remembering.* You're interrupting the autopilot mode
again, but this time you're doing so in a way that cuts through your
tendency to get lost in various experiences and your knee-jerk reactions to them. For example, if you're walking through the woods on
that beautiful Spring afternoon, it's easy to get lost and "swept away"
by the surrounding scenery. But in the Pellucid form of the reality-
check method you take a cognitive step back from this tendency and
come back to your psychic center. You're no longer lost in the experience, but centered in the Experiencer. In other words, you *remember*
your Self. This sudden and intermittent self-remembering has a
profound effect on your subconscious mind. Eventually, and with
enough practice, this mindfulness will begin to happen spontaneously
in your dreams as well. When it does, that's Pellucidity! *Pellucidity is
meditation carried into the Sleep Cycle.*

Another form of the reality-check method is performed in the
dream state and involves looking at one's hands. Of course, the aim is
to locate your Subtle Body hands, not your Gross Body hands. Once

you see them, the reality-check is to take the forefinger of your dominant hand and try to pierce it through the palm of your non-dominant hand. If it goes through, you're in your Subtle Body.

An excellent way to train Dream Control and Reality Checks at the same time is to look upon your daily perceptions and experiences *as if you're the one creating them.* One of my favorite ways of doing this is to look up at the clouds and convince my mind that I'm the one moving them. I couple this with the Reality Check of focusing on a cloud and trying to split it into two pieces.

Another one of my favorite Dream Control exercises is practiced while riding in the passenger seat of a car. I'll conjure up in vivid and full-sensory detail the feeling that I'm flying. I'll use the rapidly passing scenery as sensory input to increase the sensation of flying.

The key to making these exercises work is that you must believe it's really happening. For example, you must convince your brain that you're making the clouds move or that you're flying through space. The longer you can hold this conviction the better. That's on the Lucid side of the street. On the Pellucid side, it's not perceptual reality that you must convince your brain is a dream, but rather, that *you* are the dream! This is exceptionally difficult. The best way to train this ability is through the so-called *formless* meditations, such as *Yoga Nidra, Vedanta,* or the Gnostic *Cloud of Unknowing.*

The underlying mechanism at work in these methods combines the hypnotic *belief* of the dreaming mind with the self-awareness of the waking state. While dreaming, the brain sees nothing out of the ordinary about, say, flying over a mountaintop on a broomstick. That's one of the reasons sleepers never become Lucid: *they don't know they're dreaming and they're fine with that.* So, by combining this hypnotic belief in the absurd with the vigilance of the awake mind, you'll eventually experience it in the Lucid and Pellucid states. That is, you'll start having Reality Checks while asleep!

I've developed a powerful method which combines the reality-check with a Qigong practice, called Zhan Zhuang. Qigong (Chinese Yoga) has four "schools," and each has its own unique set of goals. The four Qigong schools are:

- Religious Qigong
- Scholarly Qigong

- Medicinal Qigong
- Martial Qigong

As a *Qigong* method, *Zhan Zhuang* is practiced in accordance with the goals of the *Qigong* school adopting it. (If you are interested in an exhaustive discussion of this topic, read *Taiji Qigong,* by Dr. Yang Jwing Ming. I learned my *Zhan Zhuang* in the lineage of Yang Jwing Ming [*Taijiquan*] and Li Gui Chang [*Xingyiquan*].)

I'm going to give detailed instructions on how to practice *Zhan Zhuang* in just a moment. But before I do, allow me to explain how this practice can help you as a Veiler.

Like all complete Yogas, the Chinese *Nei Gong* school (Internal Arts) attempts to engage the Gross, Subtle and Causal bodies all in the same exercise. There are dozens of methods, both ancient and modern, that have this holistic attitude towards the human bodymind. I'm offering the Taoist/Buddhist variety because it's the system I'm most familiar with. Once you understand how this process works, you're free to pursue other disciplines as well. The vehicle is only useful for reaching the goal. Once the goal is reached, the vehicle is no longer as important as deepening your understanding of the goal.

The first goal of *Zhan Zhuang* is to open the physical structures of the physical body through a process of relaxation and opening of the body's connective tissues. Once this has been accomplished, the Etheric energy (Qi/Prana) of the Subtle Body can be more easily sensed and led to circulate (in the 12 meridians/nadis). For this to be effective, first you must be rooted in the relaxed but focused state of *Wuji* (Causal Body). Mastery is attained when a profound cognitive shift occurs between *leading* the energy to *being* the energy. Your consciousness has now become *mobile.* If you guessed that this is the entry point to Astral Projection, you guessed right!

But that's a little ahead of our story…

For our purposes, all that's needed is to first open and consciously feel into the connective tissues of the Gross Body so that the internal energy can be detected. We're not concerned with *leading* the energy at this point, only *feeling* it. Once the energy is sensed, the bodymind must be led into deeper and deeper stages of relaxation, almost verging on sleep. We'll then focus on our outstretched hands, and utilizing a method called *Trataka,* we'll train our brains to spot our hands while in the dream state. This *looking-for-your-hands* method is actually very old. I'm simply combining it with other methods to include all three Bodies in the training.

Although proper *Zhan Zhuang* practice is a topic that demands a separate volume, I'm going to introduce you to the basics of the practice now. My reason for this is that we'll be using it in certain practices in the final section of this book. Also it can be used as a Reality Check and stabilizing technique while Lucid Dreaming.

Zhan Zhuang Practice

The following practice can be used both while awake and while Lucid Dreaming. One of the most popular methods of stabilizing the Lucid Dreaming state is to gaze intently at your hands in the dream. Combined with the full-bodied awareness of *Zhan Zhuang,* the stabilization of Lucidity can be strengthened even more. First, look closely at the following diagram. The basic rules for structural alignment of the body is as follows:

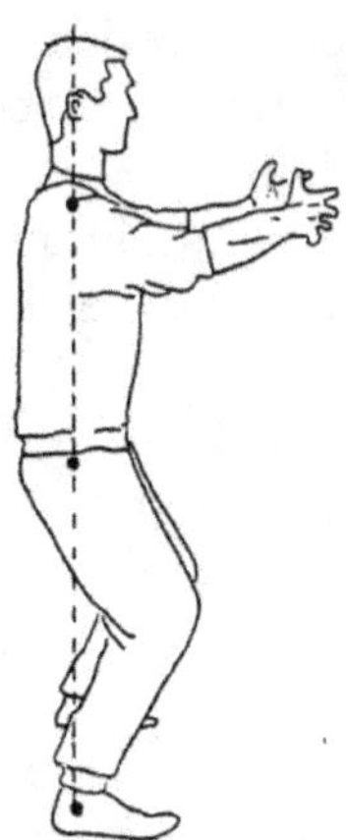

STEP ONE: Stand erect on a level surface with your feet parallel and your toes pointing forward. Bend your knees slightly with your arms akimbo. Your knees shouldn't extend past your toes!

STEP TWO: Keep your head erect, and allow your gaze to rest gently on the tip of your nose. You'll know you're doing this correctly when the tip of your nose seems to vanish. This "blind spot" keeps your *Qi* close to your body and stimulates the Brow Center.

STEP THREE: Relax your jaw muscles, but close your mouth so that teeth are lightly touching. At the same time, the tip of your tongue lightly touches the upper palate of your mouth. This is called "Building the Magpie Bridge" in *Qigong* society, and connects the Governing and Conception vessels of your Etheric Body.

STEP FOUR: Relax your shoulders so that they fall naturally downward. Also, relax your chest so that it becomes slightly concave (but not closed!)

STEP FIVE: Next, relax your lower back so the curvature of the Lumbar Region flattens. This is often misunderstood to mean that the butt must be "tucked." This is a common mistake made by beginners.

STEP SIX: Now, slowly raise both of your arms at the same time and bring them to rest at about sternum level. Your hands should be about one foot away from your body, your arms bent as if holding a large ball, and your fingers relaxed but open.

STEP SEVEN: Take a few moments to notice any tension in your body. Every time you encounter resistance or tension, simply exhale and let it go. The trick is to remain braced, without becoming tense, and relaxed without going limp.

STEP EIGHT: Breathe naturally and gently squeeze your perineum muscles at the end of each exhalation. This will lead *Qi* to your Brow Center.

STEP NINE: Staring at the tip of your nose, include also the view of your hands. With each inhalation, focus on the tip of your nose, and on each exhalation shift your attention to both of your hands. This will result in your eyes remaining totally motionless, which is crucial for stimulating your Brow Center.

STEP TEN: For the next five minutes or so, simply continue scanning your body for tension and let it go. When this is done properly, the result will be that your body *extends* rather than contracts. This has to be felt to be appreciated, but once you do, you'll see why *Zhan Zhuang* is so useful in unifying the Gross and Subtle bodies!

NOTE: When practicing *Zhan Zhuang*, go easy on yourself! If you're interested in really cultivating this practice to higher levels, I urge you to find a qualified teacher. Start off practicing for five minutes, and slowly work your way up to half an hour. In the lineage I belong to, we start with five minutes and work toward a goal of two hours. Such lengthy practice is usually reserved for martial art purposes. For our purposes, *Zhan Zhang,* when practiced in the way I just described, is great for placing the mind in a Trance-like state. When combined with Gross Body coordination, *Zhan Zhuang* is an excellent way to train Lucidity while awake. Eventually, this Gross and Subtle Body cooperation spills over into the dream state, where is can be used as a Reality Check and Lucidity stabilizer.

(10)
The WRCBTB Method: The WBTB Method Upgraded

The year was 2009. I'd awoken to the sound of rain. Thunder rolled in the distant sky, and my girlfriend stirred in the bed next to me. I tried to go back to sleep, but couldn't, so I decided to lie on my back and count the distance of time between lightning flashes and thunder. The only problem was...*I couldn't open my eyes!*

Alarmed by this, I decided to roll over onto my stomach. As soon as I began to move, I realized something wasn't right. The bed beneath me was soaking wet! Not only was it soaking wet, it was rocking!

It must've been the shock that did it, but I was now able to open my eyes. The first thing I did was look for my girlfriend.

She was gone...

My girlfriend was gone, my bedroom was gone, and in place of all things familiar was a vast sea. Oh, sure, my bed was there; but it was sinking. So it was at that moment I said to myself, *"Yup! I'm dreaming!"*

As tends to happen in such moments of dream-recognition, I woke up. I lay there for a few minutes, contemplating what had just happened. Then, having to urinate, I got up and went to the bathroom. Only, when I went to the bathroom, the lights were off, and I just started peeing in a corner. Realizing that this is quite out of character for me (rumors notwithstanding), I stopped and reached for the bathroom light.

But the wall with the light switch on it was missing...

Just then, I heard the sound of ocean waves crashing ashore. "Aha! I'm still dreaming," I said to myself, and promptly awoke in my bed.

Of course, for a moment I wasn't sure whether I was awake or still dreaming.

The technical name for this phenomenon is *False Awakening Syndrome*. And it can be a real pain in the, well, you know the rest.

It wasn't until many years later that I'd discover a powerful method of Lucid Dream induction using this phenomenon. If you look closely at it, *False Awakening Syndrome* hides a secret. It's a lesson of sorts. In fact, I've had quite a few *False Awakenings* that actually featured a guru. This teacher seems to enjoy appearing as a beautiful Creole woman with three eyes. At other times my teacher appears as a wise old man. At any rate, this dream-teacher loves to use the Socratic method! Confronting me with many *False Awakenings* in a row is his/her preferred teaching method.

The night I finally passed my exam, the lessons stopped. I realized that my Guide was trying to let me in on a little secret, and one night I figured that secret out.

Here's the skinny version of how it happened:

One night, I was having very profound *False Awakenings*. What made them so profound was I'd fall asleep in the Lucid Dream world and wake up in the "real" world. Then I'd fall back asleep in the real world and wake up in the Lucid Dream world. At one point, I was having a Lucid Dream in which I was having quite an adventure. I told one of the prison guards (it's a long story) that I'd be sleeping for at least forty-five minutes and not to wake me up until then. No sooner had I fallen asleep in the dream than I woke up in my bed.

For a moment, I couldn't tell if I was still dreaming, so I decided to try a few reality checks (more on this below). I passed with flying colors. I was awake alright.

As I lay in bed, I could feel **REM** sleep in the background of my mind. It's hard to explain, but whenever I wake up between the hours of 4:00 am–5:00 am, I can always sense the **THETA** brainwave close by. Even if I'm wide awake in bed, I can still feel its presence.

At any rate, roughly forty-five minutes later, I consciously reentered the Lucid Dream world. I didn't wake up in a prison, but in an old dilapidated house. I was all alone and a storm was raging outside. I realized I was dreaming, so I decided to wake up. I woke up, performed a reality check, and decided to reenter the Lucid Dream.

I did this cognitive pendulum act about three more times, and then it hit me: *I'd stumbled upon a new method of Lucid Dream induction!*

Well, not quite new, but an interesting combination of well-known techniques. Ladies and gentlemen! Introducing the *Wake/Reality-Check/Back-To-Bed* method (WRCBTB).

I'd like to do a little recap of the *Reality Check* and *Wake Back To Bed* methods.

Realty Checks—also called "reality-testing"—has been around for thousands of years. The most popular form of it is handed down to us from Tibet. The main purpose of Reality Checks is to get into the habit of questioning whether you're awake or dreaming. This exercise can be deepened to include seeing even your self as a dream. Eventually, this practice will spill over into your dreams and you'll suddenly find yourself questioning whether you're asleep or awake even while dreaming.

The *Wake Back To Bed* method (WBTB) works by interrupting the sleep cycle after about ninety minutes or so of natural sleep. The dreaming phase of sleep (REM) occurs roughly every ninety minutes or so in a given night's rest.

The WBTB method has been scientifically proven to induce Lucid Dreams, especially when combined with a strong intention to fall asleep consciously. One such study was conducted at the University of Adelaide, and utilized a combination of Reality Checks, Strong Intention, and the WBTB method to induce Lucid Dreams in their Australian volunteers. The results?

Seventeen percent of the volunteers experienced Lucid Dreams...

So far, the best methods for inducing Conscious Sleep involve a combination of electronic stimulation, WBTB, strong intention, Lucid Dreaming technologies like Binaural Beats, and Reality-Testing. This is especially true for beginners. Once you become more adept, however, you'll find that you can step behind the Veil at any time of the night or day.

Since most of us don't have access to electronic brain stimulators, expensive Lucid Dreaming headbands, and so forth, we must rely instead on our willpower, talent and timing.

So try it! Set your alarm for 4:00 am. Remember to use an alarm with sound settings that allow a gradual increase of volume rather than jolting you awake. Practice this until you no longer require an alarm to wake you up at 4:00 am.

Next, as soon as you wake up, train yourself to remain *completely* motionless. No fidgeting, scratching, stretching or even swallowing. Just lie there as you find yourself upon waking. I can't stress this enough.

Finally, conjure up the feeling that you may very well be dreaming at this moment. Perform a Reality Check of your choosing. Personally, I'll try to sit up using only my Astral Body. I'll also try to somersault backwards in the air. This is also my favorite method of inducing an Out of Body Experience.

This usually suffices to induce any number of behind the Veil activities. Experiment and come up with your own preferred techniques. Have fun! Also, remember to use your breathing if you find yourself too groggy to focus. As I've mentioned elsewhere, gentle *Fire Breathing* usually suffices to focus the mind just enough to keep you from falling unconscious.

You don't have to take my word for it; try it yourself and see!

CHAPTER SIX

THE IMPORTANCE OF FULL-SENSORY DREAMING (VIVID DREAMING)

Introduction
I Don't Have Dreams, I Have Movies!

By far the most unacknowledged elephant in the room is the topic of Vivid Dreaming. It's taken for granted that dreams, Lucid or not, must be sufficiently colorful if they're to be worth exploring. The presumption that anyone interested in Conscious Sleep must already have Vivid Dreams is understandable. But the truth is that this isn't always so.

In 2018, I made it a point to tackle this issue by asking for a show of hands in online Lucid Dreaming forums. My questions were simple: *How many of you regularly remember your dreams? And how colorful are the ones you do recall?* As you might imagine, answers ranged from "My dreams are like movies!" to "I know my dreams are vivid, but I often can't remember them when I wake up."

Well, if that's what you imagined the answers were, you're not entirely right. Sure, there were many such answers, but whenever I pressed someone for more details their answers often began to change slightly. For example, someone would initially claim to have dreams of epic proportions, but when asked to describe them, their "vivid" dreams were often limited to one or two of the five senses. In other words, they were having *vivid* dreams, but not *full-sensory* dreams.

In this section, I'm going to discuss this often-neglected topic of Vivid Dreaming. You may have already discovered that the capacity to have full-sensory dreams is crucial if you wish to have memorable Lucid or Pellucid Dreams. The first thing I'd like to discuss is the use of Vivid Dreaming for the purpose of better Dream Recall.

(1)
Vivid Dreaming for Dream Recall

One of my favorite activities as a child was to wake up in the morning, sit up in my bed, and watch the moving memories of the prior night's dreams dance before my closed eyes. These dreams are now memories etched into my mind, and stand out with as much color and emotional attachment as actual events. The magical creatures, the adventures, the loves and the losses—they've taken place in my dreams as much as in my waking life. Sometimes these dreams were Lucid, other times they weren't, and I had to watch them via Dream Recall when I awoke.

The way I did and still do this is by willfully but gently scanning my inner world for specific themes. These themes stimulate the archetypal and biographical elements within my psyche that regularly appear in dreams. Consequently, these common themes then evoke the prior night's dreams, and they appear before my mind's eye. It was by way of this method that I'd eventually create the *Seven Categories of Dream.*

Because dreams are mostly composed of events that occur in daily life, the fastest route to Dream Recall is to scan your dreams for biographical elements. Examples of these are work-related issues, family issues, issues pertaining to one's social circle, and so on.

Once you've scanned your dreams for biographical elements, you can then move on to biological themes, and then archetypal themes, romantic themes, spiritual themes, and so forth until you have a good picture of what last night's dreams were all about. (If you are interested in a more elaborate "dream rolodex," I urge you to read Dr. Christopher Sowton's wonderful book, *Dreamworking: How to Listen to the Inner Guidance of Your Dreams.)*

One more thing: All of this depends upon how vivid your dreams are; that is to say, how full-sensory your dreams are. It's not enough that you can see very well while dreaming. Vivid Dreaming isn't merely visualization, but rather, it's visual, auditory, tactile, olfactory and even tasty!

Guided Imagery Meditation and Full-Sensory Immersion

Guided Imagery Meditation (GIM) may be defined as the creative use of imagination to affect healing and spiritual awakening. It is, in short, self-hypnosis. But what makes for successful *GIM?* I mean, is it really as simple as downloading an APP and following the vocal narrative streaming through the headphones?

Absolutely not!

It takes far more than good visualization abilities to reap the benefits of *GIM.* Indeed, it takes full-sensory immersion in the imagined landscape to truly obtain those benefits. Try this: preheat your oven to 335° Fahrenheit (168° Celsius). Then, stand in front of it with the oven door open. (Not too close! Simply stand close enough to the oven's mouth to feel the heat emanating from it.)

Next, close your eyes and allow yourself to feel the warmth of the oven. Do this for about five minutes and then switch the oven off. Allow the heat in your body to subside. Finally, stand in a cooler room and *mentally recreate the oven's heat.* That is, try to feel the heat as acutely as you did while you were standing in front of the oven.

Most people have considerable difficulty succeeding in this simple exercise. Many find it easy to *visualize* in imagination, and even to hear and taste, but the sensation of touch is lost to them. The sense of smell suffers a similar fate in dreams and imagination.

In the *Three-Body Fitness Program (TBFP)*, I'll share with you a few methods for the cultivation of full-sensory dreaming. Also, in this section, we'll perform a few experiments as *preludes* to the *TBFP*.

The internet is replete with *GIM* apps of varying degrees of quality. I recommend https://insighttimer.com for those interested in quality recordings.

Remember these simple rules while listening to any *GIM* program:

- Sensory-withdrawal from the external environment.
- Total immersion into the inner-landscape provided by the *GIM.*
- Relax to the point of sleep, but stay alert.
- Stay alert by engaging the *GIM* narrative in a full-sensory fashion.

Following these simple guidelines will not only build the neural pathways for more Vivid Dreaming, it'll also pave the way for more memorable Lucid Dreaming.

Emotions: The True Sixth-Sense

Once you've learned to include all five senses into your imaginings, you might begin to notice some changes taking place in your nightly dreams. The most obvious of these changes will be an increase in Dream Recall. As your dreams become more colorful and full-sensory, they become easier to remember.

The you may then notice that your dreams become more emotionally evocative. You may wake up laughing, or crying, or in full orgasm! That last one is a reliable gauge of progress.

In *Behind the Veil* I offered a technique which I call *The Touchless Orgasm* which was created out of a profound breakthrough in my own practice. After many years of having sexually charged Lucid Dreams, and an equal number of years of self-experimentation (let's just call it that), it occurred to me that the ability to bring oneself to orgasm solely through full-sensory imagination represents a profound attainment in terms of Conscious Sleep. Imagine, for instance, if you could make yourself break out in a sweat by simply imagining that you're standing in front of a hot oven? Well, many Tibetan monks can do just that. They call it *Tummo.* However, for most people, performing such a feat isn't easy. Sexual arousal, though? That's typically there at the touch of a button (pun totally intended)! So, accomplishing orgasm without resorting to physical stimulation is a great starting point for dreaming while awake. This, of course, will eventually parlay into your Vivid and Lucid Dreaming. Not only that, but you'll eventually be able to branch out into making other physical and emotional changes.

The key to making *The Touchless Orgasm* work is to bring your emotions into play while practicing it. I've noticed that this is especially important to female practitioners, but many males benefit from this, too. Of course, you needn't go the sexual route to start training.

Try this: Lie down in a quiet place where you won't be disturbed. Put on some emotionally evocative music and replay a memory from your past in vivid detail. The music best suited for this exercise is instrumental, as music with lyrics tends to be distracting. And you want pure instrumentals so that you, and not a lyricist, can create the narrative. (My favorites for this purpose are movie scores of a highly emotional nature.)

Next, allow yourself to bring all your senses to bear upon the visualization. And by "all of your senses" I mean all *six* of them! What is this sixth sense, you ask? Well, it's your *emotions!* That's right, your emotions truly do account for a sixth sense. And, because it's so closely related to the sense of touch, visualizations that contain tactile experiences are best for this purpose. (Thus my inclusion of *The Touchless Orgasm* in the *120-Days Curriculum* in *Behind the Veil.*)

But you don't need to limit yourself to sexual fantasy to begin training *GIM.* In fact, any fantasy or memory that provokes an emotional response in you will do the job.

Practice this exercise for as long as you wish. Once you're finished, it doesn't hurt to perform a grounding meditation such as the *Embryonic Breathing* or *Microcosmic Orbit* meditations discussed earlier. (I recommend these because I use them to great effect in my own practice. Also, they've stood the test of time in Taoist and Buddhist traditions. Still, you can choose any practice that calms, centers, and balances you.) Remember: working with the emotions can be exhausting. It helps to know how to restore and balance your nervous system after engaging them.

(2)

Eye and Ear Exercises for the Development of Vivid Dreaming

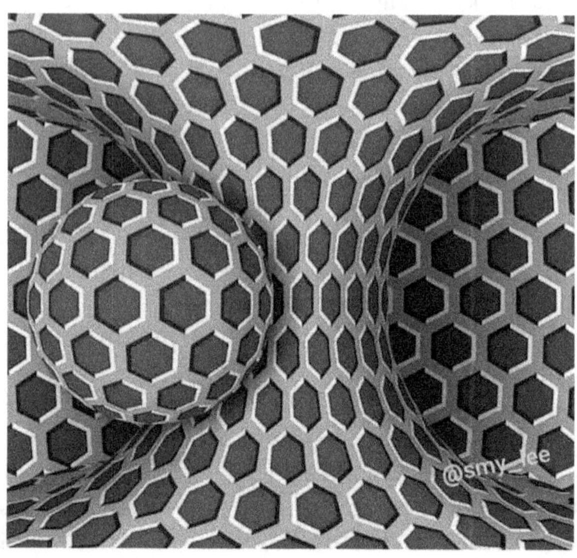

By far the most common form of Vivid Dream centers around the senses of sight and sound. So important are these two senses to Vivid Dreaming that one might think of them as doorways for full-sensory dreaming *per se*. Sight can play an important role in inducing an Out of Body Experience. Indeed, when it comes to Astral Projection and Lucid Dreaming, seeing is truly believing!

Sound, too, can have a profound impact on dream Lucidity and OOBE induction. The pioneering work of Graham Nicholls into Infra-Liminal Sound comes to mind, not to mention the ancient practice of chanting found in virtually every known culture of the world.

In this section, I'd like to explore some techniques that feature sight and sound as gateways to full-sensory dreaming, OOBE, and especially the aspect of Lucid Dreaming called Dream Control. Like all the practices included in this pages, the following exercises can be used in conjunction with the *120-Days Curriculum* of *Behind the Veil,* or the *Three-Body Fitness Program* found in the final section of this book. Don't hesitate to get creative; that's what *SCT* is all about!

Exercise One: Motion in Stillness

This first exercise is designed to cultivate how you perceive movement in dreaming. It's also designed to teach you how to control what moves and what doesn't. One of the most common problems faced by Lucid Dreamers, for example, is that whenever they try to focus on one specific item in the dreamscape, it either vanishes or changes shape entirely. This problem is also encountered during meditations that demand concentration upon a single object. While dreaming, this inscrutability of visual images is particularly irksome when the object of concentration is a pattern, such as a script or musical notation. So, this following exercise is meant to counter that tendency. Here's what to do:

First, direct your attention to the diagram above. If you're reading this on your computer or cell phone, isolate the image and place it at eye-level roughly one foot away from your face. Make sure you're comfortable and free of interruption for the next five minutes or so.

Next, stare into the image without blinking. This is called *Trataka* in the Yoga traditions of India. For the first ten seconds or so, stare only at the honeycomb-shaped background of the image. Then, suddenly shift your concentration to the ball on the left. Stare at this for about ten seconds, and then shift your attention to the hourglass-like shaped column in the center of the diagram. After ten seconds or so, shift your focus to include the entire diagram. At this point, it's okay to blink. This first part of the exercise is meant to stretch your optical muscles in a novel way.

For most people, the diagram will appear to move though some claim that it doesn't move at all. If you're of the latter type, don't worry! Simply perform the exercise up to this point, close your eyes, and then meditate on the afterimage that appears behind your eyes. But if you do see the image in motion, proceed to the next part of this technique.

As you stare at the moving image before you, try to stop it using only your willpower. Then, if you're successful, try to put it into motion again. Finally, try to stop and start it at will. Then, bring the exercise to a close by shutting your eyes and meditating on the after-image, which should appear floating in the black screen behind your closed eyes.

Exercise Two: Suriya Shabda and The Inner-Tones

As anyone who suffers from Tinnitus will tell you, the ringing, chiming, high-pitched tones, and bells heard in their ears are the last thing they want to promote. But we all have a degree of this going on, whether we have a Tinnitus diagnosis or not—and this doesn't have to be a bad thing!

The ancient Yogic practice of *Suriya Shabda* is one example of how *The Inner Tones* can be used as a meditation practice in itself. In this practice, the meditator concentrates on the subtle ringing sounds in his ears. These internal sounds are said to be the sonic expression of the "solar currents."

To experience these sounds, go into a room where there's complete silence. If this isn't possible, use earplugs. Next, sit and direct your attention to any sounds you might hear. Eventually, you'll notice high-pitched tones coming from somewhere in your head. Sometimes these tones are heard in the right or left ear only. At other times, they seem to fill the entire head or body. At any rate, once you're able to perceive them, you're ready to practice the following exercise.

STEP ONE: Calm down your body and mind. To this end, you might practice *Embryonic Breathing* for a few moments or any other technique of your choosing.

STEP TWO: Direct your attention to the sounds in your ears (or anywhere else you perceive them). Simply focus on these for a while, listening *into* the sounds with an active curiosity.

STEP THREE: Listening into these inner sounds, try to make out any voices, melodies or rhythms in them. Make a mental note of what you hear so that you can write it in your Dream Journal later.

STEP FOUR: Next, experiment with these tones. See, for example, if you can lower or raise their pitch. Then, see if you can make them into different vowel sounds, such as "Eeeeeeeee" or "Ahhhhhhhhh" sounds.

STEP FIVE: Lastly, try to send these tones to different locations in your body. I find that the easiest places are the heart and throat, but you can eventually learn to send them anywhere you wish.

Exercise Three: The Vertigo Method

WARNING: The following exercise isn't for everyone! Avoid this practice if you suffer from epilepsy, balance issues, nausea, stroke, neurological issues, or if you're taking medications that cause disorientation, vertigo or nausea. Neither the publisher nor the author are in any way responsible if you neglect this warning!

The following exercise is designed to enhance the first exercise in this section. That is, it grounds the first exercise in somatic experience, bringing the Gross, Subtle and Causal Bodies to bear.

STEP ONE: Find a room in which there's a couch or bed for you to fall onto should the need arise. Clear the area so that should you want to dance, you'll have enough room.

STEP TWO: Stand near the couch or bed. Begin spinning in the direction of your non-dominant hand. So, for example, if you're left-handed, spin to the right. Start off by spinning slowly and gradually pick up speed.

STEP THREE: Spin rapidly for about thirty seconds, and then suddenly stop. The room should now be spinning in the same direction you were spinning in.

STEP FOUR: Exhale naturally and stop breathing and moving. Become *totally* still. At the same time, try to *will* the room to stop spinning. **TIP**: If you can stop the movement of your eyes and thoughts, the room will also stop spinning.

Practice this before bed and also combine it with the *Wake Back To Bed* (WBTB) method for best results!

Exercise Four: Brow Center Method

The following exercise, though typically used to induce the first two phases of Lucidity (**LD-1** and **LD-2**), can also be used to cultivate full-sensory Vivid Dreaming. We utilize the Brow Center in many exercises in this book. The key to successful practice is involving all six senses in the experience (I call the emotions a "sixth" sense). Once you've worked with the Brow Center long enough, you'll see why it's often dubbed a "third eye." For the following practice, it may help to take a nootropic, such as *Huperzine-A* or *Galantamine* before bedtime. (But consult your doctor before taking any nutritional supplements!)

STEP ONE: On a night when you're especially tired, lie down comfortably on your back in a silent and semi-dark room. Some people fold their arms over their chest. Others find that placing their dominant hand on their chest, and their non-dominant hand on their belly greatly enhances light-phase Lucidity. Experiment with both methods to see which one works for you.

STEP TWO: Gently allow your gaze to rest upon the tip of your nose. Do *not* force this! You'll know you're doing this correctly because the tip of your nose will appear to vanish. At first your gaze will alternate between the right and left sides of your nose. This is okay, as it stimulates your optic nerve and encourages the hemispheric synchronization of your brain.

STEP THREE: Breathing naturally, become aware of the inner tones while continuing to focus on the tip of your nose. Do this for at least five minutes.

STEP FOUR: Remaining aware of the inner tones and the tip of your nose, slowly close your eyes and stare into the black field of vision before you. The goal is to continue to stare as though you're still gazing at the tip of your nose. To this end, it helps to practice in a semi-dark room, because the half-light will enable you to see the silhouette of your nose behind your eyes.

STEP FIVE: After a while, you'll begin to see shapes, psychedelic patterns, and scenery before your closed eyes. You may also hear voices, chimes, footsteps, and other auditory phenomena. Listen attentively to these, but don't become distracted by them. Just continue to gaze at the tip of your nose behind your closed eyes.

STEP SIX: Depending upon what you see and hear, try to reach out, as it were, with your senses. Do this one at a time. For example, if you see hypnagogia before hearing it, try to imagine what your visions might sound like. If, for instance, you see a natural landscape, try to hear the sound of rushing streams or waves. If you hear music, try to imagine what the sounds might look like if they were translated into color. And if you see colors, try to imagine how they might taste or smell. Lastly, bring your emotions to bear on the experience. You'll have to be very alert to accomplish this; otherwise you'll be overtaken by **NREM** or **REM** sleep.

PART THREE

MENTORING, MAGICK AND METHODS

Chapter Seven

Fear. Loss of Control. Children, Night-Terrors and Conscious Sleep

(1)
The Polar Psyche

I often encounter the following complaint from many students of Conscious Sleep. It's one of the most cited issues on internet forums, Lucid Dreaming websites, and in student/teacher correspondences. The dilemma typically reads like this:

"It seems that the more effort I put in, the less I get back; and when finally I do succeed, it's like I somehow got lucky and not as a result of my own sincere efforts."

Perhaps you've experienced something similar in your own quest? I know that I have! I began my journey into Conscious Sleep unwillingly.[10] As a child of nine summers, I was suddenly and inexplicably assaulted by spontaneous OOBE, sleep paralysis, Lucid Dreams, and assorted psychic phenomena. This lasted for about seven years before coming to a sudden halt. Unbidden it arrived, unbidden it left...

And it left me traumatized, socially alienated, and *curious*. In the end, curiosity won the day and, by the time I was sixteen years old, I made it my mission to uncover the truth about what I'd experienced. I grew up in a very strict Baptist family, so studying these topics was strictly forbidden. I had to hide all books on "the Occult" under my mattress, and when my mother found them, they were immediately burned or thrown away. It wasn't until I was removed from my home and placed into foster care that I was able to continue my studies and practices without interruption.

My practices were very specific. For starters, I intuitively understood that *fear* of these experiences was the primary reason for their sudden suppression. I call this suppression of subliminal cognition *The Psychic Moat* because the primal terror associated with OOBE and related phenomena functions as a kind of protective barrier between the conscious and subconscious regions of the psyche. So, my first order of operations was to confront this fear head on. How? Well what is the *essence* of fear of the unknown?

Total loss of control and power...

---

[10] See http://www.pixcom.com/en/productions/documentary/my-worst-nightmare-320.html for the documentary *(My Worst Nightmare)* in which my story is featured.

So long as you're afraid of losing control and confronting the unknown you'll never succeed at becoming a Veiler. It's that simple.

I experimented with LSD, magic mushrooms, formless meditations, Bhakti Yoga, and anything I could find that involved a powerful confrontation with *letting go.* Of course, these early attempts were clumsy, but I still learned a great deal from them. Not only that, but I started having *experiences* again! I took this as a sign that I was on the right path, but one problem still remained:

I had little control over how or when these experiences would occur.

A Lucid Dream here, an OOBE there, but none of it seemed to follow any clearly defined pattern. This was very frustrating, and it went on like this for about five years before the solution dawned on me. The practices I engaged in weren't the problem: how I was *employing* them was. If anything had truly helped me for those years, it was the psychedelics. I'm not saying that psychedelics are the answer, but they did teach me to get into a space where I could *allow* these experiences to surface. Literally none of the other practices I was engaged in would work if I couldn't learn this basic rule. When it comes to the skills associated with Conscious Sleep, effort only helps if it's *right* effort. It must involve a balance between the *Yin* and *Yang* of your psyche.

It was this revelation that made it easy for me to find my spiritual home in *Taoist Internal Alchemy.* Central to Taoist philosophy is the concept of the polarity of existence, *Yin* and *Yang.* But to say Yin *and* Yang is inaccurate as they're just two aspects of a singularity. *Yin/Yang* is more like it. In fact, the Chinese refer to the concept of *Yin/Yang* as *Taiji,* which means *Grand Ultimate.* This is contrasted with a transcendental concept called *Wuji,* which means *No Extremity* (between Yin or Yang). The concept of *Wuji* is very important to grasp, because it's synonymous with the skill called *Trance.* Properly understood, Trance is one of several keys to the continuity of consciousness, for which the *SCT* system was created.

The psyche also exists according to the law of *Taiji* and *Wuji.* For every action, willful or circumstantial, there's an equal and opposite reaction. So, any action one takes in the state of *Taiji* (polarity) must necessarily and unavoidably provoke its polar opposite. To illustrate how this works, let's examine the phenomenon known as *REM Rebound.*[11]

REM Rebound occurs because of the suppression of the dreaming phase of sleep. This suppression can be the result of the use of alcohol, marijuana or sleeping pills before bedtime. However, the **REM** phase is only temporarily suspended by these things, and it typically returns full-force later in the sleep cycle. Many oneironauts utilize this boomerang mechanism to enhance Vivid and Lucid Dreams.

But this approach has a downside…

I discovered that my single-minded efforts to penetrate the Veil were efficient at producing exactly the opposite result! After all, if you're working hard to stay awake, then that's a great way to tire yourself out enough to fall asleep! As most physiologists will tell you, if you're having trouble relaxing your muscles, deliberately tense them even more. Eventually, your muscles will respond by doing the opposite and they'll relax. That's one example of the skillful use of *Taiji* or *Yin/Yang.* A similar effect comes from trying to enter the sleep cycle consciously. Just as trying too hard to recall last night's dreams is a surefire way to forget them, so does too much effort prevent Conscious Sleep.

So, a skilled Veiler will utilize the polarity of *Yin/Yang* to provoke the opposite effect, but will also master *Wuji* to pierce through the Veil of *Taiji* without any effort at all. Reality Checks are one example of how this works in practice. This method utilizes *Taiji* by approaching the waking state as if it were a dream, and the dream state as though it were the waking state. That's the very essence of the Reality Check. *Wuji,* on the other hand, is utilized when one's sense of "I" jumps off of this *Taiji* ping-pong table and identifies instead with the "I" that's present throughout all states of consciousness. Once these two principles work together in a creative way, then this is *right-effort.*

This epiphany occurred when I was about twenty-one years old. I didn't refer to it then in Taoist terms, but that's essentially what the understanding was. I also joined an offshoot of the *Ordo Templi Orientis* (OTO) and the *Argentum Astrum* (A∴A∴), the *Holy Order of Ra Hoor Khuith* (HOOR), in Salem Massachusetts.[12] Alongside their

---

[11] See www.sciencedirect.com for the science behind *REM Rebound.*

[12] www.hoor.org is the website of the Thelemic Order to which I belonged.

curriculum, I was also practicing the methods of a Rosicrucian society called *The Hermetic Order of the Golden Dawn.* I found in these highly ritualistic systems a powerful bridge between *Taiji* and *Wuji,* and I eventually created another order based on a synthesis of these schools. I called it the *Collegium Cherubim* (C∴C∴), which eventually evolved into the more (shall I say) "portable" model I'd eventually dub *Subliminal Cognition Training.* The root skill of every one of these systems is the ability to bring individual and group consciousness into the deeper layers of the psyche so that the adept(s) can remain present for what they're working on. Not only that, but the attainment of alert consciousness on deeper fathoms of the psyche allows more nerve-force (by any name) to be brought to bear on the operation—whether it's Astral Projection, spiritual Initiation, or a group ceremony.

This brings me to an important point. I can't stress enough the importance of establishing a community of fellow Veilers. It often happens that the one thing preventing a student's breakthrough is lack of rapport with other Veilers at differing levels of skill. Besides the obvious benefit of having people of like mind around you who support your goals, your proficiency in Conscious Sleep will skyrocket with this kind of camaraderie! Therefore, the Buddha had a *Sangha* (group of fellow seekers), and it's why the *Milam* sect of Tibetan Dream Yoga is, well, a *sect.* Establishing a group of fellow Veilers is the lower left Quadrant of *SCT,* and is worth your serious consideration.

(2)
Teaching Children the Art of Conscious Sleep

Teaching the joys of Conscious Sleep is one of the most precious gifts we can give our children. Because they're inquisitive and playful, children often take to Conscious Sleep like ducks to water. Lucid Dreaming in particular seems especially suited to the childlike mind, though, as we'll soon see, we need not limit our kids to only one aspect of the Art. In fact, with the proper approach, your child could easily become a little Veiler, enjoying the full-spectrum of Conscious Sleep.

I'm often asked what age-group is appropriate to begin learning Conscious Sleep. In my opinion, starting at about the age of five is the ideal. My reasoning is founded on research from Developmental studies, as the "formative years" typically reach their apex at around age five. At this time, the child outgrows the "preconventional" stage and enters the "conventional" stage of development. This milestone is marked by the emergence of higher cortical functions, such as the capacity to separate Self from Other. The child's imagination also takes on a life of its own at this time, and she can now begin to "think about thinking." This is important because your child can now begin to take verbal instruction. It's difficult to teach Lucid Dreaming to a person who can't even understand what you're talking about! Also, a child at this stage is usually beginning to read, write and draw—all useful skills for training Conscious Sleep, as we'll soon learn.

I'm of the opinion that the sooner you begin teaching your child the sacredness of sleep, the better. In today's fast paced world, with its addiction to noise, digitalia, superficial pleasures, and all manner of toxic distractions, instilling in your child the importance of being able to lay quietly in the darkness, even if just to sleep soundly, is of immense value. The myriad benefits of sound sleep notwithstanding, to foster in your child a profound respect for sleep is to equip her with a secret weapon lost to a large number of folks in the modern world. Not only that, but such an attitude toward slumber provides the very foundation upon which all other skills as a Veiler are built. Indeed, without an appreciation for the sacredness of sleep, it'll be impossible to teach your child this precious art.

The Bedroom: A Sacred Space

You needn't wait until your child is five years old to begin this step! As a matter of fact, as a Conscious Sleeper yourself, your child will probably pick up your good sleep habits during his formative years. At any rate, the sooner you teach your child the importance of creating a safe, clean and sacred space to sleep in, the sooner you can begin building upon that base.

If circumstances permit, arrange your child's bed (or crib) so that it aligns with Earth's magnetic field. Her head should face magnetic North and her feet South. But if this can't be arranged, no worries! It's not absolutely necessary, but it does help.

Also, if circumstances permit, reserve your child's bedroom solely for sleep. Separate, if you can, his playroom from his bedroom. The removal of all external means of entertainment will signal to the child that her bedroom is reserved for internal entertainment only, namely dreaming. If this can't be arranged, however, decide upon a time when all toys must be put away, video games turned off, and inner games and adventures turned on.

Unplug all electronic devices, and be sure that your child doesn't sleep with any plugged in cellphones or laptops in his bedroom. ("Dirty" electricity and WiFi are a toxic source of radiation, and can negatively impact your child's bioelectrical balance, sleep quality, and overall well-being.)

Keep your child's bedroom clean, and encourage her to clean it herself. Explain the psychological effects of a clean or cluttered room, and make it a fun activity rather than a tedious chore.

Of course, your child's bedroom should be kept cool in the summer and warm in the winter. The air should be kept fresh, with plenty of circulating oxygen. An ionizer is a great way to accomplish this in cold weather when opening a window is out of the question.

When possible, your child's bedroom should be kept completely dark throughout the night. This ensures that your child's pineal gland will produce an adequate amount of melatonin, which is crucial for deep and restorative sleep. I understand that a fear of the dark is common among children, and this is a problem not easily solved without compromise. My own daughter is no exception! Eventually, her mother and I were forced to buy her a small nightlight. But I discovered that giving her the option of wearing a sleep-mask was a good compromise. In that way, she could be assured that the monsters were kept at bay by the nightlight while she enjoyed a dark field of vision as she slept. A bonus was that she'd look stylish while she slumbered!

It can also be of benefit to hang a dreamcatcher—or some other object of protection and sacredness—over your child's bed or on the door to his bedroom. This gives your child the added confidence that she's safe while sleeping, and that sleep is a sacred act. If your child chooses what this object should be, even better!

Depending upon your child's preferences, stuffed animals make great dream companions. I remember when I was a child, I had a stuffed animal, a dog named Simon. There were many times, while I was having recurring nightmares, that Simon would appear in my dreams and save the day. So allow your little one to choose his favorite dream companions, and tuck them in, too!

Lastly, the decision whether to play soft music or leave the bedroom in silence is something you might discuss with your child. As discussed earlier, should you opt to play music while your child falls asleep, select music without any vocals. As always, communicate with your child and don't be afraid to get creative. The more relaxed and excited you are about the process, the more your child will be, too.

Dream Journaling: Recording Your Adventures!

This part of the process is my personal favorite. I positively love listening to my six-year-old daughter describe her nightly dreams. As a rule, as soon as she wakes up, before she plays with her toys or watches TV, we sit on the couch or bed and take turns describing our nightly adventures. It's been such a rewarding experience, watching my daughter's deepening ability to recall the details of her dreams. In the beginning, she had great difficulty remembering her dreams at all. But gradually, with consistent effort and encouragement, my daughter eventually became adept at recalling her dreams. She even became quite a good storyteller! I watched with pride as she cultivated the ability to articulate her dreams in a way that's engaging, cogent and colorful.

It's a good rule of thumb to begin training your child to recall his dreams by asking him every morning about last night's "adventures." Asking in an excited tone, and then genuinely listening to his description, is a surefire way to get the most out of your child and to promote future cooperation. Be sure to have a notebook handy so that you can jot down any symbols or themes that stand out in your child's description. A good idea is to purchase a small diary, preferably one with your child's name on the cover, and record your notes in that. If she asks you what you're writing in, you can add mystery and suspense to the exercise and tell your child that every Veiler (or whatever title you choose) has a special book in which he records his nightly adventures. You can then hand the diary to your child and excitedly tell her that this is her special journal. Tell her that she can write, color or draw anything she remembers of her nightly dreams within the pages of her book. Encourage your little one to make a habit of recalling and recording her dreams, and to look for patterns in them. As always, make it a fun and magical exercise that both of you can share together. For example, my daughter is a huge fan of the 1980's classic film, *The NeverEnding Story*. So every morning we discuss and record last night's adventures in "Fantasia", the magical realm featured in the film. And being the loyal and fastidious "Fantastican Knight" that she is, my daughter makes it a point to recall and record her nightly "quests."

The only rules to remember while teaching your child how to journal her dreams is to be as descriptive as possible, record them first thing in the morning, and be consistent! It's okay to skip a day or two here and there, but consistency is key to cultivating your child's Dream Recall. Other than that, have fun!

Night-Terrors: Helping Your Child Creatively Cope

If you've been following this book series, you know about my own hellish childhood experiences with night-terrors. Between the sleep-clinics, psychologists and pastors, no one had the foggiest notion what to do with me! My parents were at a loss too, and everything from my schoolwork to my social life suffered as a result.

After I published my first book on Conscious Sleep, I received a handful of letters from parents with children suffering from chronic nightmares. Granted, I'm no doctor, and the following information isn't intended to replace the advice of a qualified specialist. Rather, the tips and methods I'm now going to share with you contain the timeless wisdom I wish my parents had access to. In my opinion, medication should be the *last* option when dealing with night-terrors. There are, of course, exceptions, but ruling out all other potential causes first seems wise. Diet is one good example of a potential source of night-terrors and other sleep-disorders. Trauma—physical and psychological—may also contribute to chronic nightmares. In my own case, the spontaneous occurrence of Lucid Dreaming and Astral Projection as a child frightened me so much that I soon became unwilling to fall asleep! In my case, it wasn't so obvious why I was having these experiences. My primary physician said it might be my asthma medication. My psychologist said it might be the result of my parents getting divorced. And my mother's pastor said it was a spiritual test. Well, thanks for nothing guys!

But then there are cases where the source of a child's night-terrors is easy to spot. In such cases, the solution tends also to be fairly obvious, though typically just as difficult to implement. In this section, I'll be sharing with you some strategies you can use in cases both obvious and elusive. I'd also like to emphasize that these tips and strategies are meant to be supplemental only. As always, discuss your child's night-terrors with a professional before resorting to the following methods.

Your Child's Dream Journal

The most direct route to resolving your child's night-terrors simply involves talking to her and allowing her to vent. Some children are reluctant to discuss their nightmares, though, and this is where keeping a regular Dream Journal can be a big help. Writing and telling her nightmares as a story or adventure places your child's nightmares in a creative context. This has multiple advantages. First, it gives your little one a sense of control by making her the narrator of the tale. Second, it puts both of you into conscious contact with the subconscious elements within your child's nightmares. Consequently, you can both now work creatively with those elements. You could, for example, have your child write down her nightmares in her Dream Journal and then change the way the story ends. For instance, let's imagine that your child has a nightmare about being chased my monsters. In the dream, your child simply ran away screaming and crying. So, you'd first instruct your child to write the nightmare down exactly as it occurred, and then create a section below that story in which she rewrites the ending with herself heroically facing the monsters and chasing them away! Tell your child to be as descriptive and colorful as possible with her plot-twist, and encourage her to vividly imagine every detail as she writes.

In the event that night-terrors become chronic, it's a good practice to scan your child's journal for recurring themes. This is especially helpful if your child is seeing a psychologist. I know this from personal experience. When I was about nine, my mother brought me to a child-psychologist because of my night-terrors. One of the first things the good doctor did was ask me to write down the first nightmare I could remember having. He then gave me some clay, some crayons, some paper, and told me to recreate that nightmare as best I could. And he continued with that approach every time he saw me. Eventually, a pattern emerged in my chronic nightmares. He noticed that many of my nightmares were centered around the theme of abandonment and betrayal. This is how he reasoned out that my night-terrors were probably a consequence of my parents' divorce.

So, whether the source of his nightmares are obvious or not, consider Dream Journaling as one tool you can use to help your child creatively tackle his fears. Get creative and innovative, and adjust accordingly to fit your child's unique personality. With love, patience and commitment, I'm confident you can empower your little one and get to the bottom of what's causing his sleep-disturbances.

Amulets and Power-Objects

My daughter suffers from night-terrors. Luckily, the source of her nightmares was obvious from the very beginning. You see, she suffers from psychogenic sleep-apnea, which means she stops breathing at various intervals throughout the night. The problem started when she was two years old and hasn't stopped since. She's now six. Her mother and I took her to doctors, but none were any help. One doctor told us to give her chamomile before bed. That didn't help. Another doctor told us to place a "sleep mask" on her face, a rather uncomfortable looking device designed to keep her breathing throughout the night.

So, being the Conscious Sleeper I am, I began studying her sleep cycle...

After some time, I was able to pinpoint where in my daughter's sleep cycle the attacks were occurring. Like clockwork, roughly ninety minutes or so into her sleep cycle, she'd gasp, stop breathing, then start breathing again, but with an erratic rhythm. She'd often talk in her sleep at this time, and typically began to cry at which point I'd hug her and gently wake her up. I also noticed that these attacks were especially dramatic in the early morning hours between three and five o'clock.

So what does this mean?

Because the average sleep cycle initiates the dreaming phase every ninety minutes or so, and increases in intensity and duration as the night progresses, it became obvious to me that my daughter's apnea was a symptom of her entering a round of dreaming. As we know, sleep-paralysis also sets in at these intervals. As a Conscious Sleeper, I'm well-acquainted with the fact that awareness of breathing vanished during the onset of sleep-paralysis. I believe that my daughter is on some level conscious of this transition, and this produces anxiety, which produces nightmares.

So what was my proposed solution?

Because I knew that I couldn't magically erase my daughter's apnea, nightmares or sleep-paralysis, I decided to begin training her to Lucid Dream. Since her attacks were occurring on the threshold of the dreaming phase of sleep, why not acclimate her to the nuances of that transition by teaching her to consciously engage it?

As I mentioned, my little girl is a huge fan of the film adaptation of Michael Ende's novel, *The NeverEnding Story,* so I decided to introduce her to Lucid Dreaming by using that film as a springboard. In the film, the hero wears an amulet called "Auryn", which serves as both a guide and shield. So I consulted Google, found a site that sold customized jewelry, and ordered two Auryn necklaces, one for me and the other for her. My idea was to first get her to see me wearing her favorite amulet. I knew she'd see it around my neck and ask questions, which she did. I then pulled her aside and whispered, "If I tell you a secret, do you promise to keep it?" Her eyes widened and she said, "Yeah! Yeah!" I nodded my head affirmatively. I then looked around secretively and then whispered, "I'm a Fantastican Knight. I'm a protector and defender of Fantasia." Her eyes widened even more as she reached for the amulet around my neck. I then pointed to a copy of *Behind the Veil* which was sitting on my bookshelf, and said, "I teach people how to go to Fantasia. That's my job." At that point, my little girl was beside herself. She whispered excitedly, "Can you teach me to go to Fantasia?!" To which I replied, "Of course. But first you need an Auryn. Going to Fantasia is a big quest, and you need Auryn to guide you. I'll have to ask Empress Moonchild if you can have one." With her hands on her hips, and a look of bewilderment on her face, my daughter asked, "You know the Empress?" I said, "Oh yes. Every Fantastican Knight knows the Empress, silly. I'll ask her tonight if you can have an Auryn necklace, but remember: it takes a lot of courage to wear the Auryn." She nodded.

The next morning, while she lay sleeping, I placed the necklace with the Auryn pendant around her neck. I then went about my morning routine. About half an hour later, my wife came into the kitchen and said, "Your daughter is awake. She's over the moon right now with joy." I then went into my daughter's bedroom to find an extremely elated six-year-old girl holding her Auryn up to the light pouring in through the window:

"Papa! Papa! I have an Auryn!" she exclaimed with pride.

It was such a treat to watch my daughter slowly conquer her fear of the dark because she now had an object around her neck that she associates with power and courage. It was also with pride that I watched her enthusiastically attempt to Lucid Dream every night as she fell asleep. I taught her how to play with the shifting colors behind her eyes (phosphene discharge), and to turn them into any shape she desires. I taught her some basic breathing techniques to use when she has trouble breathing at night.

To this day she asks me for more information on how to be a better "Fantastican". She even asked me to teach her how to meditate.

My daughter's night-terrors didn't vanish, but her reactions and overall attitude toward them has changed dramatically. She sees them as a sort of challenge, as part of her nightly adventures. She's even had a handful of Lucid Dreams!

If you're unsure about what kind of amulet to use, here's a list of amulets you might use:

- A Dreamcatcher. These popular talismans come down to us from the shamanic traditions of Native American peoples.
- A Cross. Besides being the central symbol of the Christian faith, the Cross is also a solar symbol. It also represents the unity of the Earthly (horizontal bar) and Heavenly (vertical bar) realms.
- A Hexagram. Also called the Star of David, this ancient symbol is also one which represents the union of the Earthly and Divine realms.
- Your Child's Birthstone. Each sign of the Zodiac is associated with its own precious stone. Your child can wear her birthstone either as a ring or necklace.
- A Photograph. Placing a picture of yourself or someone else he admires in an amulet your child can wear as a necklace is a great

way to make him feel safe at night. You could also simply place the picture in a frame and leave it on the nightstand by your child's bed.

• A Religious Icon. Any object associated with your particular faith will serve as a powerful amulet for your child.

Whichever amulet you choose, remember to allow your child to see you wearing it first. This will assure your little one of the authenticity of the power-object. Be sure to build a solid story around the amulet too, as this will give your child an example or two of how the amulet works and in what type of situations. As long as you're convincing and consistent, you'll be amazed by how well this approach works to instill confidence in your child!

Pellucidity Training For Kids

The first time I was taught anything associated with Conscious Sleep was in Kindergarten. A substitute teacher was filling in for our regular teacher, and she decided to make "nap time" a bit more interesting. She instructed us to lie down on our backs with our hand at our sides. She then asked us to watch our thoughts like birds in the sky, without engaging them. She told us to breathe naturally, and to feel our bodies melting into the floor with each exhalation. I found that I was quite the natural at this technique, and entered the first phase of the sleep cycle with full awareness.

Later on in life, I met Dr. John Mumford (Swami Anandakapila Saraswati), who taught me how to get the most out of this Yogic exercise. Known by Yoga practitioners as "Savasana", my students recognize this technique from the Pellucidity training section of the *120-Days Curriculum.* This "progressive relaxation" technique is arguably the fastest way to experience Pellucid Sleep, for beginners and advanced practitioners alike. It's also one of the best techniques to teach children, even if just to improve their overall quality of sleep. Because I've already fully discussed Pellucidity training in *Behind the Veil,* I won't be repeating the techniques here. The main thing I'd like to point out is that the exercises must be adapted to the childlike mind. For obvious reasons, you want to avoid making things too complex for your child to understand. Keep it simple. And make it fun!

Hypnagogia: Cartoons Inside the Mind

When teaching your child basic Pellucidity skills, it's best to begin with hypnagogic imagery. As a fun experiment, ask your child to close her eyes and stare into the darkness behind her eyelids. Tell her to look for colors, spots, shapes or lights. Tell her that if any distracting thoughts arise, simply watch them as she would a flight of birds or a school of fish. Tell her to allow thoughts to come, and bring her focus back to the shifting patterns behind her eyes. After a few minutes, tell her to open her eyes and tell you what she saw. Listen intently to her description, and then suggest that she try the same thing as she's falling asleep at night. If you like, you could add a magical dimension to the exercise and tell your child that those shifting patterns are the curtain that separates our world from the world of dreams. Explain that those shifting patterns of color and light open into a magical world, but she has to focus intently on them as she falls asleep.

Although this basic Pellucidity exercise can be evolved into Lucid Dreaming skills, for now simply teach your child how to concentrate on hypnagogic imagery. This will build her Causal muscles and sharpen the concentration necessary to sustain both Pellucid and Lucid Dreaming.

When I was a child, I used to cherish those moments before falling asleep or just upon waking, when hypnagogic imagery is most common. It was like watching a light-show or cartoon behind my closed eyes. After some time, I realized that I could single out a specific color or pattern in the hypnagogia and concentrate on it. This became a sort of meditation for me, one which evolved through various stages of refinement. I discovered, for example, that by concentrating on one pattern or shape behind my eyes, that I could "enter" into it and step into a Lucid Dream. From there, and as more complex dream images emerged, I could focus on one of them and stabilize my Lucid Dream. Students of my *120-Days Curriculum* recognize this as *The Hitchhiker Method* from *Behind the Veil*.

Mobile Mental Focus (MMF): Nap-Time Made Fun!

You may also recognize this technique from *Behind the Veil's* "120-Days Curriculum". I've chosen this technique because I feel it's a bedtime activity that many kids would enjoy. Why? Well, first, the

MMF technique is a perfect balance between activity and repose. Although the body is totally at rest, your attention is engaged in such a way that the restless mind is guided into a state of Conscious Sleep. And not just any old state of Conscious Sleep, but Pellucid Sleep. Of course, in the Yogic traditions, they don't refer to it as "pellucidity", but rather *Yoga Nidra* (see Chapter Four). To teach this to your child, you simply have to adapt it to the childlike mind (i.e., make it fun!)

So how to approach your child with the **MMF** exercise?

At bedtime or nap-time, tell your child to lie down on his back, eyes closed, with his hands by his sides and palms facing upward. Ask him to do a full body scan with his mind by mentally feeling into his body, starting from his head and slowly making his way down to his toes. Tell him to perform this mental body scan as slowly as possible, but not so slowly that he loses interest.

Next, have him mentally feel into his feet by asking him to bring his attention there and note any sensations he feels (e.g., warmth, coldness, tingles, the pressure of his feet against the mattress). Tell him to then imagine that his feet are getting very heavy each time he exhales. A useful tip is to ask him to imagine that the mattress is rising up to meet his feet as they relax downward. Cultivating a melting sensation in his feet might also help.

Now instruct your child to slowly work his way from his feet upward, performing the same procedure of feeling into the body part, breathing naturally, and cultivating a melting sensation with each exhalation of breath. The classic "yogic" order of ascension through the body is:

The Sixteen Marmasthanani

   1. Feet.
   2. Shins/Calves
   3. Knees (front and back)
   4. Thighs
   5. Buttocks
   6. Abdomen
   7. Chest
   8. Back
   9. Hands
  10. Forearms

11. Elbows
12. Shoulders
13. Neck
14. Jaw
15. Back of Head
16. Scalp

Although not necessary, you can expedite the relaxation process by asking your child to tense each body part while inhaling, then relaxing suddenly while exhaling. This is a great way to eliminate restlessness and bound-up energy. Feel free to repeat this procedure as often as you and your little one wish! As long as you keep your child engaged, you'll both soon discover that your child has learned to enter the first phase of sleep with awareness fully intact.

And this skill can be deepened.

Lucid Dreaming: The Inner Playground

Besides love and protection, teaching your child to Lucid Dream is arguably the best gift you can give her. In a world where kids are becoming increasingly dependent upon video games and the digital devices that house them, your child will, as a Lucid Dreamer, be capable of playing inside of her own virtual reality! Not to mention that you'll be fortifying your child with all of the benefits that come with consistent and refined Lucid Dreaming. With strategic and consistent Lucid Dreaming practice, your child will reap the following rewards:

• Access to worlds and adventures of his own creation.
• Enhanced creativity and inspiration.
• A strong intuition and heightened psychic abilities.
• A heightened ability to learn new skills and retain information.
• Access to a genuine superpower!
• And much more!

As I've said, Lucid Dreaming is especially suited to the childlike mind. It offers kids the chance to explore their imagination and actively live out the adventures they see on TV and in their own minds. Teaching your little one to Lucid Dream gives you an opportunity to foster in her the virtues of confidence, willpower, creativity, freedom and even spiritual awakening. Through Lucid Dreaming, your child will face her fears, manifest her desires and wishes, confront the archetypes of the collective human condition, and more.

In this section, we'll explore some ways in which you might teach your child how to Lucid Dream. Also, if your child is already a natural Lucid Dreamer, this section will explore ways in which you might channel her abilities toward higher development as a human being. Remember, the ability to control your nightly dreams is in many ways a direct form of self-hypnosis. If you teach your child to face her fears and manifest her wishes in the dream state, that will buttress her capacity to do so while awake.

Can you think of a better gift to give to your child?

Hypnagogia: The Colorful Curtain of Dreams

As I mentioned in the section on teaching your child the skill of Pellucidity, the phenomenon called "hypnagogia" is the fast-track to light-phase Lucidity (i.e., **LD-1** and **LD-2**). The colors, patterns, lights and images that emerge behind your child's eyes as she falls asleep is a great starting point for Lucid Dreaming. The main reason for this is that hypnagogic imagery, and even hypnagogic sound, are easily accessed while still fully awake. This active participation in sleep as it approaches, signals to your subconscious mind that you wish to remain aware in your dreams. That your child is taught to hold and sustain this intention is crucial to success in all forms of Conscious Sleep, not only Lucid Dreaming. That said, conscious intention often isn't enough for stable access to Lucid Dreaming. As we'll discuss in the next section, you must engage your child's subconscious mind as well for true success in this regard.

For now let's talk about how you might teach your child to use hypnagogic sound and imagery as a doorway to Lucid Dreaming.

Let's start with hypnagogic sound.

Students of the *120-Days Curriculum* will recognize the Yogic practice called *Surya Shabda*. This ancient meditative exercise focuses on the inner tones, ringing and other sounds you might hear in your ears if you have tinnitus. However, you needn't have tinnitus to hear these inner sounds. Almost everyone can hear them to some degree, which is why it's such a popular method in the Yogic traditions. If musically inclined, *Surya Shabda* will be a delight for your child to practice!

So how to do it?

As always, the main difference between practicing as an adult and practicing as a child is that the latter needs the session to be fun. Don't get me wrong! Adults can benefit from adopting an attitude of fun while practicing as well, but children are especially in need of this if you'd like them to practice at all. So allow me to offer a few suggestion on how to prepare the practice session in a way that'll spark your child's enthusiasm:

1. Don't underestimate the power of fantasy! For example, ask your little one if she's ever heard the fairies, angels or elves play or sing music. Tell her that you can show her how to hear it, but she needs to be very quiet and pay close attention.
2. My favorite way of getting my six-year-old daughter interested in the practice is I'll tell her that she can listen to the sounds of the stars if she knows how to listen to them. Give it try!
3. Offer to practice with your child! Be visibly excited and eager to participate. Your enthusiasm will be contagious!
4. Pick a time and date to practice together, and get creative with the times you choose. You might, for instance, begin practicing on the night of the full moon. This will lend a magical quality to the exercise.

With a little creativity and enthusiasm, you and your child could probably come up with even better ideas! But once you've established interest, and your little one is excited about practicing *Surya Shabda,* teach him the following exercise:

The Exercise

First, be sure that your child's bedroom is completely silent. If this isn't possible, ask your little one if she'd like to use earplugs. Be sure to get the softest type of plugs you can find, as harder ones might become uncomfortable for your child to wear. If you do decide to use earplugs, you'll obviously have to instruct your child on how to do the exercise before he puts the earplugs in. Also, try to make the room as dark as possible. If your child's afraid of the dark, a nightlight may be used.

Next, walk your child through a basic progressive relaxation process. You don't have to go through the entire Mobile Mental Focus process above, though, as that's likely to just put your child to sleep. Try instead to do a condensed version of **MMF**. For example, tell your child to lie down on his back with his hands by his side. Tell him to breathe naturally while focusing more on the exhalation than inhalation. At the same time, tell your child to feel himself getting heavier with each exhalation, all the while cultivating a sensation of melting downward into the bed.

Once she's sufficiently relaxed, direct your child's attention toward any sounds she might hear "inside her head." Tell her to listen closely for any ringing, buzzing, fuzzy static, or musical tones. Once she's spotted so much as one sound, tell her to relax and listen intently to the sound. Soon, more sounds will emerge. When they do, tell your child to maintain focus on the first sound, but to add the new sound into her field of attention. And so on with other sounds as they emerge.

Eventually, and with practice, an entire symphony of sound will emerge inside your child's head. Soon enough, one night, as your little one is practicing this method while dozing off, she will enter a state in which she'll be able to manipulate the sounds. This can be great fun! When I was a child, I used to enter this state and hear what sounded like radio broadcasts, melodies and even my favorite songs! I could oftentimes "switch the station" and hear whatever song I wished for.

So go ahead and get your child started on this marvelous practice. Some things need to be heard to be believed!

Phosphene Discharge: Playing with Hypnagogic Imagery

Just as you can teach your child to turn inner sounds into inner symphonies, so too can you teach your child to transform inner colors into inner movies. My daughter and I play a game at bedtime that we call "Air Painting." The game is simple. Lying next to each other in bed, we'll close our eyes and stare at the colors, spots and patterns behind our eyes (phosphene discharge). Then, taking turns, we'll name a shape and challenge the other to recreate it using the phosphene discharge as "paint." We'll proceed in this manner, challenging each other with shapes and scenes of ever-increasing complexity until one of us loses the game.

As with many of the techniques I've learned throughout the years, I stumbled upon this one by accident, while practicing a different technique. The year was 2001, and I was immersed in the Yogic practice called *Dharana*. Generally speaking, the aim of *Dharana* is sustained concentration upon a single object to the exclusion of all else. The object can be anything of your choosing, but the goal is to first conjure the image up in your mind's eye and sustain concentration upon it. I chose a red triangle.

After about three months of daily practice, I began to notice that the phosphene discharge behind my eyes was shaping itself according to my intention. That is, it was turning into a red triangle! And, although this traditionally counts as a "break" in concentration, the red triangle would open up into dream scenarios. Soon, I was able to sustain concentration into the dream state while sitting up. As an added perk, I was quickly becoming skilled at manipulating the dream world. Of course, I could only do this up to the point of sleep paralysis, at which point I'd fall over or gasp or in some other way snap back to full consciousness. Years later I would come to refer to these states of light-phase Lucidity as **LD-1** and **LD-2**.

So how do you introduce your child to **LD-1** and **LD-2**?

First, you must acclimate your little one to her capacity to sustain attention on internal imagery. If you've taught your child any of the exercises already covered in this section, this shouldn't be a problem. Try this:

Candle Gazing: A Yogic Practice Made Fun and Easy

For this simple exercise, all you'll need is a candle and a dark and quiet room for you and your child to practice in. Called "Tratak" or "Trataka" in the Yoga tradition, this deceptively simply practice offers manifold benefits to the consistent practitioner. *Tratak* gradually teaches you the balance between effort and relaxation required for successful *Dharana* (meditative concentration). Not only that, but *Tratak* also cultivates your skill in Vivid Dreaming by gradually cultivating your capacity to generate and sustain mental images. A little-known secret of *Tratak* is that the practice can be expanded to include all five senses, and not just the sense of sight.

In this section, we'll be learning how you might teach your child this invaluable skill. *Tratak* is especially beneficial to children with a deficit in concentration or Vivid Dreaming. And for kids with an obvious aptitude in this regard, *Tratak* is a powerful tool for refining her natural talent.

So let's begin!

Begin by placing a candle about two feet away and at eye-level in front of you and your child. Be sure to sit on a comfortable surface, one that minimizes restlessness and back pain.

Next, ask your child to close his eyes and relax his body. At the same time, instruct him to focus on the natural rhythm of his breathing and the field of vision behind his closed eyes. It's important to deliver these instructions in a manner that doesn't make the practice feel like a chore. This is especially true in the beginning phases of practice. Later on, as the practice develops, you can slowly emphasize the "discipline" of consistent practice.

After a few minutes have passed, and your child is sufficiently re-laxed, you may move on to *Tratak* proper. Ask your child to open her eyes and gently focus on the candle flame. For the first minute or so, blinking is permitted; afterwards, instruct your child to stop blinking altogether for a slow count of twenty seconds while staring gently into the candle flame. After twenty seconds have passed, tell your child to close his eyes and wait for the afterimage of the flame to appear behind his eyes. Once the afterimage appears, instruct your child to relax his facial muscles from the scalp down to his jaw as much as possible, and to stare intently at the afterimage of the candle flame. This relaxation/concentration mechanism is important, as increased relaxation will increase the time in which the afterimage will remain visible. The moment your child becomes too tense, the afterimage will begin to disappear. The goal is to sustain the afterimage, and concen-tration upon it, for as long as possible.

Once the afterimage fades away completely, ask your child to recreate the candle flame in her imagination. The mental recreation of the candle flame must look exactly like the afterimage! This consis-tency in appearance is crucial, as any change in appearance counts as a "break" in concentration. The goal is to sustain concentration upon the mental recreation of the candle flame for at least two minutes with-out a break in concentration. If this proves too difficult for your child, one minute will suffice as a starting goal. As always, you want these practices to be challenging but doable.

Lastly, to shake things up a bit, you can expand this practice to include the other senses. The trick is to engage a particular sense, such as smell, by confronting it with a stimulus specific to it, and then recreate the stimulus in feeling and imagination. Finally, you want to teach your child to focus on the recreation for as long as possible. The following list contains my own suggestions, but I'm sure you can come up with many of your own ideas for sense-objects. You might also ask your child to pick them herself:

- **Sight**: Candle flame. The moon. A familiar face. A geometric shape. Your child's own hands.
- **Sound**: A musical note or even an entire song. Ocean waves. The wind. Chirping birds. Drums. Laughter. Clapping.
- **Smell**: Lavender. Freshly cleaned laundry. Mommy's perfume or daddy's cologne.
- **Taste**: Chocolate. Fruit (especially sour). Salt or pepper. Ice cream.
- **Touch**: Cool or warm water. The breeze. A hug or kiss.

As always, involve your child and get creative. Go on a hunt for new and more complex objects for your child to concentrate upon.

Deep-Phase Lucidity and Astral Projection for Kids

Teaching your child how to enter full-fledged Lucid Dreaming is much like learning it yourself. On the one hand, you must consciously engage your intention to Lucid Dream. Also, you must match your conscious intention with subconscious cooperation, which is to say, you must convince your subconscious mind to want to Lucid Dream. Oftentimes, this second step is merely a question of convincing yourself that Lucid Dreaming is even possible.

Teaching your child is no different.

A good way to introduce your little one to deep-phase Lucidity (**LD-3**) is through books on the subject written specifically for kids. One such book is *The Goodnight Fairy*, by Renee Frances. And for parents with children suffering from night-terrors, I highly recommend *The Cupboard of Fear* by Stewart Bell. You'll soon discover that reading a book that features Lucid Dreaming is a powerful and fun way to get the idea into your child's mind that such a thing is possible, and even desirable.

Another great way for your child to train Lucid Dreaming is through affirmations. At bedtime, your child can recite these affirmations as she falls asleep. You can create the affirmations with your child, or allow her to come up with her own. Here are some suggestions:

- "Things aren't always what they seem, I'm awake inside my dream!"
- "Swimming birds and flying fish, I can dream up any wish!"
- "What is real and what is fake? In my dreams I'm wide awake!"
- "Am I dreaming or am I awake?"

Combining affirmations with reading books about Lucid Dreaming is a potent combination. Whether you're an adult or child, this approach is time-tested and is used by seasoned Lucid Dreamers all over the world.

Teaching Your Child the Proper Posture for Lucid Dreaming

Although Lucid Dreaming can happen in any posture, the "supine" posture is most effective. Many people have their first Lucid Dreaming or Astral Projection experience while sleeping in this posture. Oftentimes these experiences occur without any intention to have them. A person simply falls asleep while lying on his back and has a Lucid Dream or Astral Projection experience.

There are, however, a few common problems when it comes to the supine posture. Some people find that the symptoms of sleep paralysis tend to be more severe in this posture. In any case, trying to teach your child to sleep on her back can be a formidable task, as many children toss and turn throughout the night. Still, it's worth a try!

For children with respiration issues, I find that providing them with a Memory Foam wedge helps alleviate breathing complications while still providing the Lucid Dreaming potential of the supine posture. These wedges allow you to sleep much like you would on a reclining chair. This happy medium between sitting erect and lying supine signals the mind to enter an alert but relaxed state. I suggest using the wedge for naps rather than at bedtime. An afternoon nap is an ideal time to teach your child how to enter deep-phase Lucidity.

After years of practice, your child will grow to Lucid Dream in any posture. Once her bodymind learns the skill, the sky is truly the limit!

Teaching Your Child the Reality Check Method

This is arguably the most fun of all the ways to teach kids to Lucid Dream! It's also the only method that can be practiced at any time of the day or night.

The best way to introduce your child to the Reality Check method is to ask her to periodically check if she's dreaming throughout the day. A very popular method involves trying to stick the index finger of your dominant hand through the palm of your non-dominant one. This method is typically practiced within the dream-state itself, but it can also be used while awake. The more spontaneous your child can be with this the better.

The best time of day to do a Reality Check is as soon as your child wakes up. Instruct her to examine her thoughts and sensations immediately upon waking, and ask herself if she might be dreaming. It's even better if she can learn to remain completely still as soon as she wakes up, and then perform a Reality Check. The moment the physical body is engaged, sleep paralysis fades and the dream world fades with it. So complete stillness of the body is ideal for entering a Lucid Dream through an early morning Reality Check.

Looking for odd features in the environment is also a great way to enhance the effects of the Reality Check. Tell your child to look for odd features in things in her daily life—things that look like omens or signs. For example, clouds that form an odd shape. Or a flight of birds that form a strange pattern against the sky. Actively scanning the environment for atypical features encourages a conscious link between the conscious and subconscious regions of the psyche. Eventually, this will become a habit and spill over into your child's dream life. One night, while dreaming, your child will spot something that seems to stand out as bizarre and this will trigger a Lucid Dream.

The Hitchhiker Method: Stabilizing a Lucid Dream

The Hitchhiker Method is my personal favorite method for stabilizing Lucidity within the dream. When performed properly, this technique is a powerful way to transition into the Lucid Dream state. Also, it's a great practice for kids!

Although this method can be used at any time throughout the night, the best time to practice is in the early morning hours when dreaming tends to be most powerful and vivid.

The Hitchhiker Method is best employed during the initial stages of a Lucid Dream. Sometimes this is as easy as staring into hypnagogic imagery while you fall asleep, although that's very rare. More often this method is best employed when you become spontaneously aware that you're dreaming. The reason for this is that when you become spontaneously Lucid in the dream, you typically wake up soon after.

The basic goal of *The Hitchhiker Method* is to focus on one dream-object to the exclusion of all others and "ride" it into full immersion in the Lucid Dream state. For example, let's assume you become Lucid in the middle of a dream and the dream environment begins to shake or fade away. You then actively focus on any prominent object in the dream and concentrate on it as best you can. This will have the effect of rooting you in the dream world. Thus rooted, you can then examine the subtler details of the dreamscape. This will have the effect of stabilizing the Lucid Dream so that you can continue to explore it without the threat of waking up.

Simply instruct your child to keep alert to when he becomes Lucid within the dream, and to then concentrate on one object within the dream as best he can. With a little practice, he'll be able to use this powerful method of dream stabilization whenever the opportunity presents itself.

Astral Projection for Kids!

Here we come to the most complicated aspect of Conscious Sleep that you can teach your child. Successful Astral Projection tends to combine elements of Pellucidity and Lucidity, hence its complexity. Unless your child has a natural talent for it, Astral Projection is a skill that takes time and dedicated practice to experience regularly.

Astral Projection is best taught to children who've had a spontaneous Astral experience and are trying to make sense of it. Sometimes the experience is magical, and sometimes terrifying. In either case, should your child communicate to you that she's had such an experience, it's helpful to ask her if it's an experience she'd like to repeat. If the experience was a frightening one, talk it over with your child. It may be wise to wait until a later date to reintroduce the idea to him. All it takes is a few bad experiences to slam the door shut on future success with Astral Projection, so tread softly.

If your child has been keeping a regular diary of her dreams, you can expect to eventually stumble upon an Astral Projection experience or two in the entries. This is especially true for kids who practice Lucid Dreaming on a consistent basis. This is perfectly normal, as Lucid Dreaming and Astral Projection have more similarities than not. So be on the lookout for Astral experiences if and while your child is practicing Lucid Dreaming. Remember, though, that it's possible to have access to Lucid Dreaming and still never experience Astral Projection, and vice versa. As always, it takes commitment, good techniques, and a bit of natural talent to experience these two aspects of Conscious Sleep.

Introducing Your Child to Astral Projection

A great way to introduce kids to Astral Projection is through the extremely common phenomenon called "hypnic jerks." It's likely that you've experienced these pre-sleep twitches and falling sensations yourself. Ask your child if she's ever felt like she was falling off her bed during the onset of sleep. If she says yes, instruct her to allow it to happen. Explain that you know it can be unpleasant, but that if she allows it to happen a magical experience awaits her!

In the meantime, it helps to know a few techniques.

Remember that training Astral Projection is mostly a process of teaching your nervous system how to recognize and promote what might be called "Astral Movement." That is, how to manufacture and recreate physicals movements, such as spinning, walking, swinging, falling or jumping at the exact moment when sleep paralysis sets in. That's not to say that you can't induce Astral Projection at any other phase of sleep, but the onset of sleep paralysis is a particularly potent time to practice.

It's important to understand that Astral Movement isn't the same thing as imagining the act of moving. In other words, you're not merely watching yourself move as if in a dream. Rather, you're keeping your physical body motionless while recreating all the sensations associated with actual motion. For example, if you're astrally "jumping," you should really feel as though you're jumping.

When I was a child, my two favorite methods of inducing Astral Projection were to recreate the sensations of swinging on a swing set or riding in an elevator. You know the sinking feeling you get in your gut when riding on an elevator? Have you ever stepped off an elevator and felt as if you were still in the thing? Recreating that sensation as you're falling asleep is a powerful way of inducing Astral Projection.

In my opinion, the best place to start teaching your child Astral Movement is at your local park. Give her a few pushes on the swing set and then ask her to recreate the sensations of swinging later on at bedtime. Instruct her to lie down in a supine posture, remain completely still, and then conjure up the sensation of swinging. Tell your child to feel, as vividly as possible, the rising and falling sensations as though she were actually on the swing set. Tell her to continue this activity as she falls asleep. Explain to your child that if she sees, hears or feels anything strange or frightening, that she's perfectly safe. Assure her that these experiences are very common, and that they're even a good sign of approaching success in Astral Projection.

It's also important to experiment with Astral Movements other than swinging. The goal should be to recreate movements of increasing complexity and vividness. Everyone has his or her own preferred Astral Movement that best triggers Astral Projection. Ask your child to experiment with as many Astral Movements as possible, until he finds the one that works best for him.

Lastly, deal with any fears your child might have in a calm and reassuring way. Astral Projection, especially the eerie phenomena that often accompanies sleep paralysis, can be rather frightening at times. Reassuring your child that he has nothing to fear, and arming him with the confidence necessary to confront those fears, is the best way to ensure successful Astral Projection. Otherwise the fear will bring progress to a screeching halt, often forever. As always, present Astral Projection to your little one as an exciting adventure.

Happy travels!

CHAPTER EIGHT

SEXUALITY, MAGICK AND CONSCIOUS SLEEP

(1)
Lucid Dreaming versus Enlightened Dreaming
*(The Sexual, Sensational and Spiritual Dimensions
of Conscious Sleep)*

Much has been written regarding the exhilarating adventures associated with Lucid Dreaming and Astral Projection. Whether it's beating up that annoying coworker you put up with every day, having a sexual liaison with your celebrity crush, or flying to the moon in your Astral Body:

The prospect of fulfilling one's most cherished fantasies is undoubtedly the most popular reason people learn the skill of Conscious Sleep.

But there's another side to this coin—a spiritual side—one motivated by a strong desire to transcend the merely hedonistic pursuits of the ego.

We encounter this flipside of being a Veiler in some of the practices of the early Christian Church (St. John the Divine). It was also the central focus of early Hebrew mysticism *(Merkabah)*. We see traces of it in Shamanic practices throughout the world (all of them); and it forms the foundation of many schools of Tibetan Buddhism *(Milam)*.

Generally speaking, there are two expressions of Enlightened Sleep: the *Visionary* and the *Contemplative*. We see examples of the latter in the Gnostic practice of *Via Negativa* and *The Cloud of Unknowing*. We see it in the *Clear Light* practice of Tibetan Dream Yoga. We see examples of the former in the *Seven Interior Castles* of St. Theresa of Avila. We see it also in the *Bardo Thodol* (Tibetan Book of the Dead) and in the *Soul-Retrieval* practices of many Shamanic traditions.

To be clear, I see nothing wrong with pursuing Conscious Sleep to "get off." It can be highly therapeutic! However, if pushed too far, this can actually get in the way of Conscious Sleep itself. But why? How?

In this section, I'm going to explain what I've verified through my own years of practicing Conscious Sleep. Of course, my own experience comes on the heels of innumerable fellow explorers. I stand on the shoulders of giants!

As someone who's practiced a variety of spiritual, physical and psychological disciplines consistently for many years, I feel I'm qualified to weigh in on this debate. For starters, I never adopt any discipline in a half-hearted way. When I decide to do something, I do it, and I do it to the best of my capabilities.

One such discipline I adopted is an ancient two-tiered Taoist/Buddhist practice called *Yi Jin Jing* and *Xi Sui Jing*. One of the fundamental rigors of this practice involves three months of regulating sexual behavior. I should point out that there's no moral reason for this enforced sexual abstinence. In fact, the sex drive is actively enhanced in this training. Rather, the purpose of this abstinence is in the interest of conserving nerve-force. This energy is then employed in the service of opening the Third Eye (conscious sleep). This newly opened Third Eye is then put to the task of total spiritual liberation.

One theory I have as to how and why this works centers on the obvious polar relationship shared by Eros (sex) and Psyche (cognition). This seems to apply especially to men. How and if the same rule applies to women, I can't say, but I see no reason to assume that women aren't built the same as men in this regard.

My theory is that, due to the suppression of dopamine usually triggered by sexual release, the "reward mechanism" typically reserved for orgasm (and thoughts leading to orgasm) are shunted away from Eros and sublimate upward toward Psyche. The results are increased capacity for concentration, invigorated willpower, increased personal magnetism, and more frequent spontaneous Vivid and Lucid Dreams, as well as Out of Body Experiences.

The One Hundred Days of Laying the Foundation[13]

Like most Taoist practices, the *Yi Jin Jing* and *Xi Sui Jing* observe a period of time in which the neophyte builds the new habits associated with the goals of longevity, increased willpower, physical strength, conscious sleep, and even immortality. Taoists refer to this period as *One Hundred Days of Laying the Foundation.* In one sense, this is a no-brainer. After all, it does take roughly ninety days to build a new habit.[14]

But there's more to it than that…

During this three-month learning-curve you're also building new neural connections in your brain, establishing an upgraded status of lifeforce economy (converting *Jing* to *Qi* to *Shen),* and then widening your Subtle Body circuitry to encourage a smoother and more vigorous *Qi* flow.

While this foundation is being laid, "getting laid" is out of the question. Well, to be more specific, "getting off" is out of the question.

You must avoid ejaculation at all cost…

Not only that, but sexual thoughts and fantasies must also be regulated, which is where meditation comes in:

---

[13] For a full curriculum of the Western Magickal Tradition, see *Modern Magick: Twelve Lessons in the High Magickal Arts,* by Donald Michael Kraig (Llewellyn Publications, 2010).

[14] See *Qigong: The Secret of Youth,* by Dr. Yang Jwing Ming (YMAA Publication Center, 2000).

Without a refined capacity to bear with equanimity the primal urges, recurrent thought-loops, and the nagging desire to indulge old bad habits, you'll never succeed in the One Hundred Days of Laying the (new) Foundation.

From the beginning of this practice, your *spirit* is called to task, and a war ensues between the drives of your ego and the strivings of your soul. I've come out of it fully convinced that you simply can't advance past a certain point unless this bridge has been crossed. Whether your goal is Lucid Dreaming, Astral Projection, Remote Viewing, or Conscious Dying, unless you get past the point of doing it just to have a good time, your adventures behind the Veil will eventually come to a screeching halt *or* you'll just get bored. At the very least, you'll be missing out on an entirely new dimension of Conscious Sleep.

My First Month of Laying the Foundation

So there I was. I had everything I needed to see this thing through to the end:

- A firm resolve.
- An understanding wife.
- Clear instructions.
- A conducive environment.
- A strong background in meditation.

The first few weeks were the most challenging. I had to continually remind myself to regulate my thoughts and emotions. Thankfully, this training was not new to me. Over the course of two decades, I'd gone on lengthy *Vipassana* retreats, Hermetic "retirements" and had already gained a measure of skill in carrying mindfulness into both the waking and sleeping worlds.

But this was a bit different…

To begin with, I found it very difficult to regulate my sex drive and the thoughts associated with it. To make matters worse, the practices of the *Yi Jin Jing* and *Xi Sui Jing* are designed to actually increase your sex drive! This is because of the *Qigong* discovery that sexual energy can be converted into surplus *Qi*. Think of the concept of Kundalini, practiced in the Yoga traditions of India and Tibet, and you'll have a good understanding of what's being aimed at here.

The first thing I noticed was an increase in physical and mental stamina. At both the workplace and the gym, I experienced a noticeable boost in workload capacity. Not only that, but I taught myself to read musical notation, began learning a second language, started writing a book, and generally turned up the dial on my overall quality of life. This energetic upgrade was without doubt due to the combination of celibacy, energy work, and mental/emotional regulation.

It is also worth noting that my depression lifted. I've suffered from bouts of depression my entire life. So much so that as a teenager, I did a two-month stint in an institution because of it. I'd be remiss if I didn't mention that I was highly promiscuous as a teenager, which may or may not have contributed to my low resilience threshold.

At any rate, my depression had vanished!

I also switched my diet from a generally unhealthy one to that of an organic, non-GMO diet (and, eventually, Vegan), as is recommended by the aforementioned Taoist/Buddhist classics.

There was a phase where I became irritable, though. It soon became clear to me that the buildup of psychosexual energy has to be continuously balanced by an increased capacity to circulate that energy. Thankfully, this little experiment includes exercises designed to do just that. Techniques like *Small Heavenly Circulation* (Microcosmic Orbit), *Grand Heavenly Circulation,* the neutralizing effect of *Thrusting Vessel* meditations, and mutual energy exchanges with the Natural world, all serve to maintain a healthy internal energetic balance.

My Second Month of Laying the Foundation

This is where things became more difficult. New challenges and setbacks presented themselves, and I often wanted to quit the whole project. For starters, I began having difficulty falling asleep at night. This was a problem because I have to wake up at 5:30 am for work every day.

The second issue was that my Lucid Dreams became *very* sexually explicit. I don't mean that they merely became more erotic, but more erotically *charged.* That is, I didn't necessarily have more sexual dreams, but the dreamworld itself had an orgiastic tone to it. The very fabric of the *Veil of Dreams* appeared to be a cosmic dance of erotic energy.

During this second week, I also enjoyed a veritable smorgasbord of strange sensations within and around my body. My lower Dantian—the energy center located two inches below the navel and two finger-widths inward toward the spine—would tremble and become suddenly hot. At times I'd be awakened in the middle of the night to what felt like insects crawling on my skin, or static electricity raising the hairs on my body. This sensation was particularly noticeable on the Third Eye area between my eyebrows.

Perhaps the most enjoyable change at this time was a newfound capacity to maintain deep-phase Lucid Dreaming (**LD-3**) for longer periods.

There was only one minor setback: *I began having wet dreams!*

Besides the fact that I hadn't had one of those since age sixteen, the loss of semen equals a loss of Etheric force *(Qi)*. Of course, I'd read about this theory before, but I wasn't sure whether there was any truth to the claim. But after almost two months of celibacy coupled with rigorous meditation, and with the loss of Etheric force due to the nocturnal emissions, I knew for sure that there's some truth behind it. The odd effect that these nocturnal ejaculations had on my *Qi* meridians (which I could now feel) were obvious and astounding. Although this didn't stop me from Lucid Dreaming, I did notice that it affected their duration, quality and overall clarity.

My Third Month of Laying the Foundation

By this time I'd firmly established a regular habit of practicing Microcosmic Orbit, Embryonic Breathing, Vegan diet, Sexual Abstinence, Mindfulness, and the myriad hormone stimulation exercises outlined in the *Yi Jin Jing* and *Xi Sui Jing*. I was able to gain some control over the nocturnal ejaculations as well, and my training was progressing.

About three weeks into this last month of Laying the Foundation, the breakthrough came! At first, I simply noticed an increase in spontaneous rather than manufactured Lucid and Pellucid Dreams, but then came the spontaneous Out of Body Experiences.

I'd be sleeping soundly in my bed when, all of sudden, I'd be awoken by powerful vibrations coursing through my body. I'd also hear my breathing as if it were coming from the other side of the room.

There was also the regular appearance of a blinding light which began as yellow for the first few nights, then progressed to blue and finally white. This light was like staring into the sun itself.

At one point, I was having a very pleasant Lucid Dream, when it was interrupted by a full-blown Astral Projection that ended with me suspended in a strange limbo filled with magnificent electric-blue grid patterns filling up the entire universe.

In the distance stood an enormous castle or a mansion, made of what looked like marble. An enormous staircase led up to a large brass door that opened before me. But as soon as I decided to approach it, I was thrown onto my back. Light rained down on me as if it were a hail storm, and I heard a man's voice say, "This is what men call *Ether*, and is to us as water is to you."

By this time I was utterly speechless. Nor could I move an inch. Just then, a large hand, translucent and shining with a pale blue light, pierced through the blinding light and reached down towards me. I, in turn, reached upward to meet its grip but felt an enormous gravity pulling my limbs downward. Even my very thoughts felt heavy.

Then the vision ended, and I was standing in the kitchen of my brother's house. He was folding a towel and I tried to alert him to my presence by putting my face very close to his, but he was totally unaware of me.

I then decided to go outside and fly around. I played at this for a while and then returned, very consciously, to my physical body.

The Final Confirmation

My experiment with the *Yi Jin Jing* and *Xi Sui Jing* described above was undertaken three years ago. Since then I've tested it again and again so as to eliminate any lingering doubts I had. What I noticed is that too much ejaculation definitely affects Conscious Sleep. I also noticed that being stressed out, overworked, excessively hedonistic, and unwilling to try new things all have deleterious effects on the more sublime aspects of Conscious Sleep.

One of the reasons for this, in my opinion, is that the overall strength of the adrenal glands plays a pivotal role in the functioning of these skills. This would explain why many oneironauts and Astral

Projectors have noted that excess caffeine and alcohol consumption negatively impacts these capabilities.

There may be a peculiar dynamic between the voluntary rerouting of the "pleasure principle" away from its usual hedonistic and sensory outlets and toward the pleasures of the soul rather than the physical body. As the old adage goes:

"The soul becomes like unto that which it loves most."

(2)

The Powers that Be: Conscious Sleep and the Magickal Arts

Many of the insights and practices that contributed to the creation of *SCT* are rooted in the *Western Magickal Tradition.* That said, it may now come as a surprise to you when I say that I hesitated to include the word "magick" in this book.

My ambivalence was due to the unfortunate stigma placed upon the magickal arts. Although the latter is, in essence, no different than any other spiritual path, the New Age movement has turned this ancient art into a parody of itself in modern times. Don't get me wrong: I believe that the original intentions of the New Age movement were noble ones. Still, what began as a hearty attempt to bridge ancient wisdom to modern science has failed miserably. In the first place, many advanced adepts depend for the virility of their Will upon a metaphysics so divorced from modern science that any successful result of their skill is immediately dismissed as hogwash. Sure, we can point to recent attempts at reconciliation—to books like *The Secret,* or documentaries like *What The Bleep Do We Know Anyway?* But neither of these works are taken seriously by the greater scientific community.

In my opinion, it's a shame that otherwise significant systems aren't taken seriously merely because they're speaking a language deemed anathema by modern science. But that shouldn't stop us from unpacking this ancient art to see if we might tease the truth from the trickery.

Do What Thou Wilt!

What, if anything, is at the root of the art and science called Magick? Is it just a vestigial hangover from the preconventional stages of human evolution? Or is there something more to it? Perhaps, once you divest it from its cultural baggage, taboos and superstitions, the ancient art of Magick might work via mechanisms that will one day be explainable in purely scientific terms.

Or perhaps not.

In either case, it can't be disputed that the complex ceremonies, symbols and practices associated with the magickal arts continue to be a source of profound spiritual meaning for many people today. Far from being a merely *translative* discipline, Magick takes as its primary objective a *transformative* approach to life. In other words, Magick doesn't ask its adherents to passively imbibe a set of beliefs. On the contrary! Magick is predicated upon the discovery of natural laws, and a bending of those laws to the Will. In fact, the infamous occultist, Aleister Crowley, defined Magick as *"The art and science of causing change to occur in conformity with Will."* (This same Crowley is credited with the novel spelling of the word "magick" with a "k" to distinguish it from the charlatanry of the illusionist.)

What is this "Will" that Crowley speaks of?

First, it must be understood that Will isn't a synonym for Desire. Desires, it can be said, are the enemy of the Will. Well, at least when it comes to Magick, desires are the enemy. Why? Because desires are fleeting, whereas the Will is enduring. In fact, the very hallmark of the Will is that it *endures*. Allow me to explain.

Have you ever known anyone with an ironclad will? Such persons may start out with a goal in mind, one that may seem far-fetched. The entire world may scoff at this person, accusing him of being quixotic and unrealistic, but he pays these naysayers no mind. Eventually, by degrees, this intrepid soul ascends the steps leading to the realization of his goal. At some point in his journey, the obstacles still arise, but something begins to change. Slowly, but consistently, the universe seems to clear a path for him. Not only that, but the exact types of people, carrying the exact type of assistance needed, seem to appear from out of the blue to help him. Finally, a threshold is crossed in which his goal seems to fall into place by its own weight, as it were. His progress takes on a life of its own, and his goal is finally realized as if by...*magick!*

Certainly, there's nothing supernatural about the success of our hypothetical over-achiever. After all, if you faithfully pursue a goal, success is inevitable, right? Wrong!

One of the core tenets of the Magickal philosophy is that of the *True Will* which may be defined as the underlying key to the evolution of one's genius. This formula applies to individuals and cultures alike. For example, it was the True Will of ancient Rome to conquer empires and absorb them into their own body-politic. To this end they worshipped gods and goddesses, adorned themselves with garments and symbols, all of which consistently reiterated this Will. In the same way, the early Christians adopted an opposite but equally driven morality, and to this end worshipped a God, adorned themselves with symbols, and took up practices that reiterated this Will. The end result? Christianity overtook the same Roman empire that crucified Christ himself!

This is the essence of True Will. This is the essence of Magick.

But how does one discover and cultivate this True Will? Moreover, can the True Will apply to any goal of one's choosing? Or is it a matter of uncovering one specific talent in oneself and developing it at the exclusion of all others?

To answer these questions in their respective order, how one comes across his or her True Will is a very personal affair. For me, it revealed itself after all else was stripped away. Lesser wills and desires either came to serve my True Will, or else they fell by the wayside and were abandoned. Also, I noticed that this Will was often transferrable. That is to say, once I learned how to align my behavior with the goals that were arising in me, I found that I could sometimes apply my Will to areas of endeavor that normally seemed quite *other* to me. Be that as it may, I'd always find in retrospect that these extraneous pursuits only seemed *other* to me on the surface. A little analysis always revealed the subtle thread that bound the projects to me. Having said that, it's worth mentioning that even when your Will is transferrable, there always remains a core Will that drives you relentlessly onward and upward. Like a tree growing toward sunlight, your every thought, deed and dream steers faithfully toward that guiding star, the beacon of your *True Will*.

One way to uncover your True Will and to put it to work is to become conscious on all levels of your being. In my opinion, to be able to evoke the potent forces of the Unconscious and meet them half-way is the very *raison d'être* of the Western Magickal Tradition. And what better way to accomplish this than to become conscious throughout the Waking, Dreaming and Dreamless sleep states?

Think about it: What is the purpose behind the intense visualizations, altered states of consciousness, Astral voyages, and psychotropic plants used in most Magickal ceremonies? If not to induce a specific aspect of Conscious Sleep, what possible reason would there be for these prescriptions? I posit that these practices were created to produce, in the individual (ritual) or group (ceremony), a deliberately *willed* Lucid Dream or Astral experience.

In my many years of Magickal practice I've confirmed this theory for myself. To this day I perform specific banishing and invoking rituals in my Lucid Dreams to great effect. These effects, it must be pointed out, often spill over into my daily life without any conscious effort on my part in the wake-a-day world. What further proof do you need? What better word for it than "magick"?

Try This!

One of the most common symptoms of stepping behind the Veil is the appearance of bright lights behind the eyes. For some people, these appear as bright camera flashes. For others, it seems as if they're staring directly into the sun. Most common is the appearance of a white, golden or blue light behind the closed eyes. Accounts of these interior illuminations fill the religious and mystical tomes of the world. For me, I've noticed a parallel between the color and intensity of the lights, and my state of health. When overtired, sick or depressed, I notice that these lights tends to be murky, dim and of orange or brownish hue. When I'm healthy and happy, though, the lights tend to be bright white, yellow or lilac.

At any rate, here's a little trick you can use to invoke your Higher Self when you see these interior lights:

First, choose a divinity that possesses characteristics you'd like to invoke. For example, I might choose the archangel Gabriel if I want to be inspired as a musician. Or, you may wish for your subconscious or superconscious mind to pick the divinity for you. In this case, I recommend laying out a series of pictures or names of divinities in a circle or line. Next, use a pendulum to decide which divinity to invoke. (For instructions on how to use a pendulum, visit my website or simply look it up online.)

Next, as you're meditating or falling asleep, perform the Brow Center activation exercise from *Chapter Six*. Or, you can simply wait for a night when these inner lights appear. In either case, once the light appears, begin mentally intoning the name of your chosen divinity. My favorite method of chanting during these times is to use the inner tones and ringing in my ears. I simply *bend* the tones to form the name of my chosen divinity, and that usually suffices.

If nothing happens right away, don't write it off as a failure! Instead, take note of the dreams you had that night and write them down in your Dream Journal. Also, pay attention to any synchronicities that occur throughout the next day. There may be messages waiting for you in unexpected places. The more you practice this technique, the more successful you'll be.

Oh! By the way, congratulations! You just performed the magickal operation known as *Invocation*.

CHAPTER NINE

THE THREE-BODY FITNESS PROGRAM

Introduction
Integral Methods for the Attainment
of the Continuity of Consciousness

I originally created the *Three-Body Fitness Program* (TBFP) to be an expansion of the *120-Days Curriculum* presented in *Behind the Veil*. On the other hand, I've also structured it to be a unique curriculum in its own right. As you'll soon discover, this course includes some of the more advanced exercises of the *120-Days Curriculum,* and adds new techniques that build upon those skills.

The following techniques have been taken from a variety of sources. This program is an *Integral* one, which means it takes the methods, minds and theories that have stood the test of time and lays them out like a multi-tiered tapestry. Because there are as many methods as there are types of practitioners, my work has been to create a system comprised of methods which yield the most benefits for the greatest number of personality types. To this end I've drawn on the teachings of other Veilers, both ancient and contemporary, and then woven them into the tapestry I lay before you now. The following list shows just a few of the more prominent sources I've drawn from:

• Classics like the *Vigyan Bhairav Tantra,* the practicing of which has provided years of endless delight and illumination for me and countless other souls throughout the centuries.

• The Taoist/Buddhist Classics, *Yi Jin Jing* and *Xi Sui Jing,* which continue to challenge both my will and my body. From these I've gathered the pollen that gradually became the honey I offer in the *TBFP.* In particular I owe my unearthing of the influence of sexual economy on Conscious Sleep to my long practice of these Classics.

• The timeless and elegant cartography of the Vedantic school of Yoga. From this rich garden of spiritual gymnastics I picked the fruit that became the very structure of *SCT* and *TBFP.*

• To my two decades of involvement in the Western Esoteric Tradition of *Hermetics,* I owe a debt of gratitude. Particularly my ongoing exploration of that gray area where Dream and Astral meet and overlap.

Before diving into the Program, I'd like to offer a helpful tip: The key to accessing the Gross, Subtle and Causal bodies in a full-sensory and "embodied" fashion is to gradually reduce the movements of the physical body to the point of micro-movement.

In disciplines like *Tai Chi Chuan,* for example, the goal of practicing the long form sequence is to make each physical movement smooth and seamless. The next step is to slow those movements down to the point where you can no longer tell which moves, the energy of intended movement or actual physical motion. At this point, *Physical* movement shades into *Etheric* movement, which is experienced as the motion of Etheric energy in and around the physical body. Once this has been accomplished, you can take it a step further *and become the Etheric movement.* At this point, Etheric movement has now become Astral motion. This typically begins with what's been called *Etheric Projection,* which can best be described as the ability to move one's self-awareness within the body and slightly beyond it. Eventually, with practice, this evolves into Astral Projection. This is the secret relationship between subtle arts like *Tai Chi Chuan, Qigong* and the various forms of Yoga. Success in this regard is 100% dependent upon your conscious sensitivity to the liminal transitions between Awake and Asleep. To this end I've created the *Three-Body Fitness Program.*

Before bringing this Introduction to a close, I'd like to point out that it's not enough merely to learn how to acquire the skills associated with Conscious Sleep. You must also learn how to do so in a balanced and healthy manner.

Remember at all times that Lucid Dreaming and Astral Projection require energy. They are, as it were, the *Yang* aspects of Conscious Sleep, just as Pellucidity and non-Lucid Dreaming are the *Yin* aspects. Attaining and sustaining this *Yin/Yang* balance is very important to your development as a Veiler, and you should make it a top priority.

This balancing of Etheric force must also extend to the activities of Lucid Dreaming and Astral Projection themselves, as too much of a given emotion or Astral movement can harm its corresponding internal organ within the Gross Body. What follows is a list of each general Astral movement along with their corresponding internal organ and primordial Element:

- Spinning = Stomach/Spleen/Earth
- Rising, Falling, Flying = Heart/Fire
- Expanding and Shrinking = Lungs/Metal or Air
- Forward and Backwards = Liver/Wood
- Rolling and Somersaulting = Kidneys/Water

A powerful practice involves balancing each Astral movement with its Elemental opposite. You might, for example, practice Astral spinning to counterbalance Astral expanding or shrinking. Because full-bodied Lucid Dreaming has the same effect on your internal organs and *Qi* as Astral motion, this Elemental balancing also applies during Lucid Dreaming, especially *Wake Induced Lucid Dreaming (WILD).*

(1)
Malleable Proprioception

It often comes as a shock to some of my readers when I discuss the neurological underpinnings of OOBE. This is due to the popular notion that OOBE is strictly a psychic or spiritual phenomenon and has nothing to do with biology. As understandable as this metaphysical belief may be, it's still just that: a *belief.* Although I do respect this belief, I still regard it as presumptuous. For even if it proves to be true, it doesn't negate the fact that there's a neurological correlate to OOBE.

The problem lies in the tendency among New Agers to see any insertion of biology into the "supernatural" as material reductionism. To be fair, this antipathy toward the hard sciences isn't, in this instance, entirely unfounded. After all, the Newtonian/Cartesian view of the cosmos has been reducing everyone and everything to machines and matter since the separation of Church and State. Be that as it may, this reductionistic worldview has done much good for humanity. One such boon of the Enlightenment era has been the discovery of the human nervous system and its many mysteries. I'm not going to go into detail about the nervous system here. I simply wish to highlight the symbiotic relationship of the Subtle Body and Gross Body and, most importantly, that clandestine bridge between them called the *Nervous System.* For you see, between the Gross and Subtle bodies there extends a vast network of telephone wire, as it were, and the primary language used during these phone calls is *feeling.* Whether it's the sensation of heat, cold, lightness, heaviness, dizziness, tingling, flying, falling, flipping, flailing or any other "F" word, *your nervous system records all of it.* It communicates these things so efficiently that most of it goes completely undetected by the conscious mind. But the thing to remember is this:

If the nervous system can record these sensations, then it can also recreate them.

By recreating these sensations you can then unlock the secret powers of the Gross, Subtle and even Causal bodies. You can then use these neurologically recorded sensations as primers for OOBE and other forms of Conscious Sleep.

In this section, I'm going to introduce you to three common activities you can use to train your nervous system to act as *biofeedback* for inducing OOBE. All you require for these exercises is the willingness to try the techniques and apply them at the optimal time for the desired effect, in this case OOBE.

Method One: The Swing-Set

Have you heard of *The Tetris Effect*? It's a neurological reflection of a stimulus to which the bodymind has been exposed for a prolonged period of time. For example, have you ever driven a long distance on the highway, only to fall asleep later that night to find you can still see the road behind your closed eyes?

Well, that's the *Tetris Effect.*

Or perhaps you've been out dancing all night at a club only to hear the thump of the bass as you're falling asleep later that evening.

That, too, is the *Tetris Effect.*

Or have you ever been on an elevator and, when you step out of it, feel as though you're still rising or falling?

You get the point…

The Tetris Effect, besides being a strange anomaly of the nervous system, holds a secret key to inducing OOBE, and I'm presently going to share this secret with you.

During your quest for handy instructions on how to induce an OOBE, you'll sooner or later come across the exhortation to bring yourself to the point of light sleep and then "imagine" that you're swimming or flying or rolling like a large beach ball. These are all viable ways to have an OOBE. The problem is that most people can't truly conjure up these sensations to a sufficient degree. So I've devised biofeedback methods to satisfy this lack. I call it *Malleable Proprioception Training* (MPT). I like this term because it sounds more scientific than metaphysical (no disrespect to metaphysicians).

This first trick demands nothing more than a swing-set. So all you parents and babysitters with a penchant for OOBE, this one's for you.

I accidentally stumbled upon this trick while at the park with my five-year old daughter. After pushing her for nearly half an hour, my little one asked me if I'd like a push on the swing too. Wanting to build my daughter's confidence and muscular strength, I agreed. I just wanted to feel like a kid again for a few minutes!

Later that evening as I lay in bed drifting off to sleep, I suddenly felt myself swinging as if I were still at the park. This induced a full-fledged OOBE! Inspired by this, I decided to take it to the next level and recreate the sensation of being on a rollercoaster. Not just any rollercoaster, but the Black Widow rollercoaster of Riverside Park, which I used to occasionally visit as a teenager. This particular rollercoaster featured a loop that momentarily puts you into an upside-down position before whipping you back down into a forward spiral. So, as I lay in bed the following night, I conjured up the lifelike sensations of being on the Black Widow. Sure enough, this also induced an OOBE.

So, if you can't find a swing-set, find an amusement park! The trick is to take note of the sensations and recreate them as you're falling asleep *and* immediately after you wake up. I say "immediately" because you want to catch the tail end of a REM cycle and follow it into sleep paralysis while practicing this technique.

I noticed that the visceral sensations created by the downward arc while swinging proves to be a powerful trigger for OOBE. This is the same sensation you get during the free-fall of a rollercoaster ride, though to a lesser degree. You might look for other activities that produce this butterflies-in-the-stomach feeling, and reproduce it at bedtime and while waking up. Remember that this exercise affects stomach and liver *Qi,* so be sure to practice Embryonic Breathing for a few minutes after practicing it.

Method Two: The Swimming Pool

This technique involves conjuring up the sensations associated with swimming. If you've never been in a Floatation Tank, I highly recommend you try it. The feeling of being suspended, weightless in space, is a powerful primer for OOBE. Scuba-diving is another excellent way to experience weightlessness. But if you can't access a Sensory Deprivation Tank or scuba-diving gear, then a swimming pool is the next best thing. And if you don't have access to a swimming pool, then find a lake or pond. Of course, you must be able to swim!

The instructions are straightforward: first, focus on the feeling of weightlessness. Close your eyes and float on your back. Take note of any rocking sensations you feel and try to mentally increase them.

Then, get out of the water, lie on the ground or in a lawn chair, and then try to reproduce the rocking sensation using only your mind.

Next, get back into the water and practice somersaulting forward and backwards under the water. Be very mindful of these sensations, especially the sensation of being upside down. Then, once again, get out of the water, lie down, and try to mentally recreate the sensations associated with somersaulting under water.

Finally, go back into the water and do a slow breaststroke, taking note of every sensation. Then, again, remove yourself from the water, lie down and recreate it. Later that night, as you're falling asleep, follow this same procedure. Start with the feeling of weightlessness and rocking, followed by somersaults, and ending with the breast-stroke. Then cycle through them again until one "clicks." You may experience an OOBE your first try! Sometimes it takes a bit of prac-tice, until your nervous system understands what you're trying to do. Lastly, because these exercises affect kidney, stomach and lung *Qi,* be sure to practice Embryonic Breathing and Microcosmic Orbit for a few minutes after this exercise.

Method Three: The Trailing Method

This technique is also included in the *120-Days Curriculum.* I call it *The Trailing Method.* The purpose of this exercise is to train your consciousness to move without having to use your physical body. The ability to play with your proprioception while remaining physically motionless is the basic skill required for successful OOBE. For exam-ple, can you convince your nervous system that your body is upside down, with your feet to the sky and your head toward the ground? Can you conjure up the feeling of spinning in a circle without moving your body? If so, then you've acquired the fundamental skill of "malleable proprioception."

The Trailing Method is designed to teach your nervous system that your consciousness can spin on its axis without having to actually move the physical body.

Here's how it works: The practice can be divided into two main parts. All you'll need is a dark and quiet room, a candle, and freedom from interruptions. The first part is as follows:

STEP ONE: Go into a dark room and light the candle. Hold it at eye level and roughly one foot away from your face.

STEP TWO: Stare into the candle flame without blinking for a slow count of thirty. In yoga, this is called *Trataka*.

STEP THREE: Keep your eyes open, blow out the candle and remain standing. Continue to stare into the dark space about one foot in front of you. Soon, an afterimage of the candle flame will appear before you.

STEP FOUR: Without blinking, observe the behavior of the afterimage. Eventually the image will begin to move downward and slightly to the left or right of your vision. Follow it! Not just with your eyes, but also with your body. If it moves to the right, then move to the right. If it moves to the left, move to the left.

The first time I practiced this technique, I was astonished to find the afterimage morphing into all kinds of mythological creatures. At one point, it transformed into a unicorn and rested in the palm of my right hand!

You may continue with this practice for as long as you wish. When you're finished, proceed with the second part of the practice. It goes as follows:

STEP ONE: Keep the light off and remaining standing. Take a few slow deep breaths and feel yourself balanced and rooted to the floor. Be sure that nothing in your space could cause injury should you fall and take note of where your bed is. It's a good idea to practice this section next to your mattress.

STEP TWO: Next, begin spinning in the direction opposite to that of your dominant hand. That is, if you're left-handed, spin to your right (i.e., clockwise); if you're right-handed, spin to your left. Start off by spinning slowly and gradually pick up speed until you feel yourself getting dizzy.

STEP THREE: Once the dizziness kicks in, stop spinning and sit down quickly on your mattress or a nearby chair. Close your eyes and relax. Remain completely motionless! Now, feel your awareness spinning, all the while trying to conjure of the feeling of physically moving in the direction of the spin.

CAUTION: This exercise disturbs stomach *Qi!* Some sensitive individuals may get nauseous while practicing this technique. To avoid this problem, it's a good rule of thumb to avoid eating anything for an hour or so before practicing *The Trailing Method.*

I'd like to close this section by pointing out that OOBE is largely the domain of three Chakras, namely the Solar Plexus (Manipura), the Heart (Anahata), and the Head (Ajna and Sahasrara). As long as you can engage sensations of motion in these areas, especially during the onset of Sleep Paralysis, you've discovered the trick of OOBE.

Method Four: The Balloon Method

The Balloon Method is one of the most ancient methods of inducing OOBE. It also happens to be one of the most difficult. The difficulty stems from the fact that many people have little or no experience of the sensations required to effectively employ it. Sensations, such as those experienced while rising in the air, or of expanding outward or shrinking inward aren't exactly common.

Be that as it may, there are a few things you can do to train your nervous system to reproduce these sensations at will. Of course, if you're not afraid to go skydiving, parachuting, floating in a hot-air balloon, or taking a rocket to outer space, you should be able to reproduce these feelings easily! But if you're like most people, your experience of these activities is probably nil.

So how does one reproduce these sensations?

Before I answer this question, I'd like to point out that the following exercises stimulate Heart *Qi*. Be sure to practice while in a relaxed state of mind and in an area where you'll remain undisturbed for the duration of the practice. Any sudden shock can adversely affect the functioning of your heart. That said, the exercise is as follows:

STEP ONE: Stand erect with your arms akimbo and your knees slightly bent *(Zhan Zhuang)*. Breathe naturally and through your nose. Your eyes should be half closed, and your gaze should gently rest upon the tip of your nose. You'll know your gaze is correct when the tip of your nose vanishes from sight. This is known as the "basilisk gaze" and is a means of activating your brow chakra.

STEP TWO: Relax your body from head to toe so your posture is braced but not tense, relaxed but not limp. Relax your facial muscles, your shoulders, and your lower back (so the curvature of your lower back is flat).

STEP THREE: Next, conjure the feeling that your head is a helium balloon. Your head should feel light, as though it were floating on a string attached to your spine. Feel it wobbling and rocking gently as if swayed by a gentle breeze. You can assist these sensation by performing these motions as micro-movements. For example, by gently extending your neck upward, you can simulate the sensation of rising. Add to this a gentle rocking from side to side, front to back, and the rising will feel more like floating.

STEP FOUR: With each natural exhalation of breath, cultivate a feeling that your entire body is elongating. Then, as you inhale, feel as though your body is shrinking back to normal size. The way that works best for me is to feel my torso, head, arms and legs elongating all at once. I'll help this feeling along by gently extending my extremities as I exhale. It's very important to perform these micro-movements *smoothly*. Any jerky movements and the practice will be in vain. Picture your body as a human-shaped balloon that elongates as you exhale and shrinks when you inhale. Lastly, gently push your perineum down when you exhale, and squeeze it gently when you inhale. As I pointed out in the section on Embryonic Breathing, this area *(Huiyin)* controls the *Qi* status of the Etheric Body, namely that of Yin (tightening) and Yang (pushing down).

STEP FIVE: Finally, upon exhalation, feel your entire body rise into the air. This tends to be the most difficult step for most people, so here's a tip to make it easier for you. Instead of rising in a straight line, rise as though you're being pulled and pushed by a wayward breeze and imagine—*feel*—that you're rising in a spiral or a staggered manner, at once rising and *drifting* in different directions. I find that this makes the sensation of rising into the air much more accessible.

(2)

The Causal Body: Stabilizer Muscles of Conscious Sleep

The Causal state of consciousness and its corresponding *Embodiment Zone*, the *Causal Body,* function as a sort of fertile womb for the gestation of new skills. I can't prove this, but I believe it to be the crossroads where experience, intention and understanding meet. That is to say, the Causal Body is where new information is logged by the nervous system and stored for future use. When, for example, you're truly paying attention to a lecture, a book, or a new hands-on activity, your mind is totally silent. This is the ideal state to be in if you really want to learn something new. Soon, and with repeated practice, new knowledge eventually becomes "second-nature" and begins to function naturally…*causally.*

Causal Body practices are effective in inducing spontaneous Lucid Dreams and OOBE, and I believe this may be due to this womb-like characteristic of the Causal state. The "right-mindfulness" taught by the Buddha, and the "self-remembering" practiced by the Sufi, are for this reason among the most powerful methods of training Conscious Sleep. It's worth emphasizing that the Causal state can be experienced in all three Bodies (Gross, Subtle, Causal). It is, after all, the root of egoic consciousness itself. However, the phenomenology of the Causal state will differ depending upon which of the three Bodies you're occupying in a given moment. If, for instance, you're in the Gross Body (awake), you'll experience the Causal state as the simple feeling of being—of "I Am-ness." While in the Subtle Body (dreaming), the Causal state will be experienced as Pellucid Dreaming or perhaps the "exit-symptoms" of an impending OOBE. Lastly, while in the Causal Body (dreamless sleep), the Causal state might be experienced as pure formless bliss or full-blown Astral Projection.

So how do you begin training the Causal state specifically for Lucid Dreaming and Astral Projection?

Though Lucid Dreaming and Astral Projection may not be the same thing, they definitely follow similar neuropathways in the physical body and share a similar phenomenology. We might say that they travel the same highway but toward different destinations.

The similarities between Astral Projection and Lucid Dreaming being what they are, we shouldn't be surprised that the methods of training them are also similar in many respects. Both skills require that consciousness be capable of mobility without the necessity of physical motion. Also, both demand a heightened sensitivity to the emotions as well as the five senses, which must be particularly vivid for full effect. In fact, a heightened sense of awareness is absolutely indispensable to the stability of Lucid Dreaming and Astral Projection. Without it, Conscious Sleep wouldn't be very *conscious* at all! This heightened awareness must begin with the Causal Body.

The Causal Body are the "stabilizer muscles" of consciousness. This means that all experience and learning consolidate in the Causal Body—not necessarily in the Causal *state,* but in the Causal *Body.* That is to say, you don't have to be in deep Dreamless Sleep or one of the formless "Jhanas" of Yoga to access the Causal state. On the other hand, you do have to be fully embodied in the Causal Body to, say, Astral Project or experience Pellucid Dreaming. This rule doesn't apply to Lucid Dreaming, which requires Subtle Body engagement, though a degree of heightened Causal awareness is necessary for profound and stable Lucidity.

As with all exercises in *The Three Body Fitness Program,* the following techniques are designed to strengthen the Gross, Subtle and Causal bodies. The way this works is that you must cycle through all three Bodies, engaging each in a unique and specific way. As with most of the exercises in this Program, the following methods begin with the Gross Body, then include the Subtle Body, and conclude by planting the skills honed by the exercises in the Causal Body. The new skills are then wired to and grounded in the nervous system of the Gross Body, which makes them available for future use. That's *SCT* in a nutshell!

Exercise One: Stationary Recreation of Environment.

The following exercise accomplishes two things. First, it serves as a gauge for how developed your Vivid Dreaming muscles are. Second, it trains those muscles.

STEP ONE: First silence your body and mind. Be sure that you'll remain undisturbed for at least fifteen to twenty minutes. Your environment should be quiet, peaceful, with a decor that's not "loud" or intricate—at least not at first. Use earplugs to block out any sounds in your environment.

STEP TWO: Sit down comfortably and take a few minutes to relax your mind and body. Breathe slowly and evenly and feel into your physical body with an inner smile. Then take a panoramic view of the room you're in. Notice every little detail of the room. Simply look around and take it all in. Also, take note of any sounds, smells and physical sensations you experience.

STEP THREE: Close your eyes. Now, recreate in your mind's eye an exact replica of the room you're in. Include all of your senses in the mental recreation if you can!

STEP FOUR: Try to sustain a relaxed but unwavering concentration on this mental simulation of the room you're in. Once you're able to sustain concentration for at least five minutes, you've succeeded in this exercise.

STEP FIVE: Lastly, relax your concentration and rest in the simple feeling of pure being. Enjoy the feeling of *I Am-ness* and rest in the Causal state. This step is very important, for it plants the seed of your practice in the rich soil of your subconscious mind.

Practice for at least one week before proceeding to the next exercise. If, however, you find this exercise too easy, you may proceed to the following technique.

Exercise Two: Mobile Recreation of Environment

STEP ONE: Repeat steps 1–2 of Exercise One.

STEP TWO: Stare straight ahead and, without blinking, slowly raise both of your hands to eye level and slowly rub them together at an even pace. Rub them together twenty times and then bring them to rest on your lap. Repeat this process two times.

STEP THREE: Close your eyes and repeat step two *in your imagination.* Do *not* actually move your physical body. Remain as motionless as possible. Try to recreate every sensation exactly as you experienced them when you physically performed the motions. Do *not* merely visualize the movements. Repeat this process two times.

STEP FOUR: Open your eyes and once again take in the details of the room you're in, only don't move your eyes or head. Rather, stare straight ahead without blinking and use your peripheral vision.

STEP FIVE: Slowly stand up and pay attention to every sensation you feel while doing so. Then, slowly sit back down. Repeat this two times.

STEP SIX: Close your eyes and repeat step five, only this time do so in your imagination. Be sure to include every little sensation exactly as you felt them when physically performing the motions. Repeat two times.

STEP SEVEN: Repeat step four.

STEP EIGHT: As in step five, slowly stand up and pay attention to every sensation you feel while doing so. This time, however, don't sit back down right away. Instead, slowly walk your physical body toward an object in the room, touch it, and then slowly walk back to your seat and sit down. Be aware of every little nuance of sensation as you move.

STEP NINE: Repeat step four using only your imagination. That is, try to see the room in vivid detail behind your closed eyes.

STEP TEN: Now recreate step eight, but do so using only your full-sensory imagination. Really feel as though you're physically moving as you recreate the motions. The more you can bring your five senses and heightened awareness to the imagining, the more results you'll see. Finish the exercise by resting in pure Causal mindfulness for at least five to ten minutes.

In closing, don't underestimate the effectiveness of these techniques. Performed rightly and consistently, they train the very muscles needed to become a true Veiler.

(3)
On *This* Side of My Skin:
The Ultimate Method of Conscious Sleep

This is the most powerful method I've ever encountered for waking up from both our nighttime and daytime slumber. Like all of the techniques in the ancient Tantric Classic, the *Vigyan Bhairav Tantra,* this method has no proper name. You see, the techniques offered in this document are formulated as answers to questions. The two players in this divine dialogue are none other than *Shiva* and his consort, *Devi,* of Hinduism. *Devi,* wanting to find and unite with *Shiva,* asks questions of the god in order to receive instruction on how best to discover his whereabouts. Of course, *Shiva* is symbolic of ultimate Enlightenment. *Devi,* also an Enlightened being, is asking *Shiva* these questions on behalf of humanity. *Devi* asks,

> *"O Shiva, what is your reality?*
> *"What is this wonder-filled universe?*
> *"What constitutes seed?*
> *"Who centers the universal wheel?*

"What is this life beyond form pervading forms?

"How may we enter it consciously, above space and time, names and descriptions?

"Let my doubts be cleared!"

Shiva then answers the goddess with techniques like:

"With intangible breath in center of forehead, as this reaches the heart at the moment of sleep, have direction over dreams and over death itself."

Or this one:

"Gracious one, pretend the universe is an empty vessel wherein your mind frolics infinitely."

Or this perfect summary of *SCT* practice:

"Waking, sleeping, dreaming, know yourself as Light."

Or this gem of Pellucidity practice:

"At the point of sleep when sleep has not yet come and external wakefulness vanishes, at this moment Being is revealed."

Regarding the particular method I'm sharing with you here, *Shiva* replies:

"See all space as if already absorbed in your own head."

And again:

"In truth forms are inseparate. Inseparate are omnipresent being and your own form. Realize each as made of Consciousness."

Those last two techniques utilize the same principle in practice. I call this the *Ultimate Method of Conscious Sleep* because it literally transcends the apparent divisions among the Gross, Subtle and Causal bodies and, most importantly, between these "bodies" and their respective environments (Veils).

It's quite difficult to describe in words what the proper execution of this method feels like as it transcends, but includes, all five of the physical senses. I say it "transcends" them in that it's a sensation experienced in and as consciousness, and not merely the Gross, Subtle or Causal senses (though those can and should be included). A good way to understand how this works is to imagine your consciousness as an empty vessel. Whenever something "comes into" your awareness, your consciousness takes that something's shape in the same way that water takes the shape of the empty vessel it's poured into. In terms of consciousness, this amounts to a Nondual experience in which subject *in here* isn't separate from the objects *out there.*

How It's Done

Although the following technique uses the Causal Body as a vehicle, the result is Nondual. The primary distinction between Causal and Nondual experience is that the former tends to be negative whereas the latter is inclusive. Put another way, the Causal realm is less immanent and more transcendental, whereas the Nondual experience is transcendental and immanent at the same time, hence the term "Nondual". Yet another form of the Nondual experience occurs when you can fully and consciously occupy your Gross, Subtle and Causal bodies as one seamless Body.

What makes the following method so powerful for training Conscious Sleep is this: When you experience the world *out there* as a world *in here,* you begin to see it as a dream. If practiced long enough, this new way of looking at the world begins to seep its way into your subconscious mind and operate there as Conscious Sleep. In Taoism, this is called *Tian Ren,* the union of Heaven and Human. In Yoga and Buddhism this state is called *Savikalpa Samadhi.*

So here's what to do.

STEP ONE: Find a place out in nature where you can be alone and undisturbed for at least half an hour. Choose a day with agreeable weather conditions and bring music if you'd like to add an emotional/inspirational dimension to the practice. Choose music without lyrics as these tend to distract attention. Choose instead some classical music. Personally, I love piano and violin.

STEP TWO: Choose a natural landscape to focus on. For now, keep the panorama as vast as possible. Don't narrow your attention down to one object. This is *not* a concentration exercise in that sense. You do *not* want to use "spotlight" attention, but rather, "floodlight" attention for this exercise. Personally, my favorite is to use the sky of a partly cloudy afternoon as my preferred scenery.

STEP THREE: Assuming you've chosen the sky as your object, lie down and relax for a few minutes, and simply quiet your mind. Don't force this. Otherwise you'll end up damming the energy and provoking spotlight instead of floodlight attention.

STEP FOUR: Without blinking, take in a full view of the sky. Include both your frontal *and* peripheral vision. This will have the effect of stopping the movement of your eyes, for the most part.

STEP FIVE: Next, try to feel the drifting clouds as if your consciousness were assuming their shape (i.e., the water/empty vessel analogy). When the clouds move, so does your consciousness. Try to feel the point of contact between the clouds and your sense of sight. Try to imagine what they must smell like. Then, finally, *become those clouds*.

NOTE: The same technique can be practiced with trees. I went through a phase where I became obsessed with experiencing trees in this regard. The point is to first orient yourself to the Nondual feeling. Then, expand on this by carrying this perspective everywhere you go. For me, it took about a week of consistent practice to begin noticing the effects.

First, all anxiety disappeared. (For me that was a pretty big deal as I've suffered from debilitating anxiety my whole life.) But here I was feeling a profound peace and silent joy. My theory is that this was due to the fact that anxiety is, by and large, a pushing away of the environment. It's an attempt to keep the Other on the far side of the self/other boundary. So, when you feel as though everything and everyone *is* your very consciousness, anxiety has no room left in which to thrive.

The second thing I noticed was that my Lucid Dreams became more frequent and intense. My *subconscious* seemed to take a back seat to the far more potent *unconscious,* and archetypes began asserting themselves with more urgency and clarity of meaning. I also noted that my sleep was more peaceful, and my creative inspiration soared to unprecedented heights of potency.

So what are you waiting for? Go ahead and give it a shot! Soon enough you'll see why I call it the *Ultimate Method of Conscious Sleep.*

(4)
Creating Your Biochemistry: Dream Control in Waking Life

Mind Over Matter

Have you ever had a dream of ingesting a psychotropic substance only to awaken with the actual cognitive and physical symptoms of being under the influence?

I have…

In fact, this phenomenon is common among Lucid Dreamers. So common is this ability, in fact, that Oneironauts of all times and places have made a spiritual sacrament out of it—e.g., Shamanism!

This ability to create genuine biological changes in the body using one's Will is also the key to many of the *Siddhas* (supernormal powers) of the Indian and Tibetan Yogi. A proper scientific study of the biochemical changes caused by these powers of the human bodymind is still forthcoming, but there have already been some great strides made in this regard.

On a personal level, I've stopped asthma attacks, warmed my body in the cold, created opiate and serotonin highs, and even stopped withdrawal symptoms in their tracks, all by using the methods I'm going to share with you. Also, as someone who has struggled with severe bouts of depression and anxiety, these methods have all but eliminated the need for pharmaceuticals in my life. To be clear, I'm not recommending that anyone go against the advice of their physician. That said, the techniques I'm going to share with you here can serve as powerful supplements to an otherwise toxic medical regimen.

Dream Control While Awake

What do the Waking and Dream states have in common? While their differences are fairly obvious, what is their common ground? After all, in waking life I can't fly like Superman, shoot lightning bolts out of my eyes, or land a date with Cate Blanchett; but in dreams I can do all these things and more. However, the commonalities shared by dreams and the wake-a-day-world aren't readily apparent. On the scientific side of this question, **REM** sleep (dreaming) is called "paradoxical sleep" due to the fact that the dreaming brain shows patterns of activity similar to that of the waking state. In dreams, we experience this as the absolute certainty that what we're experiencing and perceiving is *real*. In other words, we're *hypnotized*. Whether dreaming or awake, we unconsciously "buy into" the narrative we're presented with.

Let's formulate that as an axiom:

The dreaming and awake states share a common bond in which the facts of the perceived environment are unquestioningly believed to be real.

A good example of this mechanism at work in the waking world is when a convincing and charismatic speaker charms us into believing his every word, thereby winning us over to his side. Or when we convince ourselves through self-talk that we're a certain type of person, that people love or hate us, and so forth. This is a form of self-hypnosis. What we all too easily forget is that our biochemistry changes every time we do these things. Do them long enough and you may even create or cure diseases within yourself.

The Technique

The first time I became aware of this phenomenon I was thirty-six years old. It was around 2:00 am and I had to wake up at around 5:00 am for work. The problem was that I couldn't breathe, and therefore, I couldn't sleep. I've suffered from chronic respiratory issues my entire life. Especially in the dry months of the year, it's been a living hell trying to breathe without recourse to an inhaler pump or steroidal medication.

This was one of those Autumn nights…

As any asthmatic will tell you, lying on your back is one of the worst things you can do during an attack. The only position that brings a measure of comfort is sitting up. Of course, that's also the best position to adopt if you want to get zero sleep! But there I was, wheezing, sitting on the couch in the dark living room, miserable.

After what seemed an eternity, I had the bright idea to close my eyes and attempt to gain some mental control over my recalcitrant lungs. At first, I steadied my breathing. I relaxed my body from the inside out and tried to make my breathing smooth and uniform. That helped a little, but not totally, and I desperately wanted to go to sleep. But then I decided to take my meditation a step further and practice

Embryonic Breathing, a *Qigong* exercise I'd been practicing regularly for about seven years. In almost every form of meditation I practice, the first thing I do is something called *The Inner Smile.* This simple gesture of internally turning the optimism dial up as high as it goes serves a dual purpose. On the one hand, it enables me to relax even further by elevating my mood from one of work to one of playfulness. The second thing it does is it changes my biochemistry! If you're interested in learning this technique yourself, read on!

The Inner Smile

As soon as I began *The Inner Smile,* my lungs and sinuses cleared up to a noticeable degree. It wasn't a total cure, but it was enough to get me to sleep that night and up for work the next morning. So blown away was I by this that I made it a point to research it the following afternoon. Up until that point, I'd only practiced *The Inner Smile* to induce the relaxation necessary for meditation and proper *Qi* flow. That it had the potential to stop an asthma attack or clear the sinuses never occurred to me. What I uncovered in my research shocked me. Here's a perfect example of how you can essentially dream your way to desired changes in your biochemistry:

Thirty or so years ago, the professor and author, Jon Kabat-Zinn, created his now famous *Mindfulness-Based Stress Reduction Program.* He guided individuals with chronic pain and depression through a six-week meditation regimen in the basement of the University of Massachusetts. Kabat-Zinn became the first practitioner to record meditation-related health improvements in patients with chronic pain and debilitating depression. His stress-reduction techniques are now used in hospitals, clinics and by HMOs all over the world.

Speaking of depression, did you know that many lung diseases are linked to states of depression? Melancholy actually depresses the chest *visibly.* The next time you feel down in the doldrums, find a full-length mirror and look at a side profile of your body. The first thing you'll notice is that your shoulders are hunched over, and your chest is sunken inward toward your spine. So you can imagine what your lungs look and feel like when you're chronically depressed!

The Taoists note that depression and fear produce longer inhalations of breath. Sighing, yawning and a general moving inward of breath and *Qi* occurs as a consequence of profound sadness. In his biography of Aleister Crowley, *The Eye in the Triangle,* the famous occultist, Israel Regardie, observed that almost everyone with real talent he's ever met in the esoteric sciences has suffered from debilitating asthma. It's no secret that the degree of world-weariness that gives rise to the religious quest is a species of the most profound sorrow.

I guess I'm no exception…

So how and when should you practice *The Inner Smile*? In my opinion, the best time to begin training is at bedtime as you're falling asleep, and immediately upon waking up. This has a few benefits that become apparent almost immediately. First, when you practice at bedtime, you're setting the stage for Conscious Sleep of all types. In Taoist terms, smiling is a *Yang* activity, whereas sleep is a *Yin* activity. Combining these two activities balances your Etheric energy *(Qi)* and psychologically stacks the deck in your favor with regards to Conscious Sleep. Here's how it's done:

STEP ONE: Begin by lying in bed in your most comfortable position. If you like, you may play some soothing instrumental music.

STEP TWO: There are many ways to induce the inner smile. My favorite is to conjure up the feeling of having attained every goal I've ever desired—immediate and long-term goals alike. For example, if I have to work the next day, I'll convince myself that I'm a millionaire and no longer have to work a job. Or I'll convince myself that I'm in perfect health, immortal, impervious, and that there's nothing left to worry about. This has the immediate effect of quieting the mind, emotions and body. Another favorite of mine is to conjure up the feeling of being head-over-heals in love with someone. Experiment and see what works best for you. You can even cycle through many methods in a given session. The point is to first convince yourself of total joy, safety and health and then…SMILE! Literally put a smile on your face and feel that smile spread to every internal organ in your body. Feel it circulating in your veins and emanating from the pores of your skin. When you breathe, imagine that you're breathing in pure sunshine.

STEP THREE: Lastly, carry this inner joy with you as you're falling asleep. Feel the warmth of your bed, the softness of your pillow, and feel a sense of gratitude and excitement about your approaching dreams. I've even gone to sleep with *The Inner Smile* and awoken the following morning with a smile still on my face! *The Inner Smile* is especially powerful when practiced in times of genuine sorrow or anxiety. It quickly becomes an internal sanctuary that you take with you everywhere you go.

So what's happening within the body when you practice *The Inner Smile*? Only a handful of studies have been conducted, and nothing conclusive has been found. Personally, I think that the brain produces more of the neurotransmitter called *serotonin* when *The Inner Smile* is properly practiced. Serotonin is, among other things, responsible for feelings of happiness and well-being. Endogenous *cannabinoids* and oxytocin are probably stimulated by this practice as well. The key to successful practice of the Inner Smile is sustained concentration. It's not enough to merely conjure up the desired feelings—you must be able to sustain them as well. Naturally, this takes practice. And it's totally worth the effort. Try it and see!

One Last Thing

Once you gain some skill in practicing *The Inner Smile* this can possibly be extended to induce, not just Serotonin, but even Endorphin and Adrenaline! This may sound like a tall order, but most of us actually do this all the time. The only difference is that our concentration and imagination need training to induce it at will and sustain it.

How do we normally alter our own biochemistry with our minds? Well, whenever you think about sex and become aroused, that's one prominent example of how this is done. In fact, such visualizations produce everything from Testosterone to Endorphins to Oxytocin. That's quite a feat!

Another example of mentally induced biochemical changes is *self-talk*. The internal dialogue we maintain is a powerful stimulator of mood and therefore of biochemistry. I'm reminded of when I became addicted to a pain-killing plant called Kratom. This plant acts on the opioid receptors in the brain, thus its potentially addictive nature. Anyway, I began taking Kratom to numb the chronic pain of a bulging disk in the thoracic area of my spine. As someone who observes a strictly organic vegetarian diet, I thought Kratom would be the smarter choice when compared with prescription opiates. So I ingested roughly 10 grams of the plant every day for about six months. But when I tried to discontinue its use, I was hit with some fairly severe withdrawals.

So I kept taking it!

Finally, one day, I decided to quit Kratom "cold turkey." I knew that the withdrawals were going to be awful. Regardless, I decided to see this thing through, so I sat down to meditate and talk to my body. I practiced the Inner Smile and, once I was feeling centered and relaxed, I told my body what I planned to do. I told it I was quitting Kratom and that the withdrawals would feel as though I'm taking away a vital nutrient, but that it's a lie. I assured my body that it has the power to produce its own opiates (endorphins), and that it should begin to do so as soon as the Kratom was withdrawn.

The withdrawal symptoms never came...

A similar thing occurs when you tell yourself to awaken in the morning at a specific time, without the use of an alarm clock. Like clockwork, your body will start waking you up at your designated time. For me, this often happens as accurately as to the minute. What this means is that you're actually placing your "wake up biochemicals" on a timer, like a coffee-maker with a timer on it.

This ability to change your internal chemistry isn't unlike Dream Control. Both require a powerful Will, a razor-sharp concentration, and the confidence that you can do the impossible. Now ask yourself: What type of dream (life) do *you* want to have?

Afterword

The Future of Subliminal Cognition Training

Throughout this book, I've tried to emphasize the importance of an Integral approach to Conscious Sleep. I hope I was successful in convincing you to expand your horizons, and to take the leap from *Oneironaut* to *Veiler*. While there certainly are many benefits to be had from focusing exclusively on any one aspect of the Conscious Sleep spectrum, they pale in comparison to the treasure trove buried in the rich soil of an Integral methodology. Hopefully, by now, you've proven this to yourself.

If, by reading this book, I've helped you advance a few paces in your own quest for the continuity of consciousness, then I'll consider my work accomplished.

In these pages we've explored what an Integral approach to Conscious Sleep might look like. We've navigated the Five Veils of consciousness together in a comprehensive fashion. We've exercised and cultivated our Gross, Subtle and Causal bodies, thereby building the necessary anatomy to transform passing *states* into enduring *traits* of consciousness. We've checked in with modern scientific research, and we've included the ancient Wisdom Traditions in the conversation. We've explored our Etheric anatomy and learned how we might use it to bolster and balance our excursions behind the Veil. We've also listened to some of the other voices in the Veiler community, and we learned some of the more common experiences people have on this path. We've seen the benefits and pathologies that can occur on such a quest, and we've offered some advice on how to encourage the former and sidestep the latter.

But we've also learned an even more important lesson:

We've learned how to use Conscious Sleep as an authentic spiritual path!

It's my most sincere hope that the *SCT* system, and others like it, will be used by more and more practitioners of Conscious Sleep in the years to come. Through it, I strongly believe that the Lucid Dreamer, the Astral Projector, the Meditator, and even the Psychologist, will find a powerful ally in their own fields of endeavor.

I carry the conviction of one who's tried more exclusive and specialized systems only to come out more confused and frustrated than before I adopted them. I don't *believe* that an Integral approach is the better option, I *know* it is!

And now you know it, too.

It takes hard and consistent work, not just to see results from these esoteric disciplines, but to see the results you're *really* after. I'm referring to the kind of results that foster a true joy for having put in so much effort for a reward that surpassed all of your expectations.

And above and below all this effort is an overarching love, an embrace that includes your total being.

The inner demons I've faced in my own quest for the continuity of consciousness are reminders of how much work I've done. That's a true hallmark of progress in this life: How sincerely you can look at those monsters and smile. Those monsters *are* you.

Monsters are rarely born, they're made. They're constructed using very specific materials: ridicule, neglect, heartbreak, alienation—every conceivable species of abuse goes into that mortar. So many materials go into the making of monsters, and the miracle is that it takes only one thing to unmake them.

Love. Genuine love.

GLOSSARY

Ashwagandha: It has been shown to have anti-inflammatory effects and relax the central nervous system in animals.

Astral Body: The projectable double of the Gross and Etheric Bodies.

Astral Plane: The "Veil of Ghosts". A realm inhabited by the collective thoughtforms of the entire planet.

Astral Projection: Out of Body Experience (OOBE). The act of separating the Astral Body from the Gross and Etheric body.

Brahmamuhurt: Dawn. Between the hours of 3:00 am and sunrise.

Brainwaves (ALPHA, BETA, THETA, DELTA and GAMMA): The bioelectrical correlates of states of consciousness and unconsciousness. Generally speaking, **ALPHA** is "relaxed wakefulness"; **BETA** is "alert wakefulness"; **THETA** is "dreaming awareness"; **DELTA** is "deep dreamless sleep" and coma; **GAMMA** is deep "creative meditation" (as opposed to passive mediation).

Causal Body: The "embodiment zone" or "feeling zone" associated with formless awareness, deep dreamless sleep, the *Veil of Bliss,* and formless absorption meditation. The Causal Body is the "stabilizer muscles" of conscious awareness and the root of self-consciousness.

Chakras: Centers of concentrated energy situated along the spine in alignment with various internal organs.

Channeling Intensity: The skill and practice of training oneself to open up to and refine evermore powerful sensations and emotions.

Clairaudience: The ability to hear on the Astral Plane.

Clairvoyance: The ability to see on the Astral Plane.

Conscious Sleep: The act of carrying awareness into the sleep cycle.

Dantian (Lower, Upper): The Taoist term for Centers found in the Gross and Etheric Bodies capable of storing Etheric energy. The Lower Dantian is located in the gut, and the Upper Dantian is located in the brain.

EEG (Electroencephalograph): A device used to map, monitor and record changes and patterns in the five basic brainwaves.

Embryonic Breathing: The art of building and storing Etheric force in the Lower Dantian.

Etheric Body: The bioelectrical energy that circulates within and around the Gross body.

Etheric Energy: Bioelectricity.

Holon: A term coined by Arthur Koestler to describe a whole which is also part of a larger whole. Everything in the conceivable universe is a Holon.

Huiyin: From the Chinese, meaning "meet yin." The location between the genitals and anus. The perineum.

Hypnagogia: The psychedelic sensory phenomena of approaching sleep.

Hypopompia: The psychedelic sensory phenomena of exiting sleep.

K-complexes: A unique pattern of brainwaves that occur during stage two **NREM** sleep. They serve the dual function of memory consolidation and suppression of cortical arousal due to external stimuli.

Lucid Dreaming: The ability to remain conscious during **REM** sleep (dreaming) and to exert a degree of control over the narrative of the dream experience.

Microcosmic Orbit: A Taoist/Buddhist meditation practice designed to increase energy flow along the meridians situated on the back and front of the spine.

NREM (Non-Rapid Eye Movement) sleep: A slow wave/high voltage brainwave occurring during deep dreamless sleep.

Oneironaut: An individual who can navigate the *Veil of Dreams*. See also **Veiler**.

OOBE (Out of Body Experiences): Astral Projection. The subjective experience of one's consciousness separating from the Gross physical body.

Parietal Lobe: The portion of the brain situated behind the frontal lobe and above the occipital lobe. The parietal lobe is involved in rendering sensory input coherent, especially in terms of spatial orientation and direction (proprioception).

Pellucid Dreaming: Meditation carried into the sleep cycle. Pellucid Dreaming is to be distinguished from Pellucid Sleep, in that the former involves passive contemplation of the phenomena of **REM,** and the latter with conscious absorption in **NREM** (dreamless sleep).

PGO-waves: Phase-specific brainwaves that occur at the onset of **REM** sleep (dreaming). PGO-waves appear to promote longer and more vivid dreams, and they also play a pivotal role in memory consolidation.

Physical Body: The material biological organism. The "Gross" body.

Pineal Gland: A small pinecone-shaped gland situated at the center of the brain, the pineal gland regulates the wake and sleep cycles.

***Qi,* Prana, Orgone, Bioelectricity:** The electrical current circulating within and around the body. Although terms like 'Qi", "Prana", and "Orgone" can have other connotations depending upon context, for our purposes they refer to the bioelectrical energy created by the chemical, neurological and cognitive activities associated with being a living, thinking organism.

Qigong: Literally "energy work." Created in ancient China, there are several schools of *Qigong*: the Religious, Scholarly, Medical and Martial schools. Despite their differences, each school emphasizes the utilization of natural and biological life-force to achieve its goals. Some scholars refer to *Qigong* as "Chinese Yoga".

REM (Rapid Eye Movement) sleep: That phase of the sleep cycle associated with dreaming.

Shen: Depending upon the context in which the word is used, *Shen* is one of the traditional "three treasures" of *Qigong* practice. It represents one's overall mood (e.g., happy, depressed). When someone has made their unconscious elements conscious, this is known in *Qigong* society as "raising one's *Shen."* You might think of *Shen* as individual consciousness itself, especially the overall expression of that consciousness.

Shilajit **resin:** A mineral substance high in concentrations of fulvic acid and sold as an elixir in India and Tibet.

Sleep-spindles: Bursts of electrical activity that occur in the brain during stage two **NREM** (dreamless) sleep. Sleep-spindles share much in common with K-complexes, particularly their participation in memory consolidation and cortical suppression during **NREM** sleep. Also called "sigma waves," sleep-spindles follow K-complexes in sequence as the brain tries to remain asleep and undisturbed by external stimuli. I believe that both K-complexes and Sleep-spindles are responsible for the short microbursts of dreaming we often experience in **NREM**.

*Tai Chi Chuan***:** An ancient Chinese "internal" Martial Art that has been adapted in modern times as an alternative form of exercise. *Tai Chi Chuan* is also a form of *Qigong* ("energy work") and moving meditation. As such, its sincere practice can buttress your experience of Conscious Sleep, especially Astral Projection.

*Tantra***:** An ancient Indian school of thought and practice which aims at total purity through transcendence of opposites. Far from being merely a doctrine of "enlightened sexuality," the Tantric school uses any and all means to achieve nondual enlightenment.

Veils of Consciousness: The layers of conscious embodied experience as postulated by the myriad forms of the Perennial Philosophy—Body, Mind and Spirit being the most prominent example. In the *SCT* system, we qualify five Veils of conscious experience that closely resemble the "koshas" of the Vedantic school of thought. The term "Veil" is employed to emphasize that these seemingly discreet regions of conscious experience are actually limbs of a single unified bodymind. And the liminal thresholds that appear to separate these realms are but veils of blindness, environments which the undeveloped "muscles" of cognition have yet to master and integrate.

Veil of Bliss: The Causal Realm. This Veil separates the root of self-awareness as an ego from the other four Veils and Bodies, as well as from the other potential "egos" one might become. The *Veil of Bliss* may also be the region that separates living and embodied self-awareness from the realms of the afterlife.

Veil of Breath: The Etheric Realm. This is the invisible realm of lifeforce and energy. This is primarily a realm of pure feeling and energetic processes hovering close to or within the Gross physical body. Dreams may be the subjective and theatrical correlate of the processes occurring behind the *Veil of Breath.*

Veil of Dreams: The Oneirautic Realm. Largely the realm of the emotions, the *Veil of Dreams* brings to theatrical life the themes and experiences and desires that affect us most deeply. The *Veil of Dreams* is often mistaken as the Astral Plane. The *Veil of Dreams* is also the realm of memory consolidation.

Veil of Ghosts: The Astral Plane. Unlike the *Veil of Dreams,* which is mostly comprised of biographical elements, the *Veil of Ghosts* is largely impersonal. Some say that the Astral Plane is synonymous with Carl Jung's idea of the Collective Unconscious, the repository of the memories and experiences and expectations of all sentient life on Earth.

Veil of Tears: The Material World. Navigated mostly by the Gross physical body, this is the realm of birth and death, society, the cosmos, and the microcosmos.

Veiler: An individual who is capable of navigating the Five Veils and their subdivisions. Not to be confused with an **Oneironaut**, who navigates the *Veil of Dreams* only.

Vivid Dreaming: The ability to dream with all five senses engaged.

WILD (Wake Induced Lucid Dream): A Lucid Dream induced from the waking state rather than while already asleep.

Yin/Yang: The ancient Chinese conception of the dual nature of existence. Female (yin)/Male (yang), Earth (yin)/Sky (yang), Asleep (yin)/Awake (yang), etc.

Zazen: Literally "sitting for Zen." Zazen is a meditation practice from the school of Zen Buddhism. It's primary method is to "just sit" without thinking or avoiding thinking. Without "doing" anything, not even "non-doing". Zazen is a powerful method for inducing the **ALPHA** brainwave and the state of Trance.

BIBLIOGRAPHY

Exploring the World of Lucid Dreaming: Stephen LaBerge/Howard Rheingold.

Journeys Out of the Body: Robert Monroe.

The Two-Week Lucid Dreamer: Derek Ralston.

Dreaming Wide Awake: David James Brown.

The Art of Dreaming: Carlos Castaneda.

One Taste: Ken Wilber.

Qigong Meditation/Embryonic Breathing: Dr. Yang Jwing Ming.

Microcosmic Orbit: Dr. Yang Jwing Ming.

Astral Dynamics: Robert Bruce.

Reflections On Life After Life: Raymond Moody.

Consciousness Beyond Life: Pim Van Lommel.

Sex, Ecology, Spirituality: Ken Wilber.

The Multi-Orgasmic Man: Mantak Chia.

Journey to Dylan: Carlos Castaneda.

Astral Projection in 90 Days: Robert Bruce.

The Book of Secrets: Osho.

The Eight-Circuit Brain: Antero Alli.

Magick in Theory and Practice: Aleister Crowley.

Undoing Yourself with Energized Meditation and Other Devices: Christopher S. Hyatt, Ph.D.

Dream Therapy: Clare Johnson, Ph.D.

Tibetan Dream Yoga: Stephen LaBerge.

Skygates of the Mind: Ivan Kos.

Integral Dreaming: A Holistic Approach to Dreaming: Fariba Bogzaran/Daniel Deslauriers.

OTHER TITLES BY DANIEL ALLEN KELLEY

Behind the Veil: The Complete Guide to Conscious Sleep (Falcon Press, 2018)

A Garden of Vines: The Collected Poetry of Daniel Allen Kelley (Independently Published, 2018)

Predicting the Present: Twenty-two Fingers Pointing at the Moon (Independently Published, 2018)

About the Author

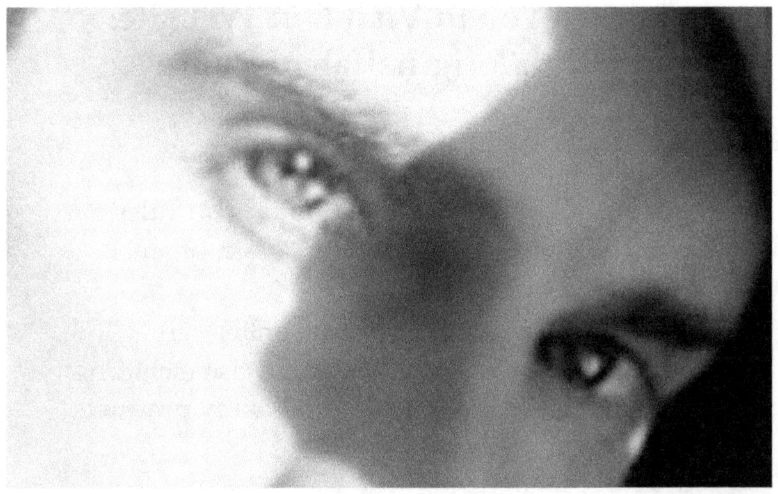

Daniel Kelley is an author, poet, musician and Integral Life Practitioner with over two decades of experience in the esoteric-arts. He is the creator of *Subliminal Cognition Training* (SCT). Daniel was born in 1979 to Baptist parents in Waterloo, Canada. His father was a Baptist preacher. After a profound and prolonged transpersonal crisis in early childhood, he broke away from his strict Christian upbringing to study the wisdom traditions of the world. At age sixteen he suffered a breakdown that culminated at age twenty-one in a transpersonal breakthrough. After joining various Hermetic societies and practicing their methods, he eventually found his spiritual home in Chinese Taoist Alchemy, Integral Life Practice, and the various Yogas of India and Tibet. He also practices and teaches Internal Chinese Martial Arts, *Qigong, Taijiquan* and *Xingyiquan*. He currently lives in upstate New York U.S.A.

http://behindtheveil.simdif.com

THE *Original* FALCON PRESS

Invites You to Visit Our Website:
http://originalfalcon.com

At our website you can:

- Browse the online catalog of all of our great titles
- Find out what's available and what's out of stock
- Get special discounts
- Order our titles through our secure online server
- Find products not available anywhere else including:
    - One of a kind and limited availability products
    - Special packages
    - Special pricing
- Get free gifts
- Join our email list for advance notice of New Releases and Special Offers
- Find out about book signings and author events
- Send email to our authors
- Read excerpts of many of our titles
- Find links to our authors' websites
- Discover links to other weird and wonderful sites
- And much, much more

Get online today at http://originalfalcon.com